MONEY AND BA

The Made Simple series
has been created
especially for self-education
but can equally well
be used as
an aid to group study.
However complex the subject,
the reader is taken
step by step,
clearly and methodically,
through the course. Each volume
has been prepared by experts,
taking account of
modern educational requirements,
to ensure the most
effective way of
acquiring knowledge.

In the same series

Accounting
Acting and Stagecraft
Additional Mathematics
Administration in Business
Advertising
Anthropology
Applied Economics
Applied Mathematics
Applied Mechanics
Art Appreciation
Art of Speaking
Art of Writing
Biology
Book-keeping
British Constitution
Business and Administrative Organisation
Business Economics
Business Statistics and Accounting
Calculus
Chemistry
Childcare
Commerce
Company Law
Computer Programming
Computers and Microprocessors
Cookery
Cost and Management Accounting
Data Processing
Dressmaking
Economic History
Economic and Social Geography
Economics
Effective Communication
Electricity
Electronic Computers
Electronics
English
English Literature
Export
Financial Management
French
Geology
German
Housing, Tenancy and Planning Law
Human Anatomy
Human Biology
Italian
Journalism
Latin
Law
Management
Marketing
Mathematics
Metalwork
Modern Biology
Modern Electronics
Modern European History
Modern Mathematics
Money and Banking
Music
New Mathematics
Office Practice
Organic Chemistry
Personnel Management
Philosophy
Photography
Physical Geography
Physics
Practical Typewriting
Psychiatry
Psychology
Public Relations
Rapid Reading
Retailing
Russian
Salesmanship
Secretarial Practice
Social Services
Sociology
Spanish
Statistics
Teeline Shorthand
Transport and Distribution
Twentieth-Century British History
Typing
Woodwork

MONEY AND BANKING Made Simple

Ken Hoyle, BSc (Econ)
Geoffrey Whitehead, BSc (Econ)

Made Simple Books
HEINEMANN : London

Printed and bound in Great Britain
by Richard Clay (The Chaucer Press) Ltd, Bungay, Suffolk
for the publishers, William Heinemann Ltd.,
10 Upper Grosvenor Street, London W1X 9PA

SBN 434 98519 8 casebound
SBN 434 98505 8 paperbound

Editorial: Robert Postema, F. G. Thomas
Cover illustration: Julia Logsdail

Foreword

This book provides a sound coverage of monetary theory, policies and institutions within a mixed economy. The whole range of banking and financial institutions is described, including the central banks of major nations, the commercial banks and the specialist banks, with special reference to the United Kingdom.

While specifically designed to cover the syllabus requirements of the Institute of Bankers Stage II examination in Applied Economics, the book will be of use to other groups—particularly intermediate and higher level students on such courses as BEC Higher National; the Diploma and Certificate Courses in Management Studies; Foundation Courses in Accounting, Insurance, Actuarial Work, etc. Undergraduates reading Applied Economics, Business Finance, Money and Banking and Government will find it invaluable.

In preparing this book we have been greatly helped by a number of trade associations, financial institutions, etc., who have kindly permitted the use of statistics and illustrations. These are acknowledged overleaf. We must express our thanks to these organisations, and also to Robert Postema, the Publisher of the Made Simple series, for his encouragement and advice on the project.

KEN HOYLE
GEOFFREY WHITEHEAD

Acknowledgments

The assistance of the following institutions and organisations is gratefully acknowledged for the use of statistical tables, diagrams and background information:

The Bank of England
The Building Societies Association
The Co-operative Bank
The European Investment Bank
The Finance Houses Association
National Girobank
The Trustee Savings Bank

Contents

Part 1

MONETARY INSTITUTIONS AND SYSTEMS

1

MONEY, BANKS AND THE ECONOMY

1.1 The Historical Development of Money

In the simplest societies there is no money. Self-sufficiency prevails, with each family or tribal unit producing for its own needs, enjoying the plenty of autumn and enduring the poverty of spring. One tribe describes a springtime dinner as 'eating another notch on one's belt'. Many tribes developed special adaptations to survive hard times, like steatopygous or fatty tissue around the buttocks, where vast meals eaten in prosperous times can be stored as fat for survival in less happy situations. The Arab found by early travellers to be crossing a vast wilderness with nothing but a handful of dates to sustain him was in reality consuming meals eaten before the journey began. Hunters travelled light; the Bushman running for hours following the spoor of an eland had no energy to carry possessions or even clothing.

Trade began as 'silent trade'. The successful hunter would leave a joint hung in a tree outside a 'foreign' kraal. The inhabitants would accept the meat, leaving agricultural produce in exchange, which the hunter would collect, unseen, at nightfall. Later, a system of open barter developed. This is the exchange of goods directly for other goods, and it presents quite serious problems to the parties trading. These problems are not a real handicap when trading is an unusual event—for example, in simple tribal societies practising autarky (self-sufficiency). To people growing their own food, keeping their own cattle and weaving their own cloth, the occasional bartering activity can usually be resolved fairly easily. The purchase of a knife or an axe, at an annual fair or from the visiting pedlar, is an event to which due time can be given.

Trade is not the only activity of mankind, however. Marriage and revenge are older practices still and appear to have played a considerable part in the development of money. Bride-price and blood-price are ancient institutions, and are often reported among primitive people. Compensation for a man's death is a sum equivalent to what his father paid as bride-price for the dead man's mother a generation before. These two activities, and barter, are matters to which serious consideration can be given, especially by peoples largely self-sufficient in ordinary bread-and-butter matters.

When we live in a community where specialisation is the rule, so that every single thing we need has to be obtained by exchange, the difficulties of barter become so onerous that a 'money' system has to be developed.

Even today it is sometimes necessary to use barter. The collapse of a currency system, such as occurred in Germany at the end of the Second World War, meant that barter took place on an extensive scale, and eventually a non-legal-tender money system developed with cigarettes acting as money. Bartering agreements at national level have also been arranged between some of the countries of the Communist bloc and Western nations in the last few years. A special class of traders, called 'barter and swap' merchants, has evolved. They make it their business to find markets for some of the products received in these 'state-trading' deals with Eastern bloc countries.

As society developed, specialisation grew. The only sensible way to create wealth is to concentrate on mastering particular skills, and thus develop real facility in a trade or service. In situations where the best hunter hunts, the best farmer tends his flocks, the goldsmith works away in his smithy all day, etc.—in short, where production is indirect and not direct—exchange becomes all important, and a medium of exchange—money—must be developed. It enables someone who has contributed usefully to the creation of wealth in one field—as a baker, farm labourer, chemical engineer, etc.—to claim a balanced 'basket of resources' from a variety of other areas. The chemical engineer exchanges the money earned by his labour in the North Sea oilfields for bread, meat, cheese, accommodation, entertainment, etc., produced by other workers.

The dawn of the money system saw many strange objects being used as a medium of exchange. Tools were widely recognised as valuable goods which could serve as money. Any such commodity will serve as money. Shells for adornment, semi-precious stones, nails, fish-hooks, compressed bricks of tea and ox-hides have all been used as money. Cattle have always been symbols of wealth, and the Mycenean talent was a bronze coin in the shape of a hide. When Jason went in search of the 'Golden Fleece' he was not looking for some exotic animal, but for gold ingots cast in the shape of hides. After the Second World War cigarettes were used as money in occupied Germany, and the British soldier who was entitled to a free issue of 50 each week was very well 'paid'. What is it that makes the best money? What characteristics does money display? These are explained in Section 1.3 below. First let us consider the development of banking.

1.2 Money and the Development of Banking

As economies grew the need for a really advanced money system increased. The use of coins made from metals of intrinsic value, such as gold, silver and copper, was for centuries the solution to the money problem, but even this was not without its disadvantages. The Portuguese discovery of a route to India round the Cape of Good Hope, and the Spanish discoveries of Mexico and Peru, brought an increased supply of precious metals into Europe at a time when the flow of goods had not similarly increased. With more money chasing the same quantity of goods prices rose and inflation caused great hardship, especially to those nations not engaged in the new territories. The ability of Spain and Portugal to purchase with their new wealth the goods and services of the rest of Europe led to the belief that nations became powerful by accumulating precious metals. The reasoning behind this belief was that supplies of precious metals allowed states to command military forces; allowed an expansion of the money supply necessary for an expanding economy; and in the process of accumulation the drain on the supplies held by rival nations had the effect of diminishing their power.

The message was clear: in the national interest there should be the maximum accumulation of gold and silver. This should be achieved by selling more abroad than was purchased, the balance being taken in precious metal. A desirable spin-off from the collection of precious metal in this way was that a surplus of exports over imports increased domestic aggregate demand. Even today the Chancellor talks of an 'export-led boom'. A strong export trade creates work for home industries.

Mercantilism was born. The operation of a state along mercantilist lines had great implications for the business community within that state. Governments in the UK, being convinced of the value of an export surplus and desirous of increasing national power, pursued a number of policies directed at promoting these ends. They found it helpful to grant monopolies to companies like the East India Company and the Hudson Bay Company; they encouraged agriculture and protected it from foreign competition and they encouraged manufacture of every sort. All these developments called for a more sophisticated money system, and gradually a class of merchant bankers grew up in every part of the country.

The first bankers in Britain began operating as early as the twelfth century. They were Lombards from the Plains of Lombardy in Northern Italy. Here had grown up a group of independent cities called the Lombard League. Merchants and traders from this cradle of European liberty came to do business in the City of London, and their home, Lombard Street, is still the centre of British banking. The Lombards, after a century or so of business in London, were eventually made bankrupt because they lent money to kings who did not repay the loans.

After the departure of the Lombards, banking came to be considered by the goldsmiths as a sideline to their normal activities in the bullion and jewellery fields. The early goldsmiths had to have large vaults which were soundly built and heavily guarded. The idea grew up of letting one of these goldsmiths take care of your wealth if you had more than you could safely defend yourself.

The person who deposited his surplus funds with the goldsmith became known as a **depositor** and naturally paid for the privilege of having his money defended in this way. These payments were the first 'bank charges'. The depositor who needed funds, to pay wages or debts, could call at the bank and collect such sums as he required.

Before long it became clear that unnecessary risks were being run by depositors who needed to pay money to creditors. The depositor had to collect the money and deliver it to the creditor who promptly had to return it to the bank. Why not simply order your banker to transfer funds from your deposit to the creditor's deposit? This was the origin of the cheque system. A cheque is an order to a banker to pay money from your account to, or into the account of, another person without the need for the money to leave the safety of the bank.

As agriculture and industry prospered banking ceased to be a prerogative of goldsmiths and other merchants engaged in banking as a sideline activity. Farmers, corn merchants, grocers, iron masters, textile manufacturers and middlemen of every sort engaged in banking. The word **broker**—commonly used today in financial and other markets—is derived from 'brogger', the man who brought raw materials to villagers all over the country, where they could be spun by the 'spinsters' into yarn, and then woven by the weavers. This was the domestic system of manufacture, before the 'dark satanic mills' replaced it with the 'factory system'. The brogger was in a useful position to develop a sideline in banking. He frequently lent money when he delivered his raw material, and took it back with interest months later when he called to collect the finished cloth, deducting it from the sums due to the weaver. As expertise grew, successful merchants undertook more and more banking for other less knowledgeable people, and the 'country-bank' system grew into a specialised activity.

The Creation of Credit

The growth of banking as a system for taking care of money was soon supplemented by a more profitable activity. The early goldsmiths had noticed that only a very small proportion, about 8 per cent, of the funds of each depositor was in use regularly, being drawn out and paid in as funds were used or received. The proportion left on permanent deposit was about 92 per cent of the average depositor's funds. It seemed sensible to lend some of this money to people anxious to borrow for industrial and commercial reasons.

However, in lending out these surplus funds the banks took a more sophisticated view of the unused balances than merely to regard them as funds available for lending. Consider a deposit of £100, of which only £8 is likely to be required to meet the customer's needs, and the balance of £92 is available. The banks did not regard this as £92 available to lend to customers, but as the **cash ratio** for loans to a much greater sum. Of what sum is £92 eight per cent? The answer is:

$$\pounds 92 \div 8 \times 100 = \pounds 1150$$

In theory the bank could lend a customer £1150. The customer has borrowed the money to spend, so let us pretend that in the eighteenth century he bought a herd of cattle for £1150. The vendor of the cattle would not know that the money was a pure invention, and would pay the cheque for £1150 into his account, but the statistical probability was that he would only then ask for 8 per cent of it, i.e. £92—the exact sum which the bank has available. We therefore see that 'loans make deposits' and also make profits for the bank. If the rate of interest was 10 per cent, and the loan was for one year, the interest earned would be £115, more than the original deposit which made the loan possible. The whole process is usually called the **creation of credit** or the **creation of money**.

This is of course an extreme example, for to rely entirely on the statistical probability might prove disastrous at certain times. For greater prudence the banks usually kept a **liquidity ratio** nearer to one third, so that a deposit of £100 would act as a liquidity ratio for total deposits of £300. This means that loans of £200 could safely be made, the other £100 being the deposit already received. While this would rarely put the banks in difficulties, at times of real national disaster the only thing to do was to close the banks, as those old enough to remember the start of either of the World Wars will recall. The first act of the Government on the declaration of war was to shut the banks, to prevent depositors drawing out money which in fact was not available.

Banks creating credit also need to pursue sound credit policies, the two requirements for which are:

(i) That the depositor whose funds are being used shall be content to leave them on deposit without making sudden demands upon the bank. To encourage this it is usual to pay him interest on the deposit.

(ii) That the borrower shall be creditworthy, and shall offer—if requested—some security. This may take the form of a guarantee from some creditworthy person, or the deeds of a house or a piece of land. The latter is sometimes called collateral security, security lying alongside the debt. Life assurance policies are often used as security for small debts, and provided the surrender value is great enough they offer good security to the banker. Stocks and shares are often used as security.

Naturally in the early days there were bankers who unwisely lent more than it was safe to lend, and were caught with depositors asking for their money back at a time when the bank had already lent the money out to someone else. Rumours of an impending bankruptcy caused panic in the countryside. Even the Bank of England on occasions made special arrangements with influential customers to restore public confidence. Famous 'names' who banked at the Bank were asked to call and collect their deposits in gold, which were carried out of the front door for all to see. The coaches then took the money round the corner and gave it back again at the back door so that the small amount of gold available could again be paid out to further depositors arriving at the front door. The manifest ability of the Bank to pay deposits restored confidence and the queues of genuinely worried customers drifted away. Today we rarely think of a bank as being involved in bankruptcy (except as a creditor who is making some unfortunate customer face up to his insolvency). As the word 'bankruptcy' implies, this has not always been the case, and even in recent times there have been spectacular bank failures, but none so serious that a rescue operation by the 'Big Four' banks has been unable to save the situation. The 'fringe-bank' failures in the mid-seventies led to the Banking Act of 1979, which called for a more careful use of the word 'bank' and restricted the ability of companies to call themselves 'banks'.

Despite the risky nature of local banking the eighteenth century bankers did much to foster the growth of industry in the years popularly known as the Industrial Revolution. They collected funds from the prosperous agricultural aristocracy and lent it to the new industrialists in the North and West of England, Scotland, Wales and Northern Ireland. This process is illustrated in Fig. 1.1 below.

This brief account of early banking is continued later in the chapter. First let us consider the characteristics of money.

1.3 The Characteristics of Money

Money must be (*a*) generally acceptable, and stable in value, (*b*) durable, (*c*) difficult to imitate, (*d*) portable, and (*e*) divisible into small units.

(*a*) **General acceptability.** There is no difficulty where coins have an intrinsic value of their own; but when that is the case, debasement of the currency may occur if people are tempted to clip precious metal from the edges of coins. Where coins are merely 'token money', i.e. the metal in the coin is worth less than the coin's so-called value, general acceptability is a matter of confidence in the coinage. Such money is called 'fiduciary money'; it depends upon trust (*fiducia* = trust (in Latin)). Where devaluation of a currency is threatened, foreigners are unwilling to accept the coinage or notes of the country in question because they have no confidence that such tokens will keep the value they are supposed to have.

Often new coins are not popular with the public, who take some time to accept the idea of an unusual shape or new metal. The British public resisted the 50-pence piece when it was first introduced in place of the 10-shilling note. Similarly, Scottish bank-notes, although acceptable throughout Britain, are so rarely seen by English and Welsh shopkeepers that the

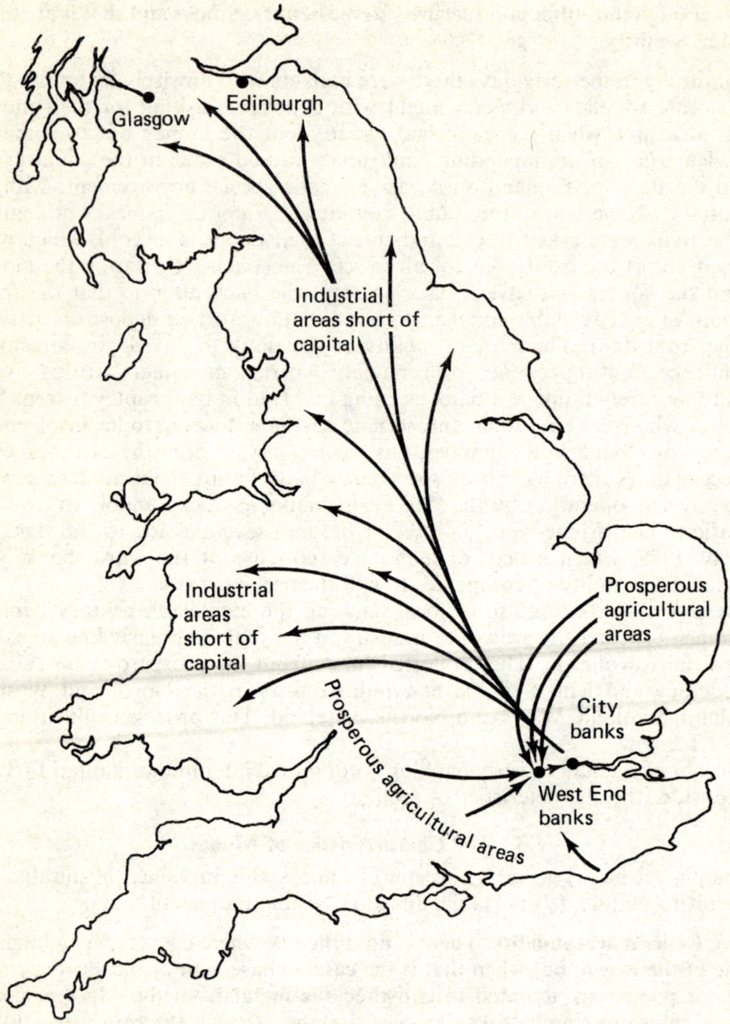

Fig. 1.1. How the banks fostered the Industrial Revolution.

Notes

The prosperous agricultural aristocracy banked with the fashionable West End banks. The West End banks loaned the money to the City of London, and the City banks loaned it to the Industrial Areas of the North of England.

production of one in a supermarket is sure to cause delay while managers are consulted.

(*b*) **Durability.** Coins and notes are expensive to produce. Most coins have a life of about 50 years, whereas notes last about three months. As a result the UK has changed over to a 50-pence cupro-nickel coin in place of a note of the same value, and a £1 coin is planned for circulation in 1983. It is also important that the metal used should not react chemically with air or with water. Such corrosion would reduce the life of the coin, and its value if it had intrinsic value. The noble metals—gold, silver—and copper are good in this respect, though silver tarnishes and copper does oxidise slowly. Aluminium alloys, being light and therefore portable, are widely used for coinage, but are less durable than cupro-nickel.

(*c*) **Ease of imitation.** Where coinage or notes are imitated, the coiner or forger obtains a claim against the available consumer goods and services. But the counterfeiter is clearly not entitled to such a claim, for he has not himself joined in any useful productive activity at all. The money system is designed to make exchanges easier between the producers of useful goods and services. Any outsider, any non-producer, who shares in the wealth created must therefore do so at the expense of honest workers who have contributed real wealth to the pool of utilities created. Counterfeiting is most likely to occur when token money is in daily use. It has sometimes been used as an instrument of policy. During the Second World War vast quantities of £1 and £5 notes were manufactured by the Germans with a view to undermining the British economy. Every effort has to be made to make coins and notes difficult to imitate. Supplies of special paper for bank-notes are strictly controlled and the destruction of dirty notes is carefully supervised.

(*d*) **Portability.** Money must be portable. One of the disadvantages of gold for coins is that it is so heavy. Notes are a great improvement in this respect, and cheques are even better. The largest cheque ever written, for £591 million, was recently paid by BP group of companies as part of its quarterly tax bill of £910 million in connection with its North Sea operations. This sum would hardly be portable, even in bank-notes, and in gold it would be extremely inconvenient.

(*e*) **Divisibility.** It is highly desirable that money should be capable of paying for the smallest transactions of everyday life. This is only possible if small units of money are available—which provides another reason why token coins have replaced coins of intrinsic value. The impossibility of making gold coins small enough to be worth a penny led to the use of copper and even less valuable metals. It has been suggested that coins should be made of plastic, which is light, durable and very cheap. The ease with which they might be imitated is the chief disadvantage of plastic tokens.

1.4 The Functions of Money

Money is (*a*) a medium of exchange, (*b*) a measure of value, (*c*) a store of value, (*d*) a standard for deferred payments, and (*e*) it facilitates one-way payments.

(*a*) **A medium of exchange.** This is the chief function of money. It overcomes one of the major disadvantages of barter as a means of carrying on trade—namely, that each of the trading partners must have what the other wants, and want what the other has: this is called the 'coincidence of wants'. Money overcomes the need for a coincidence of wants, since everyone 'wants' money, which represents a claim against any goods or services which will yield satisfaction. It does follow, though, that money must be generally acceptable. In earlier times this general acceptability was achieved by using metals which were themselves valuable: the coinage metals gold, silver and copper. Today all coins are 'token' money only—that is, they are acceptable because we all agree to accept them as being worth a certain claim against goods and services. This general acceptability is supported by a declaration by the law-making body that the tokens do constitute 'legal tender'.

(*b*) **A measure of value.** This function overcomes the difficulty met in barter of equating a decorated pot with a plump hen. The person who has made a decorated pot will exchange it for a 'fair' sum of money called the 'price' of the pot. He is then free to spend as much of the price of the pot as he likes on a plump hen, paying the fair 'price' for the hen. If hens are dear at the time, so that the money received for the pot is insufficient to purchase a hen, we can at least save the money until we can add a further sum to it. Thus the money is also useful as a store of value.

(*c*) **A store of value.** This store of value can also help us to overcome another disadvantage of barter, that some items are indivisible. If a cow is worth two sacks of wheat a farmer with one sack of wheat cannot buy half a cow, but he can save up the money he has obtained in exchange for his wheat in the hope that before long he will be able to afford a cow.

The use of money as a store of value applies only when individuals are storing it; a whole nation could not do so. Robinson Crusoe on his island found a box of gold coins which proved useless to him until he returned to civilisation. If a whole nation stored up its money and then retired simultaneously they would all starve for lack of current production. Money is only a claim against the real goods and services which are needed to support life. It is no use unless the wealth is being created which yields satisfaction of wants.

(*d*) **A standard for deferred payments.** Money is a useful unit of account, and accounts are records of debts to businesses. It follows that the money system provides a standard for deferred payments, enabling us to record debts and eventually collect them either in one payment or in a series of payments on the instalment method. It is important here, however, that the value of money is stable over reasonably lengthy periods of time.

(*e*) **One-way payments.** Some payments are not made in exchange for goods or services directly enjoyed. The benefits of peaceful existence, freedom from riot and civil disturbance are enjoyed in return for one-way payments called taxes, or rates if they are levied locally. Such one-way payments are inconvenient without a money system. In the Middle Ages the Court of England moved around the country, consuming the taxes in kind levied on the shires of England. As a result the King's Council, the forerunner of Parliament, was sometimes to be found elsewhere than at Westminster, and some famous Acts bear the names of towns where they were enacted. The Provisions of Oxford, 1258, is a well-known example. At the time His Majesty and his entourage were eating the taxed produce of Oxfordshire, which could not be transported conveniently to Westminster.

1.5 Recent Developments in the Concept of Money

Until the eighteenth century money simply meant coins, struck at the Royal Mint by authority of the Crown. During the eighteenth century there was a great shortage of coins, chiefly because the number of transactions to be financed had increased as agriculture and industry prospered. Gentlemen rode the country in search of shillings to pay their workers; some struck their own 'tokens'; some paid in notes that their bankers had written for them. The reliability of bank-notes was often in doubt; the present 'security' paper used was not available and notes were easy to forge. Even notes from reputable bankers were acceptable only as far as their reputations reached—very few notes were worth their face value all over the country. Although this was later overcome by the Bank Charter Act of 1844, which gave the Bank of England Issue Department the duty of issuing notes in such quantities and such denominations as the country required, there was still one difficulty about the money supply. Since notes were theoretically redeemable in gold, they were not supposed to be issued to a greater amount than the gold available to back them. The Bank Charter Act did permit a small **fiduciary issue** of £14 million. As explained later, a fiduciary issue is one made in good faith in the belief that, at any given moment, a great many notes will actually be out of circulation. They might, for example be in children's money boxes, or in last year's cricket flannels (reported by the dry-cleaning industry to be a major depository for crumpled £1 notes).

The purpose of the fiduciary issue, in a country which is 'on the gold standard', is to bring the notes in circulation up to the full value of the gold in the central bank's vaults, and thus finance the maximum volume of trade. Of course, this idea is really very silly. Gold is a scarce mineral, it has nothing to do with the output of goods and services, and to tie the note issue to the amount of gold is to hamstring the economy by making money scarcer than it needs to be, and therefore making business expansion more difficult. Today, as the Bank Return in Fig. 1.2 shows, the notes in circulation exceed £10 000 million, and none of them is backed with gold. Anyone who wishes to cash in notes may do so, but they can only be exchanged for other Government securities, or an entry in a National Savings Bank account.

In any case, the concept of money has changed again. Coins, and even notes, are inconvenient compared with cheques and other paper instruments. Notes are legal tender to any amount. Consider a customer who arrives at his garage to buy a £6000 car with a suitcase full of £1 notes, or even a pocket full of £20 notes. The garage proprietor not only has to check the money but he also has a security problem to get it to the bank. A cheque will be much better, so long as it is reliable, and it will present no security problems. Notes and coin are now the small change of the money system; the vast majority of accounts are settled by cheque.

In an electronic age, most paper documents are likely to be superseded by the electronic settlement of debts. This envisages not just the present-day use of plastic credit cards such as Barclaycard and Access, but more sophisticated 'on line' access to customers' accounts. Thus a customer in any major store who offers to pay by plastic card would find that the store's electronic till has access to the banking network's computer, and the sum payable will be deducted from the customer's account and acknowledged instantly.

We therefore see that 'money' is not just coins and notes in circulation, but any source of funds open to the citizen for the settlement of debts. Thus all balances in current accounts are 'money', and even balances in deposit accounts are regarded as money though technically they are not available for seven days. Any automatic credit entitlement, such as a sum available on Barclaycard if the customer wishes to use it, is similarly as good as money.

BANK OF ENGLAND

Wednesday the 2nd day of April 1980

ISSUE DEPARTMENT

	£		£
Notes Issed:		Government Debt	11 015 100
In Circulation	10086 487 814	Other Govt. Securities	7678 034 756
In Banking Department	13 512 186	Other Securities	2410 950 144
	10100 000 000		10100 000 000

BANKING DEPARTMENT

	£		£
Capital	14 553 000	Govt. Securities	663 546 810
Public Deposits— Including Exchequer, National Loans Fund, National Debt Commissioners and Dividend Accounts	44 621 613	Advances and Other Accounts	352 160 339
Special Deposits	131 835 000	Premises, Equipment and Other Securities	361 649 038
Bankers Deposits	550 789 203	Notes	13 512 186
Reserves and Other Accounts	649 324 319	Coin	254 762
	1391 123 135		1391 123 135

Dated the 3rd day of April 1980

J.G. DRAKE, Deputy Chief Cashier

Fig. 1.2. The Bank of England Return.

Small wonder the Chancellor finds it difficult to control the money supply—but this takes us ahead of our present story.

1.6 Nineteenth-Century Developments in Banking

If the eighteenth century saw the development of modern banking as an ancillary service to the agricultural and industrial revolutions, the nineteenth century saw the consolidation of the 'country banks' into a nationwide system of branch banking operated by a few major banks. This was a process of amalgamation and absorption which ended the vulnerability of small banks to local business influences. A local bank, serving a particular community, is vulnerable to changes in the local business environment. A depression in mining or textiles or shipbuilding affected everyone in the locality around the mine, mill or shipyard. With everyone in an area withdrawing funds at the same time a local bank could easily come under pressure and find itself in an illiquid position. The solution was to form links with other banks in other areas where different industries predominated, and eventually these links were formalised as amalgamations and absorptions.

The advantages of amalgamations, both with regard to the stability of the banking system and economical operation in other ways, has reduced the number of banks over the years, so that by the 1920s England had only the 'Big Five', and six smaller banks. In recent years further amalgamations have occurred. Two of the 'Big Five', Westminster and National Provincial, merged with Coutts and Co. and District to form the National Westminster Group. Another, Barclays, has merged with Martins; and the remaining three smaller banks, Glyn Mills, National and Williams Deacon's, have formed the National and Commercial Banking Group. Midland and Lloyds are the other big banks. These 11 banks were once called the clearing banks, because together, and in cooperation with the Bank of England, they operated the Bankers' Clearing House. There are now six chief clearing banks, although the clearing facility is made available to other banks.

A Sophisticated Banking System

During the nineteenth and twentieth centuries the UK developed a fully sophisticated banking system. At the top of the banking pyramid is the Bank of England, now a nationalised institution charged with the duty of controlling the banking system, in the national interest. At the grass roots level, with a widespread branch network, are the 'Big Four' commercial banks with a considerable influence over business aspects of the economy.

Two other banks which are beginning to influence the branch banking scene are the Co-operative Bank and the Trustee Savings Bank. The former is an offshoot of the Co-operative Movement, which has a vast network of local shops which can act as 'branches' for a limited range of banking activities. The Trustee Savings Banks began in the early nineteenth century as 'savings' banks. They collected small savings (often in pennies) from the very poorest people, and the 'trustee' then invested the funds at interest, the proceeds being shared among the depositors. This proved to be such a good idea that the Post Office Savings Bank was set up as a rival to the 'trustee' banks in 1861. Later this bank became the National Savings Bank. Meanwhile the 'trustee' banks continued to grow, and finally began to operate proper 'cheque' accounts as distinct from 'savings' accounts, and now offer a full banking service.

Between the Bank of England and the branch banking network are the specialised banking institutions, based chiefly in London but also in all the major regional centres. These include the discount houses, the merchant banks, the foreign banks and the financial institutions which do not merit 'bank' status under the Banking Act, 1979. This Act has only recently come into effect, and the Bank of England has not yet confirmed the status of all institutions. These specialised institutions form a large part of the subject matter of this book and the reader is referred to the index for a full account of them.

1.7 The Importance of Financial Institutions Today

We live in a world where specialisation is the essential source of all our wealth. By specialising in particular trades and services skill of every sort is encouraged and used to advantage. Any reduction in specialisation means a loss to society,

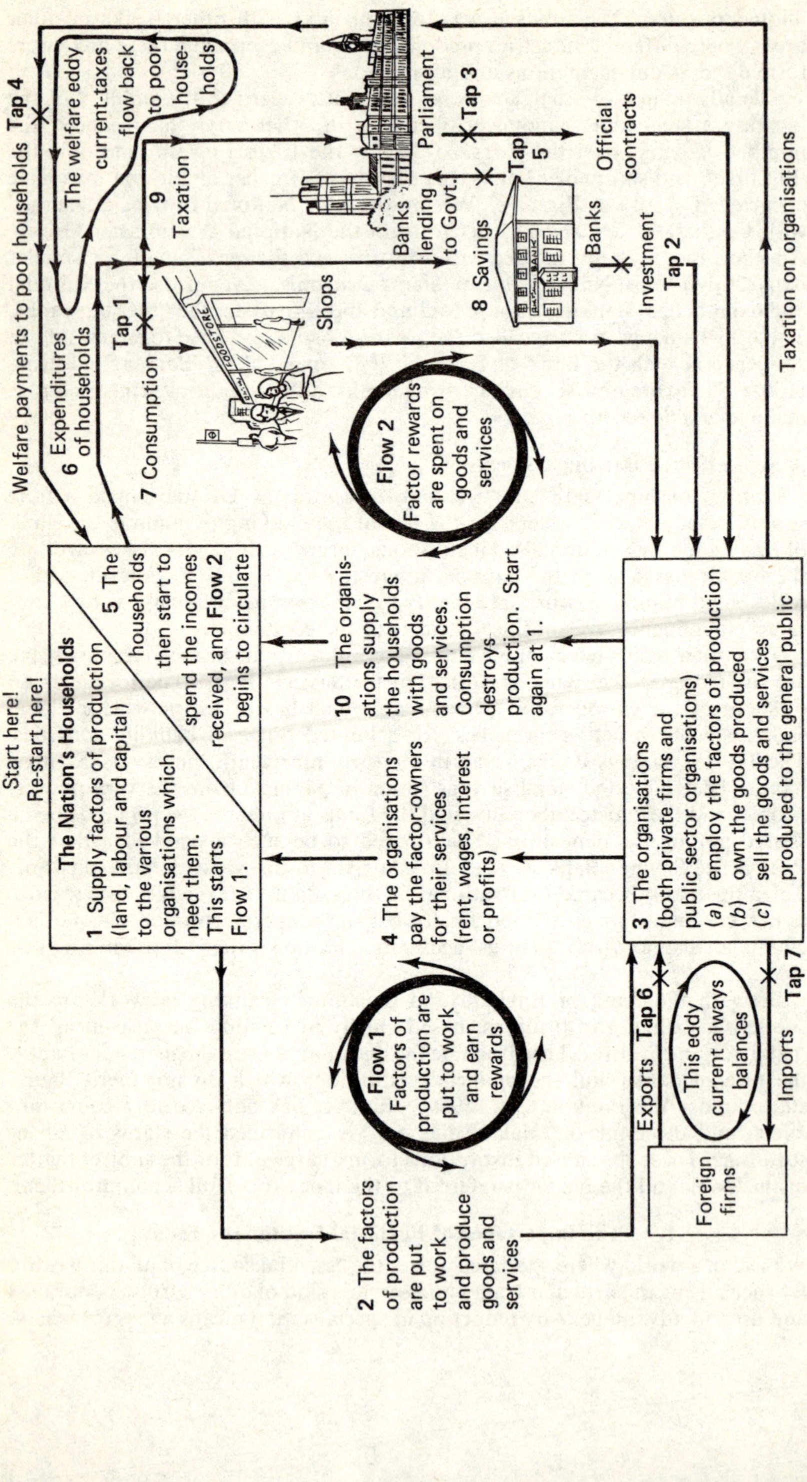
Start here!
Re-start here!
The Nation's Households
1 Supply factors of production (land, labour and capital) to the various organisations which need them. This starts Flow 1.
5 The households then start to spend the incomes received, and Flow 2 begins to circulate
Flow 1
Factors of production are put to work and earn rewards
2 The factors of production are put to work and produce goods and services
4 The organisations pay the factor-owners for their services (rent, wages, interest or profits)
10 The organisations supply the households with goods and services. Consumption destroys production. Start again at 1.
Flow 2
Factor rewards are spent on goods and services
3 The organisations (both private firms and public sector organisations)
(a) employ the factors of production
(b) own the goods produced
(c) sell the goods and services produced to the general public
Foreign firms
Exports
Tap 6
This eddy current always balances
Imports
Tap 7
Welfare payments to poor households
Tap 4
6 Expenditures of households
The welfare eddy current-taxes flow back to poor house-holds
7 Consumption
Tap 1
9 Taxation
Shops
FOODSTORE
Banks lending to Govt.
Parliament
Tap 3
Tap 5
8 Savings
BANK
Banks
Investment
Tap 2
Official contracts
Taxation on organisations

Fig. 1.3. How the mixed economy works.

Notes

(i) The first flow is of factor services into production and the payment of rewards to the factors, in the form of rent, wages, interest or profits.

(ii) Everything the firms receive in one period is paid out in the next period—either as rent, wages, interest or profits—but there is also a very large flow of taxation to the government which is used to finance the public sector services like defence, education, etc. In the first period these payments to factors must come from the capital provided by those who start the firms up. In later periods the funds come from the sales of goods and services produced in the previous period.

(iii) The second flow is the expenditure of income on goods and services. The owners of the factors spend the incomes they receive. The incomes flow through a number of taps, which influence the level of activity in the economy. If a tap is closed off for some reason activity in the economy declines (a slump). If taps are opened wide activity in the economy increases (a boom). Let us look at each tap in turn.

(iv) **Tap 1:** Consumption. If the nation's households are spending a great deal on consumer goods and services, business will be booming. If householders are pessimistic about the future and only buying essentials, Tap 1 will be partially closed and the economy will slump.

(v) **Tap 2:** The Savings-Investment Tap. If savings are high consumption will be low (Tap 1 almost closed). This will not matter if the savings are borrowed by businessmen (or by the government through Tap 5 for the public-sector borrowing requirement—PSBR). An open Tap 2 means strong investment and the economy will keep booming along.

(vi) **Tap 3** and **Tap 4:** These taps are controlled by the government. Tap 4 (welfare payments) allows tax money to flow back to poor families so that they can consume goods and services. This opens up Tap 1 and keeps the economy booming. Tap 3 allows more official contracts for all sorts of things (defence, education, health services, highways, etc.) to be placed. This gives employment to unemployed people and keeps the economy booming. If taxes are not sufficient to pay for these contracts the government borrows through Tap 5 the money that pessimistic householders are saving for a 'rainy day' when they might lose their jobs. The government contracts ensure that the 'rainy day' never comes.

(vii) Foreign trade always balances (the balance of payments) but sometimes it is a bit more difficult than others. The government does a good deal of manipulating to keep this balance right, and sometimes has to call in the International Monetary Fund to overcome a difficult period. Temporarily, it is possible for Taps 6 and 7 to affect the working of the economy. A wide-open Tap 6 gives an export-led boom (funds flowing in to UK firms). A wide-open Tap 7 gives an import-led slump (funds flowing out to foreign firms, leaving UK firms starved of orders). However, as explained above, neither of these situations can continue indefinitely. A 'balance of payments' has to be achieved. At present we are using floating exchange rates to induce a balance.

even if it benefits individuals. Finance is a service, and operates in every field of our daily struggles to create consumer goods. It provides the capital for our enterprises, collecting funds from those who do not wish to claim their full share of consumption goods at present (the savers) and making them available to those who wish to spend more funds than they have at present (the borrowers). Some of the borrowers are of course mere consumers who are borrowing to buy consumer goods and services, but the more significant group are those borrowing to set up or expand businesses, and thus create wealth for the nation.

In a sophisticated economic society financial affairs are infinitely varied and intricate. Some want money overnight, and others want a lifetime to repay. Some want to buy from the far corners of the earth and others from their local shop. Some pay in cash, some by cheque, some by credit card and some by instalments. Some institutions never deal in sums less than £10 000, and others are happy to collect halfpence. To meet these varied situations all sorts of specialist institutions have arisen—commercial banks, building societies, discount houses, merchant banks, the Post Office Giro, finance houses and moneylenders. These will carry on their specialised activities to collect funds, arrange payments both at home and abroad, loan funds and collect repayments, support sound enterprises and bring an end to unsound ones before the damage is irretrievable, or more extensive than it need be.

The whole framework of our society is financial. Not only does the wealth we create depend upon the availability of finance (the capitalist part of our mixed economy) but the distribution of that wealth is arranged through the money system. All the wealth created is distributed as rent, wages, interest or profits to those who helped provide it, the landlords, workers, investors and risk-takers. It is then subject to tax in such a way that a wide variety of social programmes can be supported. These include welfare programmes, education, health, defence, etc. (the socialist part of our mixed economy). In all these arrangements the financial institutions are playing their part, and their influence extends down to the grass roots of our society. This framework is shown in Fig. 1.3, and described in the notes below it.

1.8 Revision Test

Answers	*Questions*
—	**1.** What are the essential features of money?
1. (*a*) General acceptability, (*b*) durability, (*c*) difficult to imitate, (*d*) portability, (*e*) divisibility.	**2.** What are the functions of money?
2. To act as (*a*) a medium of exchange, (*b*) a measure of value, (*c*) a store of value, (*d*) a standard for deferred payments, (*e*) a means of settling one-way payments like taxes.	**3.** How did banking begin?
3. As a safeguarding of valuables.	**4.** What developed from this?

Answers	Questions
4. The cheque system of ordering the banker to pay money.	**5.** What is a cheque?
5. An order to a banker to pay money on demand. (The actual definition given in the Bills of Exchange Act, 1882, is: 'A cheque is a bill of exchange, drawn on a banker, payable on demand'.)	**6.** What gave rise to the idea that banks could safely lend money?
6. Experience showed that only 8 per cent of deposits were actually withdrawn.	**7.** What did this mean as far as loans were concerned?
7. That the unused portion of any deposit could be regarded as the cash ratio for a loan made to a suitably reputable borrower.	**8.** How did a loan to a borrower C return to the bank?
8. (*a*) As a deposit from D, the person with whom the borrower spent the money. (*b*) Eventually as a series of repayments with interest.	**9.** The Bank of England's note issue is entirely fiduciary. What does this mean?
9. It means that it is made in good faith, but is not backed by gold in the vaults.	**10.** Name the major financial institutions.
10. (*a*) The Bank of England, (*b*) the commercial banks, (*c*) the discount houses, (*d*) the merchant banks, (*e*) foreign banks, (*f*) the building societies, (*g*) the finance houses.	**11.** Go over the page again until you are sure of the answers. Then try the questions in Appendix 1.

2

CENTRAL BANKS

2.1 The Nature of Central Banks

Every sophisticated economy needs a developed money system and a variety of banking institutions to meet the requirements of industrial and commercial firms, local and central Government and private citizens. Such a system cannot develop overnight, and inevitably the growth has been pragmatic, meeting needs as they arise. At some point Government interest in finance develops a special relationship with a particular bank, or consortium, the Government receiving financial assistance in return for special privileges—such as a monopoly of the note issue. The Central Bank is born, and it develops to hold an influential position at the hub of domestic banking activity. Its chief functions are:

(*a*) To act as banker to the Government.
(*b*) To act as banker to the other banking institutions.
(*c*) To act as a national representative in the international banking fraternity, and as an international representative of that fraternity in advising its own domestic government.

A wide range of other functions may be performed, but they will vary from one central bank to another.

The status of central banks differs. Each is a development of national needs which has perhaps grown up over a long period of time, or has been deliberately created by an Act of the legislature at a particular moment—after a revolution, or a major financial catastrophe. The formal status of each can only be understood with reference to the constitutional arrangements of the state concerned. Since it is difficult to discuss the exact functions of a central bank in abstract terms we shall consider the Bank of England as a typical example, but the reader should bear in mind that each central bank will be operating within its own national system, to meet national needs within an international framework. Their functions will differ to suit their own national requirements, stage of development, etc., and will reflect Government views on the development of the national economy in every case. They will also change from time to time as the economy develops, to meet new difficulties or take advantage of opportunities as they arise.

2.2 The Bank of England—Its Origin and Organisation

The Bank of England was founded in 1694, to lend £1 200 000 to the Government. It was given a monopoly of joint-stock banking and the privilege of limited liability. It became the Government's bank. It was at this time not a nationalised institution but a private bank which wielded great influence because of its close relationship with the Treasury. Just over a century later Sheridan, the dramatist, described the Bank as 'an elderly lady in the City, of great credit and long standing'. Possibly this description of the Bank led James Gillray, a cartoonist of the day, to depict the Bank in a famous cartoon called 'The Old Lady of Threadneedle Street in danger.' It showed the Prime Minister, Pitt, attacking the Bank to obtain money for the Napoleonic Wars. The old lady was putting up a spirited resistance. The nickname stuck, and has been in popular use ever since.

A century and a half after its foundation, the Bank Charter Act of 1844 reorganised the Bank of England, splitting it into two parts: the Banking Department and the Issue Department. The Banking Department dealt with banking operations as they affected the Government, the commercial banks, the money market and the few private firms who banked with the Bank of England. The Issue Department was charged with seeing that bank-notes were issued as required by the public within the limits set by the gold reserves and a small fiduciary issue of £14 million.

So long as Britain kept on the gold standard the statement on a note 'I promise to pay the bearer on demand the sum of *x* pounds' meant that the customer who preferred to have gold could have it. Today the promise refers only to credit in the form of other notes and coin, or an entry in a bank account.

Today the Bank of England is a nationalised institution. The Bank of England Act, 1946, gave the Bank the status of an autonomous nationalised corporation, though its independence in running its internal affairs cannot alter the fact that it is the chief weapon of Government in controlling the financial institutions and the monetary affairs of the nation. In other countries, for example the United States, the central bank is regarded as part of the 'separation of powers'. The doctrine of the 'separation of powers' holds that in a free society it is desirable that certain powerful forces should act as checks and balances on one another. Thus the legislature, the administration and the judiciary are separate powers in the UK, each exerting a measure of control over the others. Although the Bank of England before 1946 probably exerted a strong influence on Governments, restraining them from excessive use of the printing press to finance their programmes, this function did not amount to a formal constitutional role. Indeed the Bank's restrictive economic policies of the inter-war years may have been a major cause of the continuing depression, which led to its nationalisation as the means of bringing about Governmental control of the finances of the nation. The 'managed prosperity' of the 25 years which followed the 1946 Act certainly seemed a very satisfactory period to many who advocated the policy of nationalisation. Probably the truth is that the Bank still exerts a powerful influence over the more unwise proposals of Governments, whatever the persuasion of the Government of the day, so that its role as a moderating influence has not been completely abandoned.

The Act of 1946 makes it clear that the Treasury (after consultation with the Governor of the Bank) may give the Bank such **directions** as it considers necessary in the public interest. The Bank may then **make recommendations** to the other banking institutions, and if these are not complied with it may issue **directives** to them. In fact no formal directives have ever been issued. Whatever the recommendations made by the Bank the financial institutions have done their best to cooperate, though the pace of events has sometimes revealed that the recommendations were unwise and needed adjustment if they were to achieve the original aims.

The organisation of the Bank is illustrated in Figs. 2.1 and 2.2, and the functions of the Court of Directors and the Chief officers are explained in the notes below these illustrations.

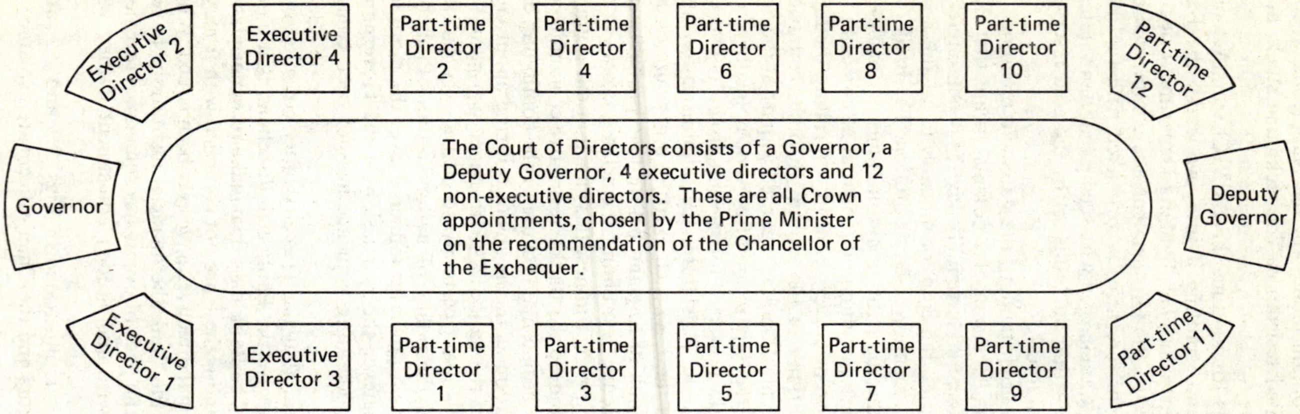

Fig. 2.1. The Court of Directors of the Bank of England.

Notes

(i) Members must be British subjects.
(ii) Members of Parliament, Ministers and civil servants are not eligible for appointment.
(iii) The Governor and Deputy Governor are appointed for five-year terms, and are eligible for reappointment in these, or some other capacities.
(iv) Not more than four executive directors may be appointed.
(v) All directors retire in rotation, and serve for four-year terms. They are also eligible for reappointment.
(vi) The Court must meet at least once a week, usually on a Thursday.
(vii) The principal standing committee is the Committee of Treasury. It consists of the Governor, the Deputy Governor and five members elected by ballot from among the Court.
(viii) All other committees report to the Committee of Treasury, and the Committee of Treasury reports to the Court.
(ix) To assist the work of the Court, in view of the charter's limit of four executive directors, posts of Associate Director and Assistant Director have been created. They carry out work in particular fields with a status equivalent to directors, but they cannot be members of the Court.

2.3 The Functions of the Bank of England

The Bank of England, as the central bank of the UK, fulfils a very wide range of functions. The Bank acts as adviser to the Government on economic and financial matters and on behalf of the Government executes its monetary policy. It has a specific responsibility under the Banking Act, 1979, for watching over the good order of the financial system as a whole. It acts as a banker to the Government and it is responsible for the note issue. It also acts as banker to all the major banking institutions.

What the Bank does is essential to the economic well-being of the nation, and even though many of its activities are routine, subtle influences can be exerted to shift the emphasis if monetary policies alter. Listing the bank's activities we find them to fall under five main headings. These are:

(*a*) The Bank's influence on monetary policy.
(*b*) Its operations in the markets.
(*c*) Its role as a banker.
(*d*) Its regulatory role.
(*e*) Its international role.

We must now consider each of these roles in turn.

(*a*) **The Bank's Influence on Monetary Policy.**

Any banker is prepared to give financial advice to his customers, and the Bank of England is banker to the Government. Since Government chiefly works through financial activities, making funds available for particular purposes, starving other areas of resources where it deems them undesirable, taxing incomes from the citizens' pockets, etc., it is clear that most Government activities have financial implications. Since the sums are so vast they must also have a profound effect on the entire nation. For better or worse, since 1945 the 'management of prosperity' has been a major concern of Governments, and if the limits of expansion appeared to have been reached in the 1970s this does not make the 'management' any less necessary. Every small shopkeeper knows that the most serious time for managing a business is when there are signs of 'overtrading'.

In offering financial advice it is essential to have a firm basis of observed data, and conclusions from a variety of research projects. These days computer simulations (economic models) can be set up which reflect the known data and simulate the effect of various policies upon the economy. The Bank has expanded its Economic Intelligence Department in recent years to enable it to give sound advice to the Treasury. Policy-making in the past has had to be rather unscientific in that control experiments cannot be set up in the real world. We cannot raise the taxes of half the nation and let the other half act as controls, so that the effects can be compared. With computer modelling, provided the model is carefully prepared, we can try out alternative policies, or even the entire range of possible policies, and see which produces the 'best' results. There are still arguments about the definition we should give to 'best', but there is much to be learned from such projects.

(*b*) **The Bank's Operations in the Markets**

In a mixed economy such as that of the UK many of the nation's activities

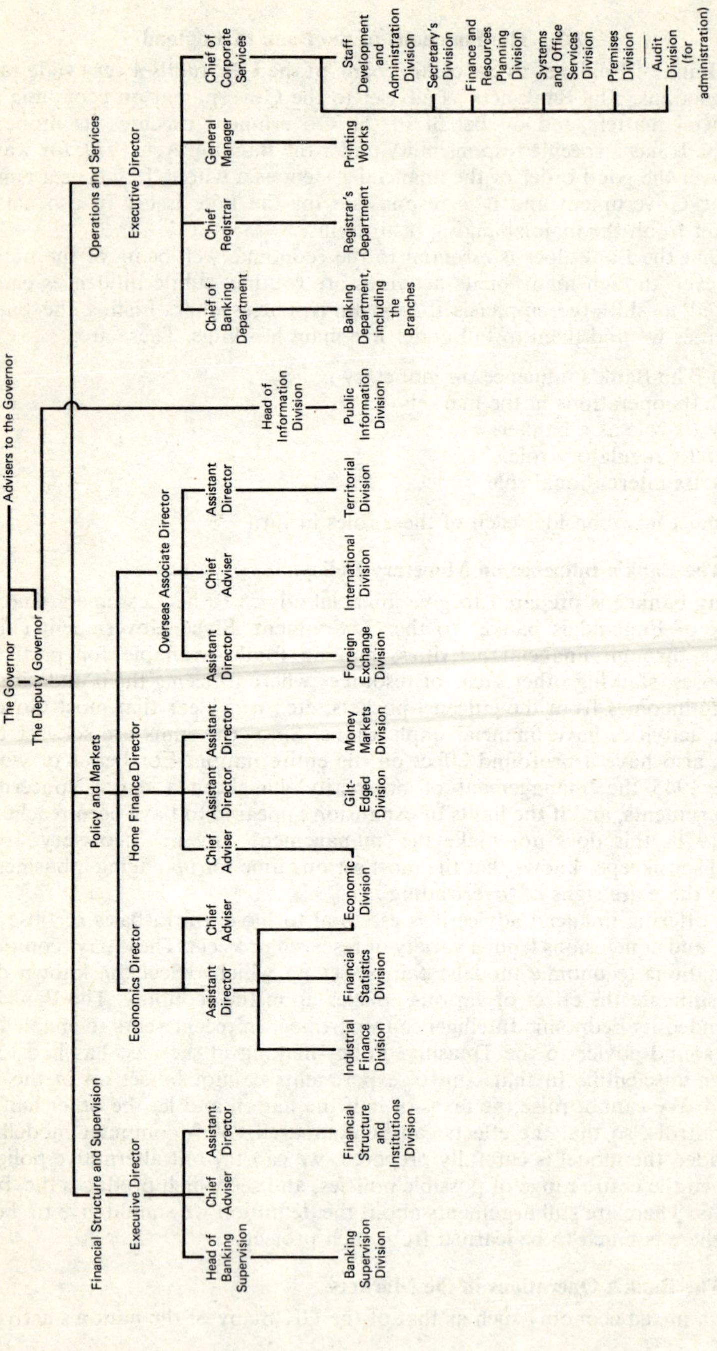
The Governor
The Deputy Governor
Advisers to the Governor
Financial Structure and Supervision
Executive Director
Head of Banking Supervision
Chief Adviser
Assistant Director
Banking Supervision Division
Financial Structure and Institutions Division
Policy and Markets
Economics Director
Assistant Director
Chief Adviser
Industrial Finance Division
Financial Statistics Division
Economic Division
Home Finance Director
Chief Adviser
Assistant Director
Assistant Director
Assistant Director
Gilt-Edged Division
Money Markets Division
Overseas Associate Director
Assistant Director
Chief Adviser
Assistant Director
Foreign Exchange Division
International Division
Territorial Division
Head of Information Division
Public Information Division
Operations and Services
Executive Director
Chief of Banking Department
Chief Registrar
General Manager
Chief of Corporate Services
Banking Department, including the Branches
Registrar's Department
Printing Works
Staff Development and Administration Division
Secretary's Division
Finance and Resources Planning Division
Systems and Office Services Division
Premises Division
Audit Division (for administration)

Fig. 2.2. The Organisation of the Bank of England (March 1980).
(*Reproduced by courtesy of the Bank of England*).

Notes

(i) Since March 1, 1980, the Bank is divided into three areas: (*a*) Policy and Markets, (*b*) Financial Structure and Supervision, (*c*) Operations and Services.

(ii) *Policy and Markets*. This area is concerned with overseas and domestic monetary policy, the associated market operations and research. It has the following divisions:

(*a*) The Industrial Finance Division: responsible for liaison with industrial and commercial companies and for monitoring the various sources of finance available to them.

(*b*) The Financial Statistics Division: collects and aggregates information from banks, discount houses and certain other financial institutions, and assembles, analyses and comments on a wide range of financial statistics—for instance on monetary aggregates, government financing and capital markets—for users inside and outside the Bank.

(*c*) The Economics Division: analyses developments in the UK economy with the object of informing, and formulating advice to the Government, particularly in the area of domestic monetary policy and external policy.

(*d*) The Gilt-Edged Division: concerned with all operations in the gilt-edged market and with other long-term borrowing operations, including borrowing in foreign currencies.

(*e*) Money Markets Division: responsible for the Bank's daily operations in and lending to the discount market, for day-to-day liaison with the discount market and the treasurers of the clearing banks and for general oversight of the short-term markets in sterling.

(*f*) Foreign Exchange Division: chiefly responsible for the operation of the Exchange Equalisation Account (EEA), the management of the UK's reserves (including gold) and the implementation of policies with respect to these two. Foreign exchange dealings are also transacted on behalf of the Bank's customers, which include Government Departments, nationalised bodies and other central banks.

(*g*) A Territorial Division.

(*h*) An International Division: these divisions (*f*, *g* and *h*) monitor developments overseas, maintaining a continuous review of economic and financial conditions abroad. They also maintain close contact with other central banks and international institutions abroad.

This area also includes the Information Division who, working direct to the Deputy Governor, deal with all matters affecting the Bank's relationships with the press and with the general public.

The Policy and Market area as a whole is co-ordinated by the Deputy Governor, assisted by the Home Finance Director, the Economic Director and the Overseas Associated Director.

(iii) *Financial Structure and Supervision*

(*a*) Banking Supervision Division: responsible for the supervision of the UK banking system. This has traditionally been based upon a close and continuous relationship between staff of the Division and senior management of the individual commercial banks. This responsibility is now exercised within the formal framework of the Banking Act, 1979.

(*b*) Financial Structure and Institutions Division: maintains relations with the securities markets, Council for the Securities Industry and the City Liaison Committee. It also exercises surveillance of the commodity markets. This division keeps itself informed about, and, where appropriate, takes an active interest in new developments and techniques in banking, clearing and transfer of funds.

(iv) *Operations and Services*

(*a*) Banking Department. This department undertakes the normal banking business for customers, including the Government and overseas central banks. It is responsible for the acceptance or delivery of stock or bills resulting from the Bank's market operations and settlement for them. The Department accounts for the Bank's operations on behalf of the EEA in gold, foreign exchange and foreign investments. It is responsible for the supply of notes to the commercial banks and for the withdrawal of used notes. This department keeps records of customers' securities and carries out customers' instructions for their purchase and sale as well as handling transfers of Government stocks for the National Debt Office. With this Department are also the eight branches of the Bank. As well as providing banking services for public and private customers, the Agents in charge of the branches maintain contact with the business community in their area and help to provide an up-to-date assessment of the state of affairs in the main industrial centres.

(*b*) Registrar's Department. This department performs the registrar function of the Bank, maintaining registers of Government and other stocks, making interest and dividend payments and repaying stocks at maturity.

(*c*) The Printing Works. The Printing Works is responsible for printing bank-notes and for their examination and destruction as they are withdrawn from circulation. The Printing Works does a limited amount of security printing (e.g. stock certificates and treasury bills).

(*d*) Corporate Service Department. This Department is responsible for staff matters and provides physical and support services to the Bank, including computer services, property management, maintenance of the Bank premises other than those of the Printing Works, the accounts of the Issue and Banking Department and the provision of secretarial services to the Governors and Directors.

are free-enterprise in nature, where businessmen are seeking to produce goods and services at the least cost to themselves; supplying their customers at the price that the market will bear, they achieve a profit (it is hoped) which is the reward for their labours. In seeking to implement Government policies in such a free-enterprise system, the Bank of England must operate in the various financial markets, influencing them in the desired direction, whatever it may be. Each of these markets is the subject of fuller discussion later in this book, and the following brief accounts cannot explain the Bank's activities fully.

Minimum Lending Rate. First, the Bank can influence the whole money market by changes in Minimum Lending Rate (MLR). This is the UK term for what is called by other central banks the **Discount Rate** or **Bank Rate**. Although regular postings of MLR were discontinued on August 5, 1981, the Bank of England reserved the right to use MLR if it was not satisfied with the levels of interest rates generally. In fact, within a few weeks it had been forced to intervene. Clearly MLR is not yet dead.

MLR is the minimum rate at which a central bank will lend to banking institutions should they get into an illiquid position. In the UK the assistance is provided via the discount houses, which are almost always the institutions that get into illiquid positions (see 'The Bill Market' below). Other central banks may loan funds directly to any bank that is in difficulties. Obviously its position as **'lender of last resort'** gives any central bank a very powerful influence over other banks, not only because of the rate of interest it can charge but also by the administrative arrangements it makes to help banks—for example the frequency with which they may call for assistance and the security to be taken for any loans made, etc.

As far as the rate of interest goes an increase in MLR raises interest rates for all other purposes. Thus a bank which, if it gets into difficulties, will need to borrow from the central bank at 17 per cent is not going to lend to its customers at less than 17 per cent unless it has a very sure source of cheaper finance which it knows will not fail it. Advances to customers tend to be made at a rate of 2–5 per cent above MLR, but this does not entirely rule out cheaper rates to some (very safe) classes of customer. A rise in interest rates to ordinary borrowers, to users of credit cards, to hire purchase customers, etc., is going to choke off many marginal projects (the least profitable ones). As a result some of the excess demand in the overheated economy will fall away.

Other ways of influencing bank lending are the **Special Deposit** and **Supplementary Special Deposit (Corset)** arrangements when these are in use. Special deposits are called for from the banks to reduce the cash available to them. The funds are deposited at the central bank (and may earn a rate of interest) but reduce the cash base available to the bank for making loans. The system is explained more fully later (see Section 11.2). Supplementary Special Deposits are a similar type of control, but are used when a bank is seen to be lending aggressively to increase its share of the loan market. In stepping outside any guidelines issued by the central bank to restrain the creation of credit, such a bank invites punishment. This takes the form of supplementary deposits which are called for on an increasing scale, according to the severity of the breach of behaviour. This squeezes the bank's cash assets more and more tightly (hence the term 'corset') and forces the erring bank to behave more sensibly.

The term 'money market' used above is a general term for the whole cross-section of institutions which supply capital or demand funds for business or domestic uses. There is no actual market in the same way that there is a Stock Exchange, or a Metal Exchange or a Corn Exchange. The market exists in a thousand banking premises of every sort, where dealers sit—with their personal switchboards at the ready—ringing around the world for money. There is no time to ask a switchboard operator to get you a number when the million pounds you need may be snapped up by another institution. However, some parts of the money market are carried on by a more limited number of institutions, though still their bargains are largely struck over the telephone. Such a market is the 'bill market'.

The 'Bill market'. Bill-brokers are people who take money from those who have a surplus temporarily available, and lend it to others who are in need of finance. They are members of the London Discount Market Association, and are collectively called 'discount houses', but some merchant bankers and other banks have money-trading departments. Those who borrow money in the discount market do so because it is cheaper than borrowing from a bank or in other ways. On the day this paragraph was written, the MLR was 17 per cent, the clearing banks' base rates were 17 per cent and most loans would be 2–5 per cent over that—say on average about 20 per cent. At such times the discount houses would be offering to buy trade bills at about 16 per cent or even less, so that borrowing from them is cheaper than borrowing from the banks; the discount they charge is less than ordinary interest rates. They are able to do this because they are borrowing the money even more cheaply from commercial banks, who are happy to lend to the discount houses 'at call or short notice'. This means that the money can be recalled by the bank at any time (at call) or within 2–7 days (short notice). The banks are happy to do this because any money thus loaned is entitled to be counted as 'secured money'—see p. 159; in other words, it is regarded as immediately available to the banks should they need it to meet the claims of customers. When banks keep cash available for customers' needs they cannot of course earn any interest on it. By lending 'at call or short notice' to the discount houses they can earn a useful rate of interest without having to bother about any loss of liquidity. How this money can be immediately available to the banks when the discount houses have lent it out to businessmen is a little difficult to understand. The discount houses are borrowing 'short' and lending 'long', the classic recipe for bankruptcy. It stands to reason that they must at times get into difficulties, with the banks calling back 'call money' which the discount houses cannot supply. To overcome the difficulty they must turn to the Bank of England which will act as 'lender of last resort' to any member of the Association that is in difficulties. This means it will lend the discount house money—but on its own terms—and this is the source of the Bank's powers in the bill market, as explained below.

Besides businessmen seeking to borrow money on 'trade bills' (bills of exchange floated to obtain finance for trading purposes), the Government is also borrowing money to meet its daily needs. Tax income may not arrive evenly, or be balanced with expenses, and any shortfall is borrowed on the bill market by issuing **treasury bills**. The discount houses have agreed to tender for the entire issue of treasury bills, which is made each Friday. They are thus committed to finding the funds the Government needs—and may even be put under pressure by the Bank of England which can always keep the market short of funds if it wishes to do so, by increasing the number of treasury bills issued. The result is that if the discount houses are being too generous with their loans (interest rates too low), and get into difficulties, the Bank of England can show its displeasure by charging a 'penal rate' when it acts as 'lender of last resort', or interferes covertly in the market. This will displease the discount houses, who have already loaned the money out at less than this rate. The next day they will push up their prices to borrowers, and some of the heat will be taken out of the economy as marginal projects are choked off because of the higher rates of interest. In this way Government policies can be implemented through the Bank of England's influence over the short-term money market.

The Gilt-Edged Market. The term 'gilt-edged' has no special significance today—it comes from the fact that in former times the issue of these Government stocks was officially recorded in a book which had gilt edges. The gilt-edged market is an active market in Government stocks. The sale of these stocks is used to finance the long-term borrowing of Government departments and nationalised industries. The 'trustee status' of such stocks assists the market in maintaining active interest in gilt-edged securities. The main object of the Bank's activities here is to promote the sale of long-term stock and keep the market healthy so that this type of long-term loan will always be available to the Government.

All purchases and sales are made through the Government Broker and are largely authorised by the Issue Department. From time to time the Bank's portfolio is restored by new issues of stock. Most of these new issues cannot be sold at once to the general public but are taken up by the Issue Department. Funding is a chief aim of the Issue Department. This may be defined as persuading citizens and institutions to lend money on a long-term basis (creating a fund) instead of only for a short term. If people lend for a short term they may spend the money when it returns to them in a few months, instead of reinvesting it. In times of inflation, when it is desirable to reduce demand, this extra spending will only aggravate the economy's problems.

While the Bank of England is active in the gilt-edged market all the time for a variety of reasons, its activities can be varied to assist the implementation of Government policies. The day-to-day activities include:

(i) The issue of new stocks as and when required to provide investors with a steady source of securities.

(ii) The purchase of stocks that are about due for redemption.

The easy way, and the economical way, for the Bank to redeem stock that is coming near to its redemption date is to buy it up on the market at the best price possible (i.e. whenever it is cheap), and thus leave only the minimum amount in the hands of investors who will need to be dealt with when redemption day arrives.

Where the Bank decides to engage in open-market operations for reasons other than (i) and (ii) above it does so in order to influence the liquidity of the commercial banks, and force them to pursue credit policies in line with Government policy. Open-market operations involve the sale or purchase of Government securities on the open market. Suppose the Government Broker sells gilt-edged securities from the Issue Department portfolio to the general public through the Stock Exchange. The buyers of these securities will pay by cheques drawn on their current accounts. This will reduce the balances deposited with the Bank of England by the commercial banks, which are part of each commercial bank's reserve ratio. There is a loss of liquidity by the banks and a consequent reduction in the loans they can make. Because the cash lost has been acting as the reserve ratio for a much larger volume of deposits, they will have to reduce loans by about three times the amount of the loss in cash. Such a credit policy would reduce inflationary pressure by reducing the amount of money consumers could obtain.

If, on the other hand, business is bad and unemployment is spreading the Bank can encourage a return to prosperity by buying Government securities on the open market. If the Government Broker buys gilt-edged securities and pays cash for them, the sellers of the securities will receive cheques from the Treasury to bank in their ordinary accounts. These increased cash deposits will encourage the bankers to go ahead with loans to businessmen wishing to expand, or private people wishing to buy cars, houses, washing machines and television sets, etc. The increased business activity resulting from this more liberal credit policy will lead to a reduction in unemployment and a return to more prosperous times.

The Foreign Exchange Market. The Bank of England was formerly very interested in everything that happened in the foreign exchange market, since for 40 years, from 1939 to 1979, all foreign exchange movements were subject to **exchange control**. There were five offices under the Chief of Exchange Control, which have been rendered obsolete by the ending of the regulations. At the same time the Bank still has an important part to play in the foreign exchange market because of the need to 'manage' the pound.

The system of fixed exchange rates which operated, with a few interruptions, from the Bretton Woods Conference in 1944 until the final breakdown in 1973, was replaced in that year by 'floating'. Floating exchange rates are the rates which are found day by day as a currency rises or falls with the prevailing economic tides. It must clearly be a very uncertain system, since contracts made at one given date may be due for settlement at a later date when the exchange rate is different. Such uncertainties are almost always harmful to trade, and business confidence depends upon some sort of stability being reached, even in a 'floating' system. We may therefore say that a fully developed 'floating' system requires that central banks, while not defending any particular value for currencies, will seek to influence their currencies in such a way as to preserve reasonable stability.

The International Monetary Fund amended its charter in 1978 to take account of the difficulties of a 'floating currency' situation by laying down certain guidelines to the policies that members should pursue. The general idea is that member nations agree to avoid 'beggar my neighbour' policies, by agreeing not to manipulate their currencies in such a way as to impose burdens on foreign trading partners for the benefit of home producers. Thus a central bank seeking to interfere on the foreign exchange market to support its own currency, or prevent it rising too much in value, would be limited in its actions by the need to conform with the amended charter.

For those not familiar with the general idea of 'managing the exchange rate' a word of explanation will be helpful. The process began in the period 1931–39 when floating exchange rates were used for the first time. The difficulty was to combat the activities of speculators, who were influencing the exchange rate for the purpose of making a quick profit—whereas the whole idea of a 'floating' currency is that it should float to a position which reflected the trading position of the nation. Thus if the demand for British goods by foreigners was small, while UK citizens were keen to buy foreign goods, the pound would float down in value, as there would be more pounds being offered on the foreign exchange market than foreigners were willing to take up. As the pound got cheaper UK goods would be better value for money and foreigners would increase their demand for them, while foreign goods would become more expensive and this would choke off the UK's demand for imports.

This 'floating to a fair value' would be hopelessly upset if speculators started to interfere with the market by selling pounds to force the price down, or buying pounds to force the price up. This is because since speculators often sell pounds they have not got, with the intention of buying them back later at a cheaper price, or buy pounds they do not want in the hope of selling them later at a profit when the price has risen, their activities adversely affect genuine traders. The solution was found by setting up a large **Exchange Equalisation Fund**, which can be used to defeat the speculators. A speculator selling pounds is given dollars, francs or whatever he wants out of the Fund, and the selling pressure is absorbed by the Fund. When he eventually decides he does need sterling again, the sterling he buys is provided by the Fund, and he will have to pay the same price, or perhaps even a higher price for it. This is called 'burning the speculator's fingers', and will deter him from dealing in 'hot' money. ('Hot' money is money flowing into, or out of, a particular currency for non-trading purposes.)

This system of managing the rate of exchange was very adaptable, because the managers of the Fund did not need to use it if the depreciation that was taking place was not a speculative one, but was the result of a genuine imbalance of payments. By refusing to buy pounds in these circumstances they could let the exchange rate depreciate to what they judged to be its true level.

The success of this Exchange Equalisation Fund led to the adoption of the same idea at the Bretton Woods Conference. The **International Monetary Fund** is exactly this kind of fund, which could be used during the 'fixed exchange rate' system set up at Bretton Woods to defeat speculators acting against a particular currency.

Today the actions of central banks under a 'floating exchange rate' system are less dramatic than in the days of speculative pressure under the Bretton Woods System, when on occasions as much as £2500 million moved through the market in a single day. The Bank of England may act on the foreign exchange market to support sterling if it is falling, or to prevent it rising more than the Bank feels to be justified by the UK's trading position, but it will not manipulate the market so as to impose 'unfair' burdens on foreign trading partners, because this would be in breach of the IMF charter. Today the Exchange Equalisation Account holds the country's reserves in the form of gold, foreign currency and Special Drawing Rights issued by the IMF. **Special Drawing Rights** are a new type of international reserve holding. At present they are not extensively used, but it is hoped they will develop as the international monetary system develops (see p. 184 for further details).

In recent years the Bank has been involved in facilitating public sector borrowing from the private sector overseas. Major use has been made over the past three years of a scheme to encourage public sector borrowing abroad with, where necessary, exchange losses being covered by the Exchange Equalisation Account.

The Bank bears responsibility for relations with other monetary authorities and participates in the work of certain international financial institutions, such as the Bank for International Settlements, the International Monetary Fund and the Organisation for Economic Cooperation and Development. With the UK's accession to the EEC the Bank has had a close and active involvement in Community affairs, including operations arising out of UK membership connected with the European Monetary System. The Bank has taken its place in the Committee of EEC Central Bank Governors, the Board of Governors of the European Monetary Cooperation Fund and, alongside Government, in meetings of the Council of Ministers (Finance). Bank representatives serve on the Monetary Committee, the Economic Policy Committee and a number of other specialist groups.

(*c*) The Bank's Role as Banker

The Bank of England is the Government's bank, and as such it must keep accounts for its customer. The chief account is the **Exchequer Account** to which all Government receipts are credited and from which all Government payments are debited.

In the year 1980 the receipts of the Government, including the National Insurance Fund, totalled £90 785 million. Its expenditure totalled £103 720 million, leaving a deficit over-all of £12 935 million. These enormous sums of money pass through the banking system in myriad different ways. The Bank of England has only a few branches—at Birmingham, Bristol, Leeds, Liverpool, Manchester, Newcastle, Southampton and a small branch near the Law Courts in London. Consequently, much of the Government revenues collected are banked in ordinary commercial accounts with the 'Big Four' banks around the country, but eventually they are all collected into the Exchequer Account. Another major account is the **National Loans Fund**, which records the money lent by the Government to nationalised industries, local authorities and other borrowers. The Bank also keeps accounts for each Government department. It is the total of these accounts which appears on the Bank Return shown in Fig. 1.2 under the heading 'Public Deposits'.

There is always finance available to cover any deficit on the Government accounts, the Bank making an automatic loan to the Government to cover any payments that have to be made. Equally, at times when there is a surplus in Government accounts the Bank will lend out the surplus at interest, as part of the general 'Debt' management policy. This is dealt with later (see Chapter 5).

The Bank's other banking activities include the keeping of accounts for a residue of private customers, for other UK banking institutions and for foreign central banks and other foreign national or international institutions.

In earlier days the Bank did accept accounts from private persons and some famous families have dealt with the Bank for over 200 years. The Bank also provides banking facilities for its own staff. This residue of private banking is at least helpful in reminding the Bank of the sorts of problems faced by the ordinary bankers. The Bank does not open new private accounts today.

The Bank of England acts as a banker to the clearing banks and the discount houses. The clearing banks have a small percentage of total assets deposited at the Bank, and these balances are used in the daily clearing to settle inter-bank indebtedness. For a full explanation of this see a companion volume, *Commerce Made Simple*.

As the Bank Return reproduced in Fig. 1.2 shows, the figure for 'Bankers' Deposits' is declared each week in the Return. The discount houses must have an account at the bank, since it is through these accounts that the 'lender of last resort' facility is extended to the discount houses. The Bank of England *Quarterly Bulletin* gives in its statistical annex comprehensive statistics for the whole banking sector. The reader is recommended to study these tables carefully.

About 90 overseas central banks and international bodies such as the IMF have accounts with the Bank of England to facilitate a wide variety of international transactions. Such central banks are primarily concerned with influencing affairs in their own countries to promote trade and prosperity. So far as possible, former Sterling-Area countries keep much of their reserves in London; others keep substantial working balances to assist home nationals desiring sterling. The Bank of England will advise on the investment and use of these funds, making arrangements of use to both Britain and the country concerned.

The biggest single task the Bank of England performs in terms of volume of work and number of employees engaged in the activity is the **note issue**. The physical labour involved is considerable, as new notes are issued daily and soiled notes are removed from circulation and destroyed. The Issue Department deals with all transactions related to note issues; the Banking Department with all other transactions. The volume of notes issued, which under the Bank Charter Act of 1844 had to be related to the quantity of gold in the vaults, plus a fiduciary issue of £14 million, now has no relation to the gold reserves. Notes are now only the 'small change' of our money system, though £10 000 million or more seems a lot of small change. Fluctuations in the note issue now reflect seasonal changes in consumer trading, and notes are issued in such a way and in such denominations as meet public demand.

The mechanism of note issue is as follows. The Issue Department prints and stores notes of such denominations and in such numbers as it deems will meet the requirements of the note-using public. These are held unissued in the Department and technically have no value (they are not backed by any Government stock until the moment of issue). The Banking Department has a float of issued notes which it issues just like any other bank to meet the needs of customers; the notes taken away by the commercial banks, being represented by a reduction in the banks' balances with the Bank of England. Of course where new notes are being exchanged for dirty notes, the notes being paid in will offset the same quantity of new notes being taken.

If an increase in public demand for notes reduces the Banking Department's float too much, an increase in the fiduciary issue will be authorised and the Banking Department will be able to buy more new notes from the Issue Department, paying for them with some of the gilt-edged securities it holds. These securities now back the note issue, but also earn interest which gives an income to the Issue Department. This income is used to pay the expenses of the Department, any surplus being paid over in full to the Exchequer. It follows that the purchase of notes by the public amounts to an investment in Government debt, which is—if not quite interest-free—at least very cheap, since the only costs incurred are the costs of the note issue itself.

Although not strictly a banking function, there is a great deal of work to be done in servicing the National Debt. The huge volume of debt, on which interest is paid twice yearly, involves the preparation of countless dividend warrants or bank transfers. Until 1869 dividends were paid in person at the Bank, and Dividend Day was a long-standing City event, with stockholders arriving in their best clothes to collect their dividends and spend an enjoyable day in town. Today the payments are by credit transfers into named bank accounts in the vast majority of cases.

(*d*) The Bank's Regulatory Role

As the *Economist* has pointed out, until the Banking Act of 1979, which came into force on October 1st of that year, the supervision of the British banking system had worked on the curious principle that the more reputable a bank was the closer the supervision required. The collapse of the 'fringe' banks in 1974, although they caused no losses to depositors because of a massive rescue operation, cost the banking community dear, and the regulatory role of the Bank of England has been extended to prevent a repetition. The Act formalises what was previously an informal role, where the Bank's status as the most important member of the financial community charged it with the duty of ensuring proper conduct by lesser institutions in the 'City'.

The Act gives the Bank of England powers to recognise institutions as 'banks'. Previously the term 'bank' had not been restricted in any way, and certain classes of deposit-taking institutions had abused the word, which implies a range of services and a degree of stability which in fact they did not have. Under the new regulations recognition will be granted to an applicant for banking status only if it offers a full range of banking services, or provides a recognised specialist service which merits the designation 'bank'.

The range of services that non-specialist banks are required to offer must be wide enough to cover the popular meaning of the word 'bank', and as a consequence some deposit-taking institutions will not be able to claim the title—for example, some finance houses.

The list of services given in Schedule 2 of the Act is as follows:

(*a*) Current account and deposit account facilities in sterling or foreign currency for the public and bodies corporate.

(*b*) Overdraft and loan facilities.

(*c*) Foreign exchange services for domestic and foreign customers.

(*d*) Finance by bills of exchange and promissory notes and the finance of foreign trade and the documentation related to it.

(*e*) Financial advice for members of the public and bodies corporate with regard to investments, and facilities for the purchase and sale of securities.

The institutions applying for licences and recognition as banks must also have an adequate capital basis, with net assets of at least £5 million for a full banking service, or £250 000 for a specialist banking service. They must be conducted by people of undoubted integrity who are professionally qualified, and have been vetted vigorously for weaknesses in their past records. Institutions which do not offer a full banking service may be licensed as 'deposit-taking institutions' but will not be able to use the word 'bank' as part of their company name, or to describe themselves as banks in their publicity literature.

That recognition as a 'deposit-taking institution' does not represent any adverse criticism of an institution was made clear by the Governor of the Bank of England in a speech to foreign bankers in May 1980. Referring to the borderline between 'banks' and 'deposit-taking institutions', he said:

> It is not intended, and was never intended, to be a great divide. We are concerned, as we have always been, to permit and encourage progression for those institutions which may wish to move from the licensed deposit-taker category to that of recognised bank. Clearly, not all will wish to make this move. For the Act provides that the distinctive attributes of a fully-fledged bank are not only, on the one hand, the high reputation and standing that it will have built up over time in the financial community, but also, on the other, the provision in reasonable depth of a wide range of banking services in this country—a criterion which many institutions will have no interest in meeting.
>
> Therefore, classification as a licensed deposit-taker is not to be seen of itself as impugning the status of an institution—and certainly not the integrity and competence of its management or the good name of the institution generally. This point is worth repetition. As further lists are published, it will be very clear that a wide variety of institutions is covered in the category of licensed deposit-taker. For example, it will include a number who, for very good reasons, have not sought or do not want to provide the range of services which go to make up the business of a fully-fledged bank. In addition it will embrace a number of institutions of overseas provenance, including branches of major foreign banks which are of undoubted standing and reputation but which have not been in business long enough in the United Kingdom to have built up their range of services here to the level required of a recognised bank. In these circumstances the Bank of England would not expect the market to make crude judgments of creditworthiness based merely on the distinction between recognised banks and licensed deposit-takers. Indeed, I should regard the market as failing in professional expertise if it were to base its assessment on this distinction alone. There can be no justification for charging a particular institution, which in every other respect remains unchanged, more for its money following publication of its name in the list of licensed deposit-taking institutions. The division between licensed deposit-takers and recognised banks has, as I have already suggested, a marked functional character and some licensed deposit-takers will undoubtedly be stronger and of greater repute than some recognised banks. This should be clearly understood by all institutions involved, both at home and abroad.
>
> (*Reproduced by courtesy of the Bank of England*)

The 'lists' to which the Governor referred are published periodically. The most recent available at the time of writing lists some 300 banks, just over 200 deposit-taking institutions, and about 150 institutions which had applied for recognition and were still under consideration.

The Bank's regulatory role, of course, goes far beyond mere registration, and is designed to prevent any repetition of the collapse of 'fringe banks' in the early 1970s. In establishing control the Bank is anxious to institute prudential controls with the cooperation of the banking system rather than as proposals from on high, and a series of consultative documents on the measurement of capital, foreign currency exposure and liquidity are under discussion at present.

Whilst the Bank's regulatory role has now been formalised by the Banking Act, 1979, so that a widespread failure of the banking system seems to be rendered highly unlikely, the Act also establishes a **Deposit Protection Board**. This Board will levy contributions upon Banks and deposit-taking institutions to create a fund for the compensation of depositors adversely affected by the failure of any institution. The levies are clearly very similar to insurance premiums, designed to spread losses that do occur fairly over the whole banking sector. In 1973–4 the failures of the fringe banks were generally borne by a few large banks in a 'lifeboat' arrangement, so preventing a major collapse of public confidence at no small expense to themselves and their shareholders. The three most powerful figures in the banking world (the Governor, Deputy Governor and Chief Cashier of the Bank of England) are *ex officio* members of the Deposit Protection Board, with the Governor of the Bank acting as Chairman of the Board. The Governor appoints three representatives of the contributory institutions as Ordinary Members, and also other Ordinary Members from the Bank of England staff.

As part of its wider responsibilities for the financial system the Bank has encouraged the adoption of common codes of practice and has promoted methods of self-regulation in a number of financial markets. In some cases, such as the foreign exchange market, responsibility for permitting new entrants to the markets resides with the Bank. The Bank has also been instrumental in forming certain regulatory bodies such as the **Panel on Take-overs and Mergers** and the **Council for the Securities Industry**.

To recapitulate the Bank's functions we may list them as follows:

(*a*) **The Bank's Influence on Monetary Policy**

(i) Its primary responsibility is to advise the Government on domestic and external monetary policy.

(ii) It monitors economic research and analyses the results.

(iii) It gives advice on financial aspects of economic modelling.

(iv) It monitors trends in industry and commodities.

(v) It advises on public finance, flows of funds, and the implications of policy on them.

(vi) It monitors the Balance of Payments (including capital movements).

(*b*) **The Bank's Operations in the Markets**

(i) The implementation of Government policy to control the economy by controlling the money market for short-term loans (**the bill market**).

(ii) The implementation of Government policy in both the long-term and short-term loan markets by influencing lending rates through overt or covert operations.

(iii) To meet the Government's long-term borrowing requirements by open-market operations in Government stocks (**the gilt-edged market**); this may also influence the lending policies of the commercial banks.

(iv) Managing the exchange rate to protect the pound (**the foreign exchange market**).

(*c*) **The Bank's Role as Banker**

(i) Bankers to the Government.

(ii) Bankers to the banks and the discount market.

(iii) Bankers to foreign central banks and international organisations.

(iv) Bankers to a residue of private customers.

(v) Managers of the note issue for the British Isles. (Scottish and Northern Ireland banks still issue their own notes, but the numbers are comparatively small.)

(vi) The registration of Government stocks and the servicing of the National Debt.

(*d*) The Bank's Regulatory Role

(i) To ensure the registration of deposit-taking institutions and publish a list of institutions licensed as banks.

(ii) To supervise the conduct of banking and other money-market institutions and review 'City' practices from time to time.

(iii) To represent the banks in its role as link with the Government, and convey the Government's views, or even directions, to the banking community.

(*e*) The Bank's International Role

(i) To participate in the international activities of such bodies as the International Monetary Fund and the International Bank for Reconstruction and Development.

(ii) To represent the views of international bankers in the representations it makes to the UK government.

2.4 The Central Bank System of the USA—The Federal Reserve System

Every sophisticated economy must run up against the difficulty that the creation of credit by the banks leaves more claims upon the 'cash in hand' than the money available. A full explanation of the creation of money is given in Chapter 6, but let us refer again to our banker who has received a deposit in cash of £100. If he relied on the probability that the owner of the £100 would demand back only the 8 per cent cash ratio, he could use the other £92 as the cash ratio for a loan of £1150. If he makes this loan by issuing a 'bank-note', it is clear that both the original depositor and the note-holder now have a claim against the deposit, and in any 'run-on-the-bank' someone is going to be disappointed. The whole banking system depends upon confidence in the value of deposits, and the chief function of the bank as far as the ordinary public is concerned is to honour its cheques by turning them into cash: under the early system its function was to honour its notes by turning them into specie (i.e. gold or silver or other coin of the realm).

In the USA at the start of the twentieth century the monetary system was inadequate to meet any loss of confidence. There was only a limited amount of specie, a limited issue of greenbacks (government paper money) and the bank-notes issued by the banks were limited to the amount of Government debt they had to back their note issues. As the US was at that time reducing its National Debt this note issue of the banks was contracting in an economy that was making a great leap forward. The solution was the Federal Reserve System.

Congress created the Federal Reserve System in 1913. It was empowered to issue notes which were 'legal tender' backed by assets other than Government bonds. This was again extended in 1933 and 1935, at the depths of the 'Great Depression'. The notes issued under the system are not obligations of the US Government, but of the Federal Reserve System. The significance of this is that the note issue, which in the UK is '*that part of the National Debt on which no interest is paid*' (Radcliffe Report 1959), is lost to the United States Government as a *direct aid* in Government activity. The proceeds of the note-issuing activity are used to buy Government bonds, and the interest paid on these is a source of income to the Federal Reserve System. This lucrative activity would of course be quite monstrous were it not for a convention by which the profits of the system are returned to the Treasury, so that the Government effectively receives back 98 per cent of the profits, and about 90 per cent of the total interest paid. The vital point constitutionally is that the note-issue is not subject to the control of the Administration but is a separate 'power' in the land—though the Fed's ability to resist a determined President bent on an inflationary policy might prove to be rather limited. At least it can argue from a position of independence, whereas the Bank of England can caution and advise only as an integral part of the 'Treasury' system.

Nature of the Federal Reserve System

The System consists of 12 regional Federal Reserve Banks, each of which has a board of nine directors. Six of the nine are elected by the stockholders, and the other three are appointed by the **Board of Governors of the Federal Reserve System**, which is based at Washington. The Board's three appointees may not be bankers, or stockholders, and one of the three takes the chair and is known as the **Federal Reserve Agent** in whose name the Federal Reserve Bank arranges the note issue for its region.

The 'stockholders' are the 'member banks', which purchase stock to the extent of 3 per cent of their own capital. This stock earns interest at 6 per cent per annum. All **'nationally chartered banks'** had to be members of the Federal Reserve System, and **'State-chartered banks'** might be members if they wished. (See p. 233 for developments in 1980.) The six directors elected by the members include three bankers and three non-bankers, so that the 'banking system' cannot be said to dominate the Federal Reserve System. One third of the directors retire each year, one from each part of the system.

The Board of Governors of the Federal Reserve System consists of seven Governors, each appointed for a non-renewable 14-year term, one Governor retiring every two years. This means that even a two-term President cannot influence the composition of the Board in time to make it his instrument, for he could only appoint a majority of the Board in the last two years of his administration. The President can appoint from among the seven members the Chairman and the Vice Chairman, who serve a four-year term once appointed. The effect of these measures is to release the 'note issue' from direct political pressures, and to enhance the status of the Federal Reserve System in the monetary affairs of the nation.

The 'New Deal' era conferred a formal recognition on a committee created in the 1920s to formulate Federal Reserve policy on open-market operations. In the essentially free-enterprise American market open-market operations are a powerful weapon for influencing the money supply, and the Federal Reserve Banks had developed an **'Open Market Investments Committee'** to formulate policy in this area. This was given legal status in the 1935 Amendment to the Federal Reserve Act. The seven members of the Board of Governors and the 12 Presidents of the regional banks meet every four weeks to decide policy. By restricting the votes to 12 the seven members of the Board of Governors maintain control (though in practice voting rarely divides upon any such harsh line). The New York Federal Reserve Bank has a vote at all times, reflecting its senior status as the bank which acts for the Committee on the New York market. The Chicago Bank and the Cleveland Bank have a vote in alternate years and the remaining nine have a vote every third year, three banks each year. The name of the Open Market Investments Committee was changed to the **Federal Open Market Committee** in the 1935 Act. The essence of open-market operations is that the Central Bank can influence bank liquidity by buying or selling securities on the open market. By buying securities the Federal Central Bank would increase the reserves of the commercial banking system, since those who sold the securities would deposit cash with the banks. This increased liquidity would make loans easier to get and cut interest rates, thus encouraging prospects of profitability. By selling securities the Fed would remove funds from the Banks as depositors reduced deposits to pay for the securities, and loans would be harder to get, while the increased interest rates would discourage entrepreneurs from proceeding with marginal projects. As is explained below, the Fed operates chiefly in the short-term market.

The procedures of the Committee take the form of a review of the economic situation, and result in a directive to the New York Fed to prescribe in a general way for its operations in the market in the weeks ahead. The Chairman of the Board of Governors or other members may be called before congressional committees to explain their actions but the monetary policy they are pursuing is largely their own responsibility. It is only reasonable to expect, though, that the views of the Administration and the Congress will be major considerations in the Committee's review of the economic situation at the monthly meetings.

The Roles of the Federal Reserve System

Policy Roles. The policy roles of the Federal Reserve System are more important economically than its regulatory and service roles, and are dominated by the Board of Governors in Washington. The original conception was that the regional Federal Reserve Banks should perform the classic functions of a central bank, which the US did not have between 1838 and 1913. These functions are (*a*) to regulate the money supply so that it expanded as trade expanded and did not act as a restraint upon wealth creation, and (*b*) to act as lender of last resort, through the 'discount window'.

(*a*) **Regulation of the Money Supply.** The money supply in the USA is regulated in rather a different way from similar controls in the UK. In particular the 'reserve requirements', which are a major way in which control of the creation of credit is established, are expressed in terms of a 'cash ratio' only, and not as 'eligible reserve assets'. Every Wednesday the banking system draws up a balance sheet showing the different types of deposit available, demand, savings and time deposits, and it is then expected to show cash reserves (a cash ratio) on a graduated scale 14 days later. The actual ratio varies from time to time, and differs for each class of liability. It may be as low as 2 per cent of the first \$2 million, 10 per cent of the next \$8 million, 12 per cent of the next \$90 million, etc. The reserves are in the form of deposits at the Bank's local Federal Reserve Bank, though it is allowed to count the cash in hand at the bank in the week of the statement with the reserves at the Fed two weeks later. It follows that in any given week a bank knows what its reserves at the Federal Reserve Bank must be (because they must comply with the statement drawn up on the Wednesday night of the week before last—except for the cash in hand during that week). Its lending policy will be influenced by the requirements.

One effect of this system of expressing reserves as a cash ratio is to increase the effectiveness of open-market operations, because these can, and do, take place largely in the short-rate market, i.e. the Treasury Bill market. In the UK dealings in bills do not affect a bank's 'eligible reserve assets', since bills count as reserves anyway, but in the US the purchase or sale of bills has a direct effect on the 'cash ratio'. It would also seem that an ability to change the reserve requirements would be a powerful weapon in the Fed's armoury, since it could affect bank liquidity in a very sudden way. In practice this has not been much used, except to take in new forms of money as they appear—for example, certificates of deposit. The trouble was that since State-chartered banks could leave the system if they liked—membership of the Federal Reserve system was compulsory only for nationally chartered banks—they tended to leave if the Fed started to interfere with the *status quo* in this respect.

During the late 1970s banks began to leave the Federal Reserve System at an alarming rate. There was simply no point in being in the Federal Reserve System and having to keep large cash reserves at no interest, when by leaving the Fed these reserves could be invested in money markets at 10 per cent or more and still be effectively 'available' in any emergency. With an increasing trend towards monetary policy, the Fed found it had a shrinking knowledge of the nation's banking affairs. The result was the introduction of two major acts, the International Banking Act, 1978, and the Depository Institutions Deregulation and Monetary Control Act, 1980. These Acts are dealt with in detail elsewhere (see Chapter 17) but the effect was to bring all banks and deposit-taking institutions into the Federal Reserve System, required to keep 3 per cent of the first $25 million of balances in cash, and 12 per cent of the rest. The system started on September 1, 1980, and will be fully implemented over a four-year period. In return all these institutions will be able to seek 'lender of last resort' facilities at the Fed's discount window.

(*b*) **Lender of Last Resort.** The use of the 'discount rate' (bank rate or minimum lending rate) as a means of controlling the money supply is largely of no importance in the USA. A traditional dislike of high interest rates means that many States have statutory rates of interest for certain types of business (for example, mortgage rates) while the 'lender of last resort' facilities are used in a rather different way than in the UK. With many thousands of 'unit' banks serving their own localities only, the need for 'lender of last resort' facilities may reflect local events rather than a nationwide situation. Natural disasters, the collapse of a powerful company or a crop failure may bring a unit bank to the 'discount window' for reasons totally unconnected with its own lending policy, and a punitive rate would be wholly inappropriate. The assistance given as 'lender of last resort' is not therefore related to the money supply in general, and any 'credit rationing' that has to be done is based upon other considerations than price. Only in the case of a general national inflation is the discount rate used for a shock effect, to bring the nation to its senses. This means that banks presenting themselves at the 'discount window' for reasons which might have been foreseen are charged a punitive rate for exercising this privilege, while at the same time other banks whose difficulties are the result of other forces are assisted at reasonable or even at very low rates. The system is therefore not strictly comparable with that of the UK.

The Regulatory Role. The regulatory role of the Federal Reserve System takes the form of a rigorous supervision of the member banks, as to liquidity, asset valuation, accounting policy generally and the probity of officers and senior staff. Its reports are exhaustive. The examination of a bank is unannounced and starts with the arrival of a team of investigators before staff arrive in the morning. Everything is then sealed, and may only be opened with the approval of, and in the presence of, an examiner. This type of investigation, which in theory takes place twice a year but in practice slightly less frequently, calls for an enormous team of investigators for the 7000 banks in the system. The costs involved are charged to the banks themselves.

The Service Role. The Federal Reserve System is in a central position in the American banking system and consequently well placed for the collection of statistical material and for research and development studies in the banking field. The one weakness in its position was the voluntary nature of the membership of State-chartered banks, which leave gaps in the statistics, though at the less important end of the banking range. This has been solved by the *Depository Institutions Deregulation Act, 1980* (see p.232).

The chief service provided is the clearing system, which operates like all clearing systems to settle only the net indebtedness of a bank with all other banks. The effect is that the daily clearing will result either in a debit balance due from a bank to the Clearing House, or a credit balance due to a bank from the Clearing House. These balances will be adjusted at the Fed as soon as the Clearing House proof sheet reaches it.

2.5 European Central Banks

France

The Banque de France. Founded by Napoleon I, the Banque de France was at one time said to 'rule the country over the heads of its chosen representatives'. Its largest shareholders were called '*Les deux cents familles*' (the 200 families) and constituted a financial oligarchy which exerted enormous influence by its ability to control credit and thus keep control of business enterprise and development. Anathematised by the left-wing, the power of the 200 families was greatly reduced by the 'Popular Front' Government of 1936, and after the Second World War the Banque de France was nationalised. Also nationalised at that time were the three largest deposit banks, *Crédit Lyonnais*, *Société Générale* and *Banque Nationale de Paris*.

The French have always had a very centralised form of government, and the holder of the purse strings, the Minister of Finance, has always been an influential minister, second only to the French Premier, and sometimes not even that. The Minister (nicknamed '*le grand argentier*') has a team of *inspecteur des finances* at the Louvre Palace, composed of the most brilliant financial minds, and their influence extends throughout France to the administrative and planning departments of all regions, and into the European institutions. This strongly centralised attitude is reinforced by the nationalisation of the four big banks. Rule by a financial technocracy does have disadvantages though, and French governments frequently have difficulty getting their financial programmes past the technocrats. There is consequently a strong call for some decrease in centralisation. The Government commission on banking recommended in 1979 that the state-run giants should be broken up into regional banks. In the event, the election of a socialist government in June 1981 has meant the opposite. The State proposes to take over control of the whole credit system, but will not nationalise foreign banks. This strengthens enormously the central control over domestic banking, paradoxically at a time when the socialist movement is talking about decentralising the system left by Napoleon by a massive devolution of powers from Paris.

With a strong centralised government the central bank is only one of the weapons available to control the economy, and in many ways it is the least influential. Direct government intervention to influence the economy is far more effective, and so is a protectionist approach to exclude imports on dubious grounds. The Barre plan, which sought between 1976 and 1979 to revitalise French industry by freer competition and reduced state intervention (on German lines), did not find it easy to overcome the inertia of a centralised system, and was unable to achieve its objectives in the face of traditionalist calls for official action and a massive programme of State investment. The devolution of powers from Paris may reduce such interference, but it is too early yet to say what success the proposed legislation will have.

Germany

The Bundesbank. Post-war Germany has risen like a phoenix from the ashes of the Second World War. Although her rapid recovery is explained partly by the fact that a defeated nation does not have to honour its war debts, the wartime destruction of the German infrastructure was enormous. The rapid recovery to a leading position in Europe reflects the hard work done and the privations borne in the immediate post-war years. The 'economic miracle' was achieved largely by concentrating upon a 'production' economy rather than a 'consumption' economy. Tax reductions and investment privileges encouraged expansion by self-financing—the need was to avoid consumption and plough profits back into expansion programmes. Niggardly handouts to war victims and pensioners contrasted with huge increases in wealth on the part of the entrepreneurial classes. This unequal distribution of wealth raised the Federal Republic to the level of an affluent nation in the 20 years from 1950 to 1970.

Preoccupation with production has led the Central Bank, the Bundesbank, to control the money supply carefully over the years, and Governments have tended to balance budgets, rather than run a deficit. This has not been difficult in a country where the labour force remembers two financial collapses in 50 years. In the 1970s the slower growth caused by increases in world oil prices and the decline in world trade led to a change in the Bundesbank's approach and the public sector deficit has been allowed to grow. The Bundesbank sets targets for growth in the Central Bank money stock and the levels of wage settlements tend to reflect this increase in the money supply. The post-war practice of inviting the unions and big business to a 'review of the economy' meeting with the Bundesbank for a programme of 'concerted action' was less influential in the 1970s, when the trade unions showed a distinct preference for increased consumption after years of a 'production' economy.

The German banking system differs from most other banking systems in the influential part it plays in industry. Not only do banks hold large shareholdings in industrial companies, and frequently appoint directors to represent their interests, but a proxy system also operates so that small investors can ask a bank to act for them in voting matters. The power of the banks is consequently much increased. Despite strong opposition by some parties, and the trade unionists, to these arrangements the strength of the German economy would appear to indicate that a strong banking sector is not harmful to industry. A nation which in the late 1970s experienced inflation rates of only $2\frac{1}{2}$–$3\frac{1}{2}$ per cent is clearly not facing an explosion in its money supply, however influential its bankers may be.

2.6 Revision Test

Answers	*Questions*
—	**1.** What is a central bank?
1. A leading bank in any nation charged with a duty to regulate the banking system in the interests of prudent financial behaviour in the national interest.	**2.** What are the central banks' chief functions?
2. (*a*) To act as bankers to the government. (*b*) To act as bankers to other banks. (*c*) To represent the nation at international meetings of bankers, and the international bankers in conveying their views to its domestic government.	**3.** What were the stages in the development of the Bank of England?
3. (*a*) Founded in 1694. (*b*) Split into two parts in 1844: the Issue Department (charged with control of the note issue) and the Banking Department (which deals with banking matters). (*c*) Nationalised in 1946. (*d*) Given extended regulatory powers under the Banking Act, 1979.	**4.** What is its chief function?
4. To advise the Government on economic and financial matters and execute the Government's monetary policy.	**5.** How is monetary supervision exercised?
5. (*a*) By day-to-day control of the short-term money market and the 'lender of last resort' mechanism. (*b*) By minimum-lending rate changes. (*c*) By open-market operations on the long-term gilt-edged market. (*d*) By special deposits (when in use). (*e*) By corset regulations (when in use).	**6.** List its other chief functions.

Answers	*Questions*
6. (*a*) To supervise and license all deposit-taking institutions. (*b*) To manage the pound on the foreign exchange market without infringing IMF regulations. (*c*) To assist the clearing mechanism for the clearing banks. (*d*) To act as banker to the Government. (*e*) To manage the note issue. (*f*) To administer the national debt. (*g*) To represent the UK in the international banking field.	**7.** What is the central bank system called in the USA?
7. The Federal Reserve System.	**8.** How does it chiefly differ from the Bank of England?
8. It is autonomous—part of the separation of powers in the US Federal System.	**9.** What is the structure of the Federal Reserve System?
9. (*a*) 12 regional Federal Reserve Banks. (*b*) A Washington-based Board of Governors of the Federal Reserve System, seven Governors appointed for a 14-year term, to make them independent of a two-term President. (*c*) A reserve requirement expressed in 'cash ratio' terms only, so that open market operations become very effective in influencing bank liquidity, since they take place in the Treasury Bill market. (*d*) A 'lender of last resort' facility which is quite different from that in the UK, where loans are made *on merit* to any class of bank in difficulties, for whatever reason. (*e*) A strict regulatory role over all banking institutions.	**10.** Go over the page again until you are sure of all the answers.

3

THE COMMERCIAL BANKS

3.1 The Nature of the Commercial Banks

Commercial banks are banks which offer a full banking service to commerce, industry and the personal sector. This 'full' service implies the following facilities:

(*a*) **A current account** facility as a means of settling indebtedness between customers through cheques, credit transfers, debit transfers and standing orders. Current accounts also enable customers to take advantages of loans and overdrafts, and use night-safe facilities if required.

(*b*) A **deposit account** facility for those who wish to leave long-term savings on deposit, at interest.

(*c*) A **savings account** facility, if required, for small regular savings out of earnings.

(*d*) Various **accreditation card services** including cheque guarantee cards, auto-bank cards for obtaining cash out of banking hours and credit cards such as Barclaycard or Access.

(*e*) Among many other services we may list assistance with export trade, foreign exchange transactions, executorship and trustee services, stockbroking services, tax advice, investment management services and many more.

Besides this widespread and personal service to a multitude of customers, the commercial banks may well have subsidiaries in more specialist fields, operating as merchant banks, finance houses, deposit-taking institutions, etc., but these subsidiaries will be arranged as separate activities of the commercial bank.

In the UK, and many other countries, the commercial banks, by a process of amalgamation and absorption, have become very large organisations with a multiple-branch system and a foot in every corner of the land, and almost every corner of the world. There are peculiar advantages in large-scale operations in banking. A broadly based bank benefits from the support it receives from region to region. If a major depression affects one industry another industry may be buoyant. A local, or unit, bank in the early days of banking frequently found itself subject to pressure from a particular depositor. If a deposit was large enough its owner could threaten withdrawal to bankrupt the bank. Personal spite was not unknown where a banker had upset a rich and powerful customer. A broadly based bank with many depositers can resist such pressures. Large scale also engenders confidence, which is the basis upon which the whole banking system rests.

Against this it has been argued that in the US the 'local bank' system has had great advantages in that it keeps banks in touch with local needs and more willing to lend money to businessmen whose 'local' expenditure will promote 'local' prosperity. This may be advantageous in a country as vast as the USA.

Large scale makes possible economies which could not be achieved in the small firm. Computer services, for example, can be organised on a nationwide scale, to effect the speedy transmission of business data and to operate cash-point and auto-bank facilities; even the automatic debiting of accounts for retail trade purposes is envisaged in the near future. The operation of investment, insurance, executorship and other services is made simpler if specialist departments can be established where staff can be trained and expertise can be acquired. The full range of services to a major industrial or commercial company requires a large organisation where no problem is too great or too specialised; the bank manager can always locate someone with the necessary knowledge and skill.

3.2 The London Clearing Banks

As a result of mergers in the 1960s the London clearing banks were reduced to six groups. The 'Big Four' (Barclays, Lloyds, Midland and National Westminster), Coutts, and Williams and Glyn's. They are also influential in three Scottish clearing banks: Midland controls Clydesdale Bank, Barclays owns 35 per cent of The Bank of Scotland and Lloyds owns 16 per cent of the Royal Bank of Scotland. In Ireland, all banks operate in both Northern Ireland and Eire. Of the two that are based in Northern Ireland, Northern Bank is owned by Midland and Ulster Bank by National Westminster. The Isle of Man Bank is owned by National Westminster.

The London clearing banks, in evidence given to the Committee to Review the Functioning of Financial Institutions in 1977, revealed that they had branch networks of 12 315 branches in 1968, which declined to 11 659 in 1976. Employees at the time of the report totalled some 225 000 with a further 50 000 employed overseas. About one quarter of UK staff were employed within three miles of Charing Cross, London. Total deposits in July 1980 were given in the *Bank of England Quarterly Bulletin* as £59 504 million. The growth of deposits is shown in Table 3.1.

Table 3.1. Growth of deposits (London Clearing Banks)

Year	*Total deposits* (£ million)
1959 (Radcliffe Report)	7 000
1972	22 854
1974	36 959
1976	45 018
1978	52 622
1980 (July)	59 504

(*Source*: Evidence of the London Clearing Banks, 1977, and *Bank of England Quarterly Bulletin*.)

Despite these impressive figures and the tremendous changes in the years between 1957 (when the Banks submitted evidence to the Radcliffe Commission) and 1977 (when they submitted evidence to the Wilson Committee), the fact remains that only half the total adult British population have bank accounts, compared with 95 per cent or more in the US, Canada and even France. Whatever the explanations, which include traditional British trade union attitudes to the payment of wages and restrictive controls on bank lending to the private sector in the post-war years, it must be said that the banks have been slow to recognise the potential of small-scale consumer savings and slow to lend to small-scale borrowers in the hire purchase and consumer durable markets.

The retail side of banking is still, therefore, relatively neglected, with the consumer and small businessman turning to the non-bank sector for the funds they require—an anomalous situation when every High Street is littered with bank premises. It is true that some of this non-bank sector is owned by the banks in the form of wholly-owned subsidiary finance houses, but this does not prevent the waste in surplus capacity that the widespread branch-banking network represents. It is time a serious attempt was made to breach traditional attitudes about the security of loans and the areas of business activity that banks are prepared to finance. Mortgage lending is one field, and the durable consumer goods field is another, where the traditional attitudes have turned business away to the benefit of non-bank competitors. Bank lending in these fields is now being developed. A serious examination of branch economics is being undertaken by the head offices of major banks as the computerisation of control procedures takes effect.

3.3 The Organisation of Domestic Banking

Domestic banking in the UK is organised on a regional basis, which lends itself easily to the delegation of decision-making. Although the arrangements vary, a system of **regional offices** which control **area offices** which control groups of branches is the typical organisation.

Management techniques have improved greatly in the last decade, with the development of computerised control systems which are just beginning to make a real impact in the management field. Computerisation, which performs basic tasks very easily and is therefore very useful for elementary banking activities, has taken rather longer to establish itself at the nerve centres of management. Crucial statistics derived from the basic activities are now making inter-branch comparisons possible, and a rationalisation of the expensive and unwieldy branch-banking networks should result. In their evidence to the Wilson Committee the Committee of London Clearing Bankers said:

> To meet the needs of their increased and more diversified business the banks have established formalised strategic planning systems, embracing the direction of future business and the allocation of capital and personal resources; at the same time the introduction by most of the banks of 'management by objectives' has given branches and departments the opportunity to assess their performance against targets set in the light of the banks' overall corporate objectives.

Some of the yardsticks to be used in measuring branch performance may be listed as follows:

(i) **Routine Statistics**
(*a*) Number of personal current accounts.
(*b*) Number of business current accounts.
(*c*) Number of personal deposit accounts.
(*d*) Number of business deposit accounts.
(*e*) Number of savings accounts.
(*f*) Number of budget accounts.
(*g*) New personal accounts opened per quarter.

(*h*) New business accounts opened per quarter.
(*i*) Private loan accounts opened per quarter.
(*j*) Overdrafts sanctioned per quarter.
(*k*) Ratio of cheque guarantee cards to the number of personal current accounts.
(*l*) Ratio of credit cards to the number of personal current accounts.
(*m*) Ratio of company credit cards to the number of business current accounts.

(ii) **Other Statistics**
(*a*) Total export business handled.
(*b*) Total import business handled.
(*c*) Ratio of export transactions to business accounts open.
(*d*) Foreign commission earned.
(*e*) Domestic commission earned.
(*f*) Specialist commission earned (insurance, executorship and similar services).
(*g*) Ratio of commission to general charges.
(*h*) Average personal lending per personal current account.
(*i*) Average business lending per business current account.
(*j*) Number of counter transactions per counter position.
(*k*) Average value of a counter transaction.
(*l*) Average cash balance.
(*m*) Cash handled as a percentage of average cash balance.
(*n*) Normal man-hours and overtime man-hours.
(*o*) Overtime as a percentage of normal man-hours.
(*p*) Commission earned per man-hour paid.

Clearly there are any number of such ratios which could in fact be calculated and would throw light on particular areas. For example, many branch premises occupy prime town centre sites with generous space allowances for customer service. While the banks have not yet descended to the level of superstores interested in how much sales are achieved per foot of counter space, they must begin to ask themselves whether there is too much space for the money being handled. In 1980 personal accounts were estimated to be costing about £750 million, of which only about £100 million could be recouped in charges. The balance had to be made up by 'lending on' the balances in the personal accounts at interest.

With the interest rates prevailing in 1980 this was not an uneconomic operation, but if interest rates fell to, say, half the 1980 levels the whole range of personal services offered would become uneconomic.

3.4 Commercial Banking as Portfolio Management

To the ordinary customer a bank appears to be merely a 'money shop' where cash can be obtained as and when required provided that due attention is given to periodic deposits, credit arrangements, etc. For the banker his business is a question of portfolio management. Certain types of money are becoming available to the banker as deposits, which the bank is then free to make available to other customers as loans. Certain problems have to be met with regard to liquidity; cash must be available in the tills in sufficient quantities to meet the needs of customers; adequate reserves must be kept to meet unforeseen circumstances and avoid a 'run on the bank'.

If these problems are successfully surmounted there remains the problem of covering the costs of the extensive range of services to be made available, and of achieving a return on capital invested. These costs and profits have to be earned out of the difference between the rate paid to depositors and the rate charged to borrowers. Despite talk of a 'cartel' in banking, which appears to imply a price-fixing agreement between the banks, the whole field is in fact intensely competitive, and the rates for money are changing constantly during the working day. The banker is therefore constantly weighing the true costs of different types of money. Thus balances in current accounts do not usually earn interest but do make enormous use of facilities such as cash-point services, credit-card facilities, etc. Even if some of these costs can be recouped by charges there are many which cannot. By contrast, deposits in deposit accounts have fewer overhead costs, but do earn interest for the depositor so that a direct charge is incurred. Money borrowed on the money markets may be more expensive but have fewer hidden costs. On the lending side some of the loans must be low-yielding loans at 'call' or 'short notice' to preserve liquidity; others will be of medium yield with high security (loans to first-class names); others will be at higher interest rates but with an element of risk over repayments. Fixed-interest rates present a problem should the levels of interest rates alter in the meantime.

As with all portfolio management the problem is to balance the various influences at work to achieve an optimum result. The major aim is to achieve a profitable pattern of activities, but profits must only be pursued where it is safe to do so. Adequate reserves must always be maintained, so that 'prudential reserves' are an essential element in a bank's calculations. An appearance of stability in banking arrangements is important; bargains made have to be carried through even though the final yield may prove to be less lucrative than was hoped. The changes in interest rates which have to be made can only be made within the pattern of existing agreements as they roll over. Fortunately many loans are of relatively short duration so that even quite sharp inflationary changes can be taken into account.

In balancing the various influences at work on their 'portfolios', the banks work within certain constraints. These may be listed as follows:

(*a*) The need to preserve liquidity.
(*b*) The need to manage liabilities.
(*c*) The need for adequate capital.
(*d*) Supervision from internal management bodies.
(*e*) Supervision from the Bank of England.

A word about each of these is appropriate.

(*a*) **The Need to Preserve Liquidity.** The banks have always exercised strict control over lending policies in order to preserve liquidity, by which we mean the ability to give cash to any depositor who wishes to withdraw funds. The whole edifice of banking is built upon confidence in the liquidity of the banks—we all expect to receive back any funds we have deposited on demand (although of course we may lose seven days' interest on the funds as a result). We persist in these expectations even though we know that in fact the greater part of our balances have been 'lent on' to borrowers and the simultaneous demand by all depositors for a return of their money would close the banks at once. The self-imposed prudential constraints on lending to preserve adequate liquidity existed long before the banks were subjected to supervision by official bodies, and would still be implemented if all controls were removed.

In ensuring adequate liquidity the maturity structure of a bank's assets and liabilities is vitally important. If all loans made were matched by deposits which had the same maturity there would be no real problem of liquidity. The fact is that banks' assets and liabilities are mismatched: they borrow short to lend long. Thus the £12 000 million in current accounts which the banks lend on to a variety of borrowers by way of overdrafts and loans is technically withdrawable on demand, and consequently very ill-matched indeed with the overdrafts and loans for which it is used.

(*b*) **The Need to Manage Liabilities.** The major liability of any bank is the sum total owed back to the depositors, a liability which is met by ensuring adequate liquidity so that demands by depositors can always be met (see (*a*) above). Other liabilities—for example, certificates of deposit, borrowing on the Interbank Market and on the Eurocurrency markets, etc.—represent what are known as 'maturity-certain' liabilities. They are the result of a specific contractual relationship with lenders of funds of various sorts. The contract to repay is in clear terms, and the date when they will fall due for repayment is known. Clearly there is a need to ensure that all such liabilities are provided for in the 'cash-flow' arrangements of the Bank. The Bank of England Green Paper on monetary control, which is dealt with more fully in Section 12.4, proposed an integrated measure of liquidity which will combine ordinary liquidity with the management of such liabilities. Besides the need to meet ordinary commercial requirements in this way there is also the need to manage liabilities in order to comply with the control procedures of central banks—for example, the monetary controls of the Bank of England in the UK. **'Eligible liabilities'** are in the process of being redefined, and are referred to later (see Section 12.4). They are liabilities which are eligible for consideration when deciding what liquid reserves it would be prudent to keep. For example, a certificate of deposit due to be repaid in two months' time is an eligible liability, but the sums owed to shareholders of the bank, while they are liabilities, are not eligible liabilities, for there is no immediate problem of repayment.

(*c*) **The Need for Adequate Capital.** Capital is the resources made available by the owners of a business to meet the requirements of the business in terms of fixed assets and working capital. Originally this capital is made available by the sale of shares to the various classes of shareholders, but in a developed business such as the major commercial banks it also consists of reserves ploughed back from profits in earlier years. These reserves really belong to the ordinary shareholders, who have taken less profit from the business over the years in the form of dividends than they might otherwise have done. The point about reserves is that they leave funds in the business which can be used to meet any unforeseen loss, and in a portfolio of assets ranging from overdrafts and loans to customers to investments in gilt-edged securities and equity shares, there will always be losses. It is part of the problem of maintaining confidence that adequate capital should be available. In former times banks held substantial 'hidden reserves' which did not appear on their balance sheets, but this is not allowed now. It follows that the true profits made have to be revealed—a process which can lead to claims from many parties. Shareholders may demand larger dividends, employees may ask for salary increases or extended 'perks', depositors may howl louder about bank charges, etc. This makes it difficult to retain an adequate capital base, despite the high profits made in recent years.

(*d*) **Supervision from Internal Management Bodies.** Portfolio management is essentially a question of estimating risk, and all the commercial banks have established computerised control and internal audit systems which make it possible to review the balance of a bank's portfolio on a day-to-day basis based upon **management by exceptions**. Thus a change in the proportion of a particular range of assets or liabilities might increase risks in a particular area and call for investigation and correction. There are also specialist staff to review individual loans and overdrafts, and the adequacy of the security taken, and an inspectorate to conduct regular and *ad hoc* investigations at all levels.

(*e*) **Supervision from the Bank of England.** This topic is a major one, and is under review at the time of writing. It is discussed elsewhere in this book (see pp. 157–63).

3.5 Revision Test

Answers	*Questions*
—	**1.** What are commercial banks?
1. Banks which offer a full banking service to the industrial, commercial and personal sectors.	**2.** Why may the retail side of banking still be said to be underdeveloped in the UK?
2. Because only about 50 per cent of the adult population have bank accounts compared with 95 per cent in some other major countries.	**3.** What is the chain of control in commercial banking?
3. (*a*) Head office, (*b*) regional offices, (*c*) area offices, (*d*) branches.	**4.** What technique is giving better control of branches today?
4. Computerised management by exceptions—which calculates a variety of ratios to detect less than optimum performance.	**5.** How does the banker view banking?
5. As portfolio management: he has a variety of investments, loans, overdrafts, etc., which have been made possible by the use of a variety of deposits. The problem is to match the assets against the liabilities in the most profitable way, while preserving a reasonable degree of security.	**6.** Now try some of the questions requiring written answers in Appendix 1.

4

DISCOUNT HOUSES AND OTHER FINANCIAL INSTITUTIONS

4.1 The Sophisticated Economy

The test of a sophisticated economy is the intricacy of its network of specialised financial institutions. Adam Smith, as long ago as 1776, pointed out that the true source of wealth in an advanced economy is the specialisation that takes place. As the scale of business activity increases, more and more specialist activities can develop. This is just as true in the 'service' industries as it is in manufacturing. Economic growth in advanced nations tends to come increasingly from improvements in services, since improvements in manufacturing have been largely achieved in earlier periods.

Prosperity, rather than necessity, is the mother of invention. To generate the wealth required by today's hugely increased populations, who raise their eyes towards ever more distant horizons of consumption, requires the most expert marshalling of financial resources. A whole range of financial institutions has come into existence to meet these requirements, and it is the diversity of these institutions and the variety of their activities which provide finance for the huge range of industrial, commercial and personal services which are made available to the general public. The consumer society may, as some say, have gone too far, and be demanding more goods and services than anyone has reason to expect can be provided. Whether this is true or not, it is certain that the modern advanced economy can be sustained only if a varied pattern of sophisticated financial services is maintained. It is now necessary to consider some of these financial institutions.

4.2 The Discount Houses

The discount houses are a group of financial houses who specialise in dealing in short-term money. They are commonly referred to as 'bill-brokers'. The 'bill' referred to is a 'bill of exchange', and the word 'broker' refers to anyone who makes it his business to know two parties who are in opposite situations, and help them out of their difficulties. We have Lloyds brokers in the insurance field and stockbrokers who assist those who have shares to sell and those who wish to buy shares. A famous definition of bill-broking was given by Samuel Gurney in 1848, in an address to the House of Lords. He said: '*My business is usually denominated that of a bill-broker, in fact a dealer in money, taking money from those who have a surplus, and distributing to those who require it.*'

Note, though, that this action as an intermediary between the leaders and the borrowers is not one where the discount houses are mere agents. They act as **principals**, not agents, borrowing the money in their own names and lending it out to borrowers in their own names. They are fully liable for the money they borrow, and run the full risk on the money they lend.

The discount houses owe their existence to the development of the country banks in the eighteenth century. These banks were 'unit' banks, serving their own localities, and had only limited financial resources. This placed them in considerable difficulty when faced with growing demands to discount bills of exchange—the main method of payment in those days. The essence of a bill of exchange is that the 'drawer' of the bill (the person who writes it out) instructs the drawee (the person who owes him money) to pay the sum named at a definite (or determinable) future date. The debtor thus has time to pay, and in due course will do so, but in the meantime his creditor cannot obtain his money, except by discounting it with a banker specialising in that sort of activity. The term 'discounting' is appropriate, since a pound sterling becoming available at some time in the future must be worth less than £1 today. The creditor who decides to discount his bill of exchange will expect to receive less than the face value. The amount of the discount will reflect (*a*) the prevailing rates of interest in the money market generally and (*b*) the quality of the debtor, since eventual payment depends upon the debtor honouring the bill on the due date.

A full understanding of bills of exchange is essential to an understanding of the work of the discount houses. The reader who is not thoroughly familiar with them, or does not know by heart the definition given in the Bills of Exchange Act, 1882, is strongly advised to read the relevant section in a companion volume, *Commerce Made Simple*.

The bill-brokers who began to specialise in this type of short-term money (bills frequently ran for only one month, though three months is about average duration in the home trade) obtained the funds to discount the bills from other bankers who had surpluses available. Thus the agricultural areas at harvest time were prosperous. Banks from these areas would lend funds to the discount houses for use in discounting bills from the industrial areas, where funds were short.

Today the London Discount Market is really based upon the business of the 11 members of the London Discount Market Association. However, though these 11 large houses are the backbone of the market there are at least a dozen smaller members involved in similar or related business. These smaller institutions though have no *automatic* right to use the Bank of England as **lender of last resort**. The Central Bank's function of acting as lender of last resort is carried out in the UK exclusively to the members of the DMA, though assistance is often more discreet under the new system (see p. 157).

4.3 The Services of the Discount Houses

Discount houses exist to borrow and lend money, hoping to make a profit out of the difference between the rate at which they borrow and the higher rate at which they lend. In doing so they render a service to both 'lenders' and 'borrowers', borrowing from the 'lenders' and then lending the funds obtained to the 'borrowers'.

The Borrowing Service

The borrowing is chiefly done from the banks, who are pleased to lend liquid funds at rates less than their base rates. The discount houses give the banks a fully secured outlet which ranks as 'secured money' under the Bank of England's 'secured money' regulations (see Section 12.4). The rate is usually at least $1\frac{5}{8}$ per cent below bank base rates, but it may be much cheaper because it reflects the supply of and demand for money. The usual way to describe this rate is to say that the discount houses 'borrow money at call and for very short periods, *at market rates*'.

The banks are not the only lenders. Many commercial companies may have a surplus of funds at particular times, and prefer to lend it to the discount houses at market rates because they do not have to give seven days' notice before withdrawing it as with a clearing bank deposit. Frequently the rate agreed is the same as the clearing-bank deposit rate, which is 2 per cent less than MLR. Other lenders may be local government departments, nationalised institutions, merchant banks and other financial institutions with temporary surpluses they wish to put out at interest, while even the Treasury has funds available at certain times of the year as tax revenues flow in. All this money is borrowed 'at call or short notice' and lent on rather longer term, three to six months in many cases. This explains the fundamental vulnerability of the bill-brokers, and the need for 'lender of last resort' facilities from the Bank of England.

In ordinary life we do not regard borrowing as a service, for when an individual needs to borrow money it is the person from whom he borrows who renders the service. In the case of the discount houses it is a positive benefit to the banks, local authorities, etc., to be able to lend money in this way at very satisfactory rates of interest for very short periods with absolute security. The discount houses are therefore assisting the lenders of money just as much as the borrowers, for to have large sums lying idle as cash assets unable to earn interest would be a very severe loss to institutions like these.

Every morning the representatives of the discount houses call on the London banks to enquire whether they need to 'call' money back, or to adjust the rates of interest agreed previously on sums lent to the discount houses. Banks usually 'call' money in the morning, when businessmen are drawing funds for such purposes as wages, cash floats for tills, etc. The money 'called' will be paid back to the banks by the discount houses almost at once, and the security lodged with the bank when the money was borrowed will be reclaimed at the same time. Interest will cease on the money called, since the discount house has lost the use of it.

Later in the day, when businessmen have takings to pay in, the banks will be flush with money and can lend it out to discount houses which cannot balance their books. These transactions are not subject to any written confirmation. There simply is no time to engage in formalities, and the whole money market operates on the principle **'My word is my bond'** (see Section 5.2).

The Lending Service

The discount houses lend money to several types of borrower, by way of discounting bills of exchange, treasury bills, certificates of deposit and other negotiable instruments. To follow the process, consider a bill of exchange drawn by T. Jones on Baker and Co. Ltd for £500 at 3 months. In three months' time this bill will be worth £500, but in the 91 days that it has to run from the starting date it is worth less than £500. Let us suppose that at prevailing rates of interest on the day it is issued the discounted value of the bill is £475. By the following day, with 90 days to run, it may be worth £475.30. Firms who draw bills of exchange upon their customers in settlement for goods or services supplied sell the 'accepted' bills (an acceptance is the signification by the debtor that he agrees to be bound by the bill) to their banks, or to the discount houses direct, for the discounted value of the bill. Such bills are called 'trade bills' and will normally be honoured by the acceptor on the due date. So the purchase of a bill by the discount houses from a commercial firm—or from a bank which has obliged a customer by discounting the bill which the bank does not wish to hold until maturity—constitutes a loan to that firm for the duration of the bill. The loan will be settled, not by the borrower, but by the original debtor when he honours the bill on the due date. The interest on the loan will be the difference between the face value of the bill (received on the due date from the debtor) and the discounted value of the bill paid to the commercial firm several months before. The profit of the discount house will be the difference between the interest earned as described above, and the interest paid for borrowing the money with which the whole arrangement was financed. Clearly this is only a small illustration of one type of transaction. A typical day's dealing on one of the discount houses would be £100 million, so the average transaction will be much larger than £500, though trade bills are occasionally handled for quite small amounts. Usually the minimum transaction is £10 000.

Funds are not only lent to trading firms but are used to purchase the whole range of short-term securities. The full list is:

(*a*) Treasury bills—virtually loans to the Government.
(*b*) Commercial bills, i.e. bank bills, trade bills and promissory notes.
(*c*) Local authority bills and promissory notes.
(*d*) Short-dated Government stocks.
(*e*) Corporation bonds, local government bonds and quoted Government, Commonwealth and similar securities.
(*f*) Negotiable certificates of deposit. These are certificates which recognise that a deposit of money has been made for a fixed period (usually one year) to earn interest at a given rate. Thus a deposit of £1 million at interest of 15 per cent would be worth £1 150 000 in a year's time. The difficulty for banks which receive deposits arises if the money is withdrawn at short notice. By issuing a negotiable certificate of deposit for £1 000 000 payable in one year's time both parties are equally secure. The bank knows that it will have the use of the money for the full period, but must provide £1 150 000 on the agreed date. The depositor may retain the certificate of deposit until maturity, but if he comes under pressure and needs funds he can sell the certificate to the discount houses at the market rate, which will be somewhere near what he hoped to receive. Thus if disposed of after six months the bill will not fetch £1 075 000, but no doubt it would be somewhere near this figure, reflecting market views of interest rates for the next six months. When these certificates were first issued in the 1960s the discount houses formed a market in them so that they should be readily saleable, and in this way added to their popularity as a short-term investment.

The short-term securities listed above become the assets of a discount house when it buys them. They are then used as security for the sums borrowed, and are lodged in 'parcels' with the various banks from whom money has been borrowed. If a bank 'calls' back a loan the discount house calls back its parcel of securities, and uses them again as security for a loan from some other institution.

4.4 Monetary Policy and the Discount Houses

In the UK the relationship between the Bank of England and the discount houses is fundamental to the management of the money supply. The Bank of England can make the Government's monetary policy effective by interfering with the money market, and a discount house which is insensitive to changes in the Bank's policy on interest rates will find its profit margins squeezed or even entirely eliminated. The directors of discount houses meet several times a day to consider what has happened on the market and adjust interest rates in line with any trends they can detect.

Suppose a 'tight money' policy is to be pursued. The Bank of England may call for **special deposits** from the banking system. This will cause a severe shortage of money in the market, and will bid up the price the discount houses must pay for the funds they borrow, and consequently raise the rates they are charging for discounting bills, etc. The special deposit system is, however, an extreme weapon and the more usual way to keep the market short of funds is to increase the Treasury Bills on offer every Friday. Since the discount houses are bound to tender for the total issue—a condition of the 'lender of last resort' facility—the Bank can make them short of funds at will. It is then for the Bank to decide how it will relieve the shortage. If it is prepared to relieve the shortage by its own operations in the market it will buy Treasury Bills at market rates. The Bank of England will buy bills for cash so that the shortage of funds reported to it by the discount houses is relieved. If it buys the bills from the discount houses this is known as 'direct assistance'; if it buys them from the banks it is known as 'indirect assistance'. The banks who have sold bills now have surplus cash available and promptly lend it to the discount houses, thus relieving the shortage. Sometimes there are insufficient Treasury bills available, and the Bank will buy corporation bills or bank bills—bills with the name of a reputable bank on them. In making funds available in this way the Bank of England is running no risk at all, for absolutely reputable corporations or banks will be honouring the bills in due course, and the Bank is earning the usual market rate of interest on its money.

If the Bank of England relieves all the shortage of funds in this way it is held to be a sign that the Bank and the Treasury are satisfied with the prevailing rates of interest. If the shortage is not relieved, and despite desperate phone calls in all directions the discount houses are unable to balance their books, they are said to be **'forced into the Bank'**. In earlier days this resulted in a procession of gentlemen in top hats wending their way from Lombard Street to the Bank of England to borrow money from the 'lender of last resort', at whatever penal rate the Bank might specify. The discount houses, who are only short of money because they have loaned it out to customers very cheaply, are now going to lose money. The Bank has indicated that it thinks prevailing interest rates too low, credit is too easy and the next day the discount houses will be raising interest rates to take account of the Bank's disapproval, and to claw back some of their losses. Today the call to the lender of last resort is not made personally by the bill-broker. He simply reports the situation by phone and is told what rate he must pay for the privilege of balancing his books.

Sometimes the situation is reversed, and there is a dearth of borrowers from the discount houses, and every institution has funds to spare which it wishes to lend to them. In this situation the discount houses are unwilling to borrow the money, even though the market rate falls, and this may have an adverse effect upon the economy, since those who cannot lend their money to the institutions to whom they normally lend it, may use it in other ways—for ostentatious spending perhaps. In this situation the Bank of England sells securities to 'mop up' the surplus, and enables the discount houses to take funds offered to them—but of course the rate will fall under the influence of market forces: small demand for money and a plentiful supply available.

The Bank of England can also influence the money market by varying the duration of the loan when it lends as 'lender of last resort'. Before 1966 the minimum period of the loan was seven days and this penalised the discount houses more than was sometimes necessary. By varying the term of the loan to a time as short as 'overnight' the Bank could fine-tune its impact upon the discount houses. It can also request the cooperation of the discount houses in implementing a certain rate of interest, the threat of a penal rate for those who do not cooperate being sufficient to ensure compliance. One does not offend the 'lender of last resort' if one can possibly avoid doing so.

Conclusion on the Discount Houses. The essential feature of the discount house system is that the discount houses lend respectability to countless business transactions by adding their names to bills of exchange which otherwise would not command respect on the money market. If a bill is dishonoured, the holder of the bill turns to the 'good name' upon the bill and is immediately put in funds by the discount house, which then pursues the question of the dishonour on its own behalf. A huge range of business activities both at home and in the export field are provided with short-term funds by the purchase of bills of exchange, which will be self-liquidating in due course as the business proceeds to the 'due date' of the bill. Because of its adaptability, and lack of formality, based upon the principle 'My word is my bond', hundreds of millions of pounds can be handled daily with very little fuss, and very economically. At the same time the system is in close control of the Bank of England, and the Treasury, and therefore however free and adaptable its working methods it cannot pursue monetary programmes which are out of step with the economic thinking of the Government of the day.

4.5 The Merchant Banks

The term 'merchant banker' is properly applied to the 17 members of the London 'Accepting Houses Committee'. It refers to their origin as important merchants in the import-export trades.

The London commodity markets still form the basis of prosperity of the nation, and some of the 17 merchant bankers are still active as merchants: one owns subsidiary companies in the timber trade; one is active in the coffee trade; one has business houses in Australia, America, and Africa. The change to banking developed as the number of firms trading with overseas territories increased. Many of these new firms found that they lacked the respect and trust enjoyed by the well-established houses, and consequently faced difficulties in making payments in international trade. The chief method of payment was the bill of exchange drawn on London, but the smaller firms found that their bills of exchange were not acceptable unless they had the name of one of the great merchant houses on them. Remember that a bill of exchange is drawn upon the debtor by the drawer of the bill, requiring the debtor to pay a sum of money at some future time. The debtor may then 'accept' the bill, by signing his name on it, though frequently a bill may not be 'presented for acceptance' to the debtor. Whether accepted or not, a bill may be passed on to third parties by endorsement, the endorser receiving the discounted value of the bill from the endorsee.

Without going into the technicalities of bills of exchange too extensively, it is clear that a bill that has not been 'accepted' by the debtor does not bear the debtor's 'assent to the bill', and the only name that it does have on it is the endorser's name. If a bill passes from hand to hand it will soon have several endorsers' names on it, and will be that much more reliable; the better the names, the more reliable it is. It follows that the name of a great merchant 'house' will make a bill a very reliable one which will discount at a fine rate—since there is little risk of dishonour. The solution to the problems of firms new to international trade was found to be the accepting of these traders' bills by one of the older well-established firms, for a consideration in the form of commission. Gradually the merchants became bankers specialising in the accepting of bills for other merchants. They also made their own expertise available in many ways to less knowledgeable importers and exporters. Today they offer the full range of banking services to individuals, manufacturing and commercial concerns, investment institutions, local authorities and national governments, while every type of financial expertise is available for in-depth analysis of a client's problems.

A second interest of these firms in former times was the issue of foreign bonds for overseas governments who lacked capital. The issue of these bonds was only possible if the names of famous houses appeared in association with the issue. The merchant bankers arranged for a quotation on the London Stock Exchange, and handled the issues which were subscribed for by British and overseas investors. The London Foreign Bond Market was an international market and a source of 'invisible earnings' of foreign exchange, but it ceased to operate when the control of foreign exchange was implemented. Today there are other ways of arranging loans to foreign governments, but we may see a return to this type of issue now that controls have been removed.

The Functions of Accepting Houses Today

(*a*) **Finance of Home and Foreign Trade.** The accepting houses are still the specialist financiers of foreign trade, and the accepting of bills of exchange drawn on London is still one of their primary functions. Alongside the foreign bills has grown up a widespread use of inland bills, as part of the commercial sector's response to the control of credit by the Bank of England in the 1960s and 1970s. This growth in inland business has occurred because of the more competitive rates of interest charged on bills of exchange, which are essentially short-term money and therefore provide a ready, and reasonably priced, source of funds to businessmen.

It must not be overlooked, however, that the essential feature of a bill is its self-liquidating nature—that is, by the time the bill falls due, the trading venture it was designed to finance should have been completed and should have provided the funds for settlement of the bill. Bills are not intended to form a long-term financial alternative to bank loans or overdraft facilities. They are simply a method whereby the manufacturer borrows short-term or the exporter receives his payment and the importer enjoys a period of credit, while the goods are in transit, being unloaded, going through customs formalities, etc. This self-liquidating nature of acceptance credits enables merchant banks to grant the facility on an unsecured basis. Bills accepted by one of the 17 members of the Accepting Houses Committee are discounted at the finest rates and consequently are one of the cheapest ways of borrowing money.

Sterling Loans. Most merchant banks lend to a wide range of customers in the short-term and medium-term, and are heavily involved in **leasing** activities. The essence of leasing is that a firm which does not have the capital it requires to expand plant, machinery, distribution fleets, etc., comes to an arrangement whereby the merchant bank buys the equipment and leases it to the manufacturer, wholesaler, etc. This means that the lease payments are provided out of the new business made possible by the new equipment, any residue being available to the manufacturer, wholesaler, etc. This service is of great benefit to the small or medium-size firms seeking to grow, and also enables them to obtain the financial advice and guidance which the merchant bank is able to offer.

Foreign Currency Loans. Now that the controls on foreign exchange have been lifted merchant banks are able to make loans in foreign currencies to facilitate import-export business, foreign investment, commodity financing, purchase of ships and aircraft, etc. This is very much the traditional field of merchant banking, and they are better equipped than anyone else to advise on patterns of overseas trade, finance particular commodity transactions and monitor political and commercial developments around the world. They usually have subsidiary companies active in the commodity fields, such as metals, timber, grain, fibres, oil and oilseeds, beverage products, sugar and chemicals. They also have distribution facilities, and links with insurance houses. Their staff or subsidiaries are therefore able to act as brokers, agents, dealers and shippers where required. They can provide forward currency transactions to businessmen wishing to 'hedge' against currency losses, and 'option' contracts for those whose business commitments may require them.

(*b*) **Issuing of New Shares.** As foreign-bond issues decreased in the unsettled international situation of the 1930s, the merchant bankers turned to home issues. Very considerable increases in the scale of British business took place before the start of the Second World War, and the demand for large sums of capital presented problems to industry. These problems were solved by handing over to the merchant bankers the new issues of shares. The Issuing Houses Association has over 50 members, so there are many issuing houses which are not accepting houses. The accepting houses had a long experience of issuing foreign bonds, which made them particularly suitable for undertaking new issues.

New issues are made by offering shares and debentures in these ways:

(i) Direct to the general public, through a prospectus.

(ii) Through an issuing house, by an 'Offer for Sale', of shares to the general public.

Either of these methods enables a 'listing' to be obtained, so that the shares can be dealt in on the stock exchanges. Once a listing has been obtained further capital may be obtained by a 'rights' issue or by the sale of loan stock (debentures) to existing shareholders.

An alternative way to obtain finance is the private placement market, which enables fixed interest securities to be 'placed' by the issuing house with institutional investors at home or abroad. The fixed-interest securities can have an element of 'equity' interest built into them in the form of conversion rights.

Apart from the detailed arrangements necessary for the actual issue, the collection of subscriptions, the issue of allotment letters, letters of regret, etc., the merchant bank will offer advice on the pricing of the issue, and may also **underwrite** the issue, making themselves responsible for the success of the issue by agreeing to buy any part of it which is not taken up by the general public.

(*c*) **Acquisitions and Mergers.** In recent years the usual way for companies to 'grow' is by the acquisition of existing firms which are already operating in the field it is desired to enter. In this way much valuable expertise may be acquired, and the economies of large scale may be achieved. The work of identifying 'target' firms and selecting from among them the one which represents the best opportunities is clearly quite specialised and the merchant banks are well placed to conduct this type of expert appraisal. They can advise on the price to be paid, the best method of payment, the tax implications and the likelihood of meeting restrictions under UK monopoly legislation. In the case of overseas acquisitions they will investigate local regulations about foreign capital, the employment of home nationals and expatriate personnel, etc. They will usually carry out detailed negotiations about the acquisition or merger, and for every merchant bank that is offering advice on a 'takeover' bid there is one giving advice on how to resist it, or secure the best terms from the bidder.

(*d*) **Portfolio Management.** In investment terms a portfolio is a collection of securities, such as shares, debentures, gilt-edged securities, certificates of deposit, etc. The yield on such securities varies from week to week, and possibly from hour to hour, so the question of portfolio management is of enormous interest to individuals and institutions. The financial expertise of the merchant banks is clearly relevant to portfolio management; profits can be made and—more importantly perhaps—losses can be avoided if the portfolio is constantly reviewed in the light of day-to-day developments on the financial markets. The merchant banks are happy to undertake such work for clients who have investment portfolios for pension funds, as trustees for wards of court, etc., or for ordinary business purposes such as investment accounts for plant replacement reserves, etc. The essential element is a 'balanced' portfolio spread over a range of stocks and shares both as to the field of industrial or commercial activity and also the date of maturity, short, medium or long-term as desired.

(*e*) **Specialist Packages.** Most merchant banks have specialist fields of interest where they have extensive contacts. Thus one merchant bank has a specialist interest in films, and has put together packages of financial assistance to producers and technicians with the necessary film-making skills but inadequate finance. Others are specialists in property development, in shipbuilding, aviation, taxation, medicare finance, etc.

(*f*) **Confirming.** A confirming house operates as an intermediary between an overseas buyer and his British supplier. It confirms the order, sending it to the British manufacturer as if it was an order from the merchant banker. The British manufacturer supplies the goods to the confirming house, which pays for them, ships them to the overseas customer, and secures payment for the goods in its own name.

(*g*) **The Gold and Silver Bullion Markets.** These markets are operated by one or two of the merchant-banking firms, in association with certain independent brokers. All the accepting houses handle bullion; the price of gold is fixed daily at a meeting whose chairman is the representative of one of them which owns a refinery. Merchant banks also offer safe custody facilities for investors who invest in gold bullion, krugerrands and similar valuables.

4.6 The Merchant Banks Today

Today the more formal regulation of banks under the Banking Act, 1979, has led to a review of the status of each bank in the banking network. Whether this will lead to any changes in the membership of the Accepting Houses Committee remains to be seen but there seems to be some prospect that membership of an exclusive club which confers the City of London's approval will be less meaningful when status has already been conferred statutorily by the Bank of England. The chief requirement for membership is that a bank should be independent, and not subject to external influences—particularly foreign external influences. This is a limiting requirement in days of international banking, with British banks buying up banks in countries like the USA and Germany, while foreign bankers are also making approaches to link up with members of the Accepting Houses Committee.

4.7 The Savings Banks

Originally the savings banks were all trustee savings banks; later the National Savings Bank was formed, originally under the title 'Post Office Savings Bank'. The original aim of the trustee savings banks was to organise savings from small investors who were not individually able to make use of banking services or invest in gilt-edged and other securities. The savings were handled on a voluntary basis by 'honorary trustees' who invested the money collected in gilt-edged securities, and shared the interest earned as interest payments to the savers. Later the position was regularised so that all deposits were paid into funds managed by the National Debt Commissioners and all withdrawals finished up as withdrawals from these funds.

Later the manifest usefulness of this class of savings in providing funds for Government use led to the starting of the Post Office Savings Bank in the mid-nineteenth century. At this time the Post Office was a Government department, with a widespread network of post offices which could provide a cheap 'branch-banking' network for the entire nation. Many savings were very small—until recently it was possible to save up 12 pennies until a 'shilling' had been collected, a shilling being the minimum deposit. Some idea of the vast number of accounts can be gathered from the fact that towards the end of the Victorian era Parliament authorised the closing of all redundant accounts with balances of less than £1, whose owners could not be traced, in order to provide the funds to build the Law Courts in London. A million pounds was provided in this way, so that the Law Courts are a monument to the thrift of the Victorians (or perhaps to their unwillingness to lose face by claiming the last few shillings in their accounts). When the Post Office Corporation was set up in 1969 the Post Office Savings Bank became the National Savings Bank.

This National Savings Bank started in 1861, and by the end of the century was offering 2½ per cent interest on deposits, a rate which prevailed until

1970. For at least some of the post-war years the drive for increased national savings, which was a such a feature of the war years for example, was reduced in the interests of Keynesian economics. Thrift was no longer a virtue; what was needed was for everyone to spend, spend, spend. It became a virtue again in the mid-1960s, when the greater equality of incomes led to 'excessive' demand as the working classes with their strong propensity to consume became affluent for the first time in history. In 1962 the London docker was still earning £12 a week; by 1967 this had risen to £35 per week and by 1974 they were asking £100 per week. Changes in personal income, consumers' expenditure and personal saving in recent years are given in Table 4.1.

Table 4.1. Personal income and savings (£ million)

	Total personal disposable income (1)	*Consumers' expenditure* (2)	*Personal saving* (1) – (2) (3)	*Personal saving as a percentage of total personal disposable income* (4)
1966	26 655	24 211	2 444	9.2
1967	27 798	25 428	2 370	8.5
1968	29 701	27 338	2 363	8.0
1969	31 663	29 102	2 561	8.1
1970	34 766	31 644	3 122	9.0
1971	38 454	35 165	3 289	8.6
1972	44 229	39 716	4 513	10.2
1973	50 954	45 044	5 910	11.6
1974	60 305	51 832	8 473	14.1
1975	73 751	63 373	10 378	14.1
1976	84 459	73 966	10 493	12.4
1977	96 854	84 010	12 844	13.3
1978	112 247	96 308	15 939	14.2
1979	133 285	112 245	21 040	15.8
1980	158 587	134 594	23 993	15.1

(Source: *Financial Statistics*)

Although actual personal savings increased eightfold in the 15 years, the percentage of income being saved increased only 1.7 times. Savings in the National Savings Bank during the late 1960s actually fell, a situation which reflected the return received: a 2½ per cent interest rate could not compete with building society rates of 6 or 7 per cent. From 1966 to 1970 there were net withdrawals from National Savings. In 1970 the 2½ per cent rate of interest was abandoned. Rates were increased, but the Page Committee reported in 1973 in favour of still higher yields, more competitive with those available to small investors in other forms of saving. An increase in the permitted size of holdings of National Savings Certificates, Premium Bonds, etc., and the introduction of index-linked Save-As-You-Earn and Retirement Certificates brought increased flows into National Savings during the later years of the decade.

By 1980, with a variety of different schemes available to savers, the total contribution of the National Savings movement to the Central Government borrowing requirement was £11 378.1 million made up as shown in Table 4.2.

Table 4.2. National Savings: 1980, First Quarter

Type of Savings	*£ million*
National Savings Certificates	4 135.0
Retirement Certificates	1 514.2
National Savings Stamps	9.3
Save-As-You-Earn Scheme	36.8
Index-linked Certificates	390.3
Savings Bonds	582.9
Premium Bonds	1 420.9
National Savings Bank	1 805.4
Other	1 483.3
	£11 378.1

Source: (*Financial Statistics*)

Meanwhile the Page Committee Report was having a more pronounced effect on the work of the trustee savings banks and led to the Trustee Savings Bank Act of 1976.

The Trustee Savings Bank Act, 1976

The Act recognised that developments in modern society had created a situation where savers required more from a bank than a mere repository for savings against a rainy day. The general public are more sophisticated in monetary matters than earlier generations, and require the full range of banking services. This had already been recognised by developments in the trustee savings bank system before 1976, but the Act recognised that a new statutory framework was desirable. Accordingly it set up a Trustee Savings Bank Central Board, which it empowered as follows:

The Central Board—

(*a*) may give directions of a general character to the trustee savings banks as to the carrying on by the trustee savings banks of their activities;

(*b*) may provide banking services for the trustee savings banks;

(*c*) may provide other common services for the trustee savings banks including data processing services and the formation, management and operation of unit trusts;

(*d*) may give directions to the trustee savings banks as to the equipment and procedures to be adopted by them in the operation of banking services, the manner in which funds are to be raised, expended, allocated to reserve and invested and the rates of interest to be paid on deposits;

(*e*) shall give directions to the trustee savings banks as to the conditions of service of persons employed by the banks.

(*Reproduced in abbreviated form by courtesy of Her Majesty's Stationery Office*)

The full effects of the 1976 Act are still being realised by the trustee savings banks, who have extended the services available to a considerable extent. They are now concerned with offering a full personal service of money management to customers, including overdrafts, personal loans, bridging loans, credit cards and personal savings. *'As they are not conducted for private profit they should be able to do this in the most convenient and economical manner to the even greater benefit of their customers and the community at large.'* So reads one of their brochures.

4.8 The National Girobank

Giro systems are usually associated with less-sophisticated economies where a fully developed branch-banking network is not available. Many European countries developed giro systems at times when their populations were peasantries associated with petty agriculture. The establishment of a Giro system did not take place in the UK until 1967. Its aim was to provide banking services for the sector of the population that has not traditionally used the branch-banking system—chiefly housewives and lower-income groups.

The essence of a giro system is that credits can be transferred from one account to another under a 'credit transfer' system. Since this term really describes what happens it is rather a pity that the banks, in order to resist competition from National Giro, adopted the term 'bank giro' to describe their 'credit transfer' systems.

In the 10 years after its creation National Giro established a firm foothold in the banking sector closest to the cash market, where less sophisticated methods of money transmission (postal orders and money orders) had traditionally been used. It grew rapidly, and extended its range of banking services to the point where, in 1978, it changed its name to National Girobank and was accorded the status of a listed bank. This status has been confirmed under the Banking Act, 1979.

The field for Girobank services has proved to be more extensive than seemed likely in 1967. The most obvious example of the use of the giro system is in the field of mail-order business, where housewives acting as agents for the mail-order houses collect weekly payments from friends and neighbours. Many such housewives do not have bank accounts and also call regularly at Post Offices to collect family allowances. They are thus able to pay in the takings from their agency at the Post Office for credit to the Giro account of the mail order house. No charge is made for such transfers and it is obviously more convenient than buying postal orders and sending the payment by post. The fact that National Giro operates through post offices is its major advantage; the use of the existing outlets avoids the heavy costs of a branch network, and this marginal activity is a source of further income to sub-postmasters and sub-postmistresses.

Other possibilities in the near-cash field have been the collection of rents for local authorities and the payment of accounts for gas, electricity and water. More than 40 million rent payments per year are made through National Girobank, and several million gas, electricity and water accounts are also paid over the counter at post offices. The service which National Girobank wishes to develop most is the credit transfer system for wage payments. Payment of wages in cash is one of the most expensive, time-consuming and risk-ridden aspects of business life, and also restricts the development and full use of advanced financial services. The conversion of wage earners into bank customers may yet be National Girobank's most valuable contribution to the economy.

Deposits from corporate customers in 1979 exceeded £18 000 million. This huge sum reflects the widespread use of the post office network to accept deposits from branches of multiple-shop concerns. A daily list identifying branches which make deposits and the longer hours for post office counter business, give head offices good control over their branch managers.

Links with European giro organisations have enabled British tourists to cash Girocheques in 80 000 post offices abroad.

4.9 The Co-operative Bank

The Co-operative Movement started in 1844 at Toad Lane, Rochdale, with 28 co-operators and a turnover in the year of £700. It grew rapidly into a nationwide institution, which not only ran retail shops but set up its own wholesale organisation, the Co-operative Wholesale Society. It turned to manufacturing as a means of providing employment for workers over-exposed to the rigours of early capitalism, and eventually the services of insurance, shipping and banking were deemed to be appropriate fields of activity for an organisation dedicated to co-operative control of every aspect of economic activity. The bank was set up originally in 1872 as the 'Loan and Deposit Department of the Co-operative Wholesale Society', since banking was not permitted by law as a co-operative activity. This restriction was removed in 1876 and the department then became the CWS Bank. Not until 1971 was the link with the Co-operative Wholesale Society finally severed, and the bank called the Co-operative Bank Ltd.

By 1882 the assets were still only £214 000, and it was 1919 before the assets reached £10 million. Today they are about £400 million, and the bank has a subsidiary company, Co-operative Commercial Bank Ltd, which operates in the City of London on the interbank lending market and the eurocurrency market. Another subsidiary is FC Finance Ltd, a medium-size finance company which handles much of the Co-operative Movement's hire purchase finance—still one of the most economical Hire Purchase activities, offering co-operative shoppers fair terms on a huge range of consumer durables.

The co-operative banking movement has always had the significant advantage of in-store banking, where premises for the banking facility could be provided at little additional cost. Banking hours were linked to retail trade hours, which are longer than normal banking hours, and convenience for the co-operator was also a consideration. Regrettably for the Co-operative Bank, the fullest extension of its banking system coincided with a decline in Co-operative trade as a percentage of total retail trade, and a decline in 'co-operator loyalty' associated with the greater affluence of working people today. The co-operative shops have always done best in bad times and less well in affluent times, when shoppers are less concerned with the real value of the goods they buy. Despite this change in the co-operatives' retail impact the 'in-store' facility is the most likely development for retail banking as a whole, and this gives the Co-operative Bank a head start. If the Big Four ever manage to overcome the inertia of a widespread branch-banking system they will move into the retail outlets in a big way, copying the Co-op's 'Cash-a-cheque' counters, available at all retail hours. The Bank's activities have expanded sufficiently in the last decade for it to become a clearing bank on the London Clearing House in its own right. The disadvantage for the Co-operative Bank at the moment is that it can only expand at the same rate as its servicing ability, and to help in this respect a new central customer service bureau has been developed at Skelmersdale in Lancashire.

Co-operative banking is well-developed in Europe, where they are called 'popular' banks or 'people's banks', and a friendly network of such banks is established through the Paris-based CICP (Conféderation Internationale de Crédit Populaire).

4.10 The Building Societies

As their name implies, the building societies were started (in the late eighteenth century) as societies of working people who pooled their resources to buy plots of land and build themselves houses. The original arrangement was to pay money regularly each month into the society until all the members were housed, when the society came to an end (a 'terminating' society). Later it became clear that a great deal of time could be saved in the accumulation of capital if members were accepted who did not wish to build houses, but simply to save surplus funds and earn interest on them. Those who did want to build a house had to pay interest on the funds borrowed, and in 1874 the Building Societies Act regularised the societies in their present form. By 1900 the societies had a total capital of £60 million, which rose to £10 000 million by 1970 and £40 000 million by 1978. So much for inflation!

The current Act of Parliament is the 1962 Building Societies Act, which sets out the functions of societies and the way they must be managed. Their functions are:

(*a*) To act as a savings organisation for individual savers.
(*b*) To provide loans to individuals wishing to buy their own homes.

A high standard of probity is called for in conducting the affairs of a building society, since the small savers who invest their funds might easily be ruined by any embezzlement. The occasional scandal does occur, the most recent being the Grays Building Society, where a particular individual over a period of 40 years embezzled several million pounds. A rescue operation organised by the big societies ensured that Grays' savers did not lose their money, the loss being shared widely over the movement as a whole. The Building Societies Association exists to represent the societies, with over 200 societies as members and 99 per cent of the total assets of the movement. It requires strict financial standards as a condition of membership and advises societies on matters of policy and practice. It acts as a link between the building societies and Government and other representative organisations. It also provides information on building societies and on the services they offer to the public.

Control of the Building Societies

The affluent society of the last quarter of the twentieth century has made huge sums available to the building societies, which have inevitably become competitors to some extent of banks and other deposit-taking institutions. They offer extremely safe investment to small savers, with a good return—income tax paid (although this arrangement can be disadvantageous to the small saver who does not pay income tax at the standard rate). The convenience of withdrawal of funds is a great incentive to savers; the offices do not work banking hours and withdrawals on demand are available up to a limit of about £200.

Because of the vulnerability of the small savers who invest with them the movement is subject to controls designed to ensure prudent behaviour. Loans may only be made against the security of a mortgage on a freehold or leasehold estate of land. The bulk of such loans (90 per cent) in any year must be less than £20 000, and made to individuals or housing associations. The other 10 per cent may be higher loans to individuals, or loans to corporations.

The societies must maintain 15 per cent of their funds in liquid or near liquid form: 7½ per cent must be as cash or deposits with named banks or in short-term Government securities; the other 7½ per cent may be in longer-term debt in Government or local government securities. The aim is to have adequate funds available to meet the needs of depositors, and to avoid any *significant* capital loss if securities have to be sold suddenly.

A further control is enacted through the Building Societies (Designation for Trustee Investments) Regulations, 1977. A trustee is someone holding funds on behalf of another (who is unable to control them personally). Thus a Trustee in Lunacy is appointed by the Courts to care for the funds of those who are insane. Such a person has a duty of care to ensure that any investment made is properly placed with a reputable institution. To comply with the regulations a society wishing to accept deposits from trustees must be of a certain size (£2½ million at present), must keep its loans within certain limits, maintain a correct degree of liquidity, etc. The Registrar has discretion to refuse 'trustee status' if he believes the affairs of a particular society are not being conducted in an appropriate manner.

There is a Joint Advisory Committee on Mortgage Finance by which the Government seeks to influence building society lending. The building societies' view of this panel is as follows:

> Through the JAC, the Government is able to make its views known to building societies and, in turn, building societies can give their opinion to Government. The JAC provides a forum in which officials from the Treasury, the Bank of England, the Registry of Friendly Societies and the Department of Environment can discuss mutual problems with building society executives. The societies recognise that this arrangement is in the national interest and that it provides an appropriate means by which Government can influence the activity of the movement.
>
> (*By courtesy of the Building Societies Association*)

The Building Societies and the Savings Market

Some idea of the relative importance of the building societies in the savings market can be gained from Table 4.3. It is essentially a 'small savers' organisation, with about 98 per cent of all shares and deposits held by the personal sector. Many of these savers have no other savings account, so that the societies claim to be introducing new funds into the banking system, rather than depriving other institutions of funds. The table illustrates the savings achieved by various sectors of the savings market.

Table 4.3. Savings balances, major institutions (March 31, 1980)

Institution	*Amount (£ million)*	*Percentage share*
National Savings	11 378	11.3
Trustee savings banks	5 495	5.4
Building societies	37 657	37.4
Commercial banks	46 234	45.9
Total	100 764	100

(Source: *Financial Statistics*)

Clearly the building societies are playing an important role in the savings field, which reflects to some extent the importance of housing to the ordinary citizen, whose house is by far the most important—and the most expensive—asset acquired during a lifetime.

4.11 The Finance Houses

There are about 40 members of the Finance Houses Association, which exists to represent its members in the complex field of retail, commercial and industrial credit. At the end of 1979 balances owed to members exceeded £5900 million, of which 60 per cent was finance provided to industry and commerce, the balance being to consumers. This field is complex because it is hedged about by a mass of legislation—some of it designed to protect the consumer; some to protect the depositor who places funds in the hands of the Finance Houses; some to levy taxation, etc.

Traditionally the organisations who provided credit were the banks, but for many people the banks were not a satisfactory source of credit. In the first place, many people could not provide any sort of security for the sums they wished to borrow, and secondly they were unable to present any sound programme of repayment in a system of society where the employer's right to 'hire and fire' was considered absolute, so that unemployment was an ever-present possibility. In the circumstances a body of non-bank financiers grew up whose methods of business were more adaptable than the traditional banking system, but whose rates of interest reflected the greater degree of risk. In most cases the goods to be purchased with the finance to be provided were the only security available, so that repossession of the goods was the finance company's only way of recovering anything from a bad debt. The retail side of this business became the 'hire purchase' system as we know it today. Countless millions of such transactions have taken place in the last half century to the general satisfaction of hirers, retailers and finance companies.

The hire purchase field is now controlled, with other forms of credit, by the Consumer Credit Act, 1974, which attempts to ensure fair trading in this important area. The important concept of 'fair trading', which is personified in the Director General of Fair Trading, has been widely accepted and is very influential in credit business today. All credit grantors must now have a licence, which can be withdrawn by the Office of Fair Trading not only for a breach of the law, but even if the Director General of Fair Trading decides that a particular practice is undesirable. The finance houses are therefore extremely careful to keep within the spirit of 'fair trading' in their activities. They are very active in the consumer field, where credit assessments are relatively easy; many consumers quickly establish a reputation for reliability and the sums involved—usually a few hundred pounds—mean that an individual bad debt is not a serious loss.

Most finance houses are recognised by the Bank of England as licensed deposit-taking institutions, although by no means all the money they use is obtained in this way. The cost of developing a wide branch network for the collection of deposits are usually greater than the costs of borrowing in the sophisticated financial markets (or parallel markets) of the City. The deposits thus become large-scale fixed-term deposits from major institutional investors, earning rates slightly above interbank lending rates. Most finance houses have a mix of funds. Some will be deposits through the interbank market, some will be deposits made against the issue of Certificates of Deposit. Other funds will be obtained by using acceptance credits, and others from accepting deposits from the general public. Where funds are taken from private depositors they tend to be from interest-sensitive sophisticated lenders who are able to invest a lump sum rather than small savings. If this type of deposit is to be stable interest rates must reflect interest rates in other fields, and exceed them, so that finance house rates tend to be adjusted reasonably quickly to achieve a balance between the funds available to them as borrowers and the demand from customers for loans.

With regard to the loans made by finance houses about half are tied to the Finance House Base Rate, so that interest rates can be adjusted according to market conditions. Where they are fixed-rate loans the profitability of the loan to the finance company is affected by changes in interest rates generally. If interest rates rise this lowers the profitability of the finance house's activities. In the rather rare circumstance of a fall in interest rates the finance house would benefit—but the tendency in recent years has been for the return on funds employed by finance houses to be inadequate in times of high rates of inflation.

The volume of business handled by the finance houses may be gathered from Tables 4.4 and 4.5.

Table 4.4. Outstanding credit to FHA members, December 31, 1981 (excluding unearned finance charges)

	£ million	*Percentage*
1. Total	10119	100.0
of which		
2. Outstanding to consumers	3008	29.7
3. Outstanding to business customers (excluding leasing)	2947	29.1
4. Leasing (written down value of leased assets)	4164	41.2

Note: These figures include all outstandings whether payable by instalments or not.

(Source: *Finance Houses Association*)

4.12 Other Non-Bank Financial Intermediaries

The non-bank financial intermediaries include the building societies and finance houses already described. Others are the unit trusts and investment trusts, the life assurance and pension funds and the local authorities. Many of these institutions lend money to individuals and firms and play an important part in the intricate monetary workings of a sophisticated economy. Their activities in certain non-bank fields are crucial to the stability of the economy—we cannot envisage a housing system without the building societies, or a hire-purchase system without the finance houses. The activites of institutional investors like unit trusts and investment trusts are extremely important on the Stock Exchange, while the contented old age of our pensioners depends upon the life assurance and pension fund operators.

Besides lending money to individuals and firms these institutions are also active in taking deposits in some cases far in excess of what they pay out.

Table 4.5. New credit extended by FHA members (excluding finance charges)

Not seasonally adjusted	Quarters ended	*1981*							*1980*
	December 31 (£m)	December 31 (%)	September 30 (£m)	September 30 (%)	June 30 (£m)	June 30 (%)	March 31 (£m)	March 31 (%)	December 31 (£m)	December 31 (%)
1. Total	1781	100.0	1596	100.0	1474		1227	100.0	1440	100.0
2. To consumers	596	33.5	685	42.9	590	40.0	501	40.8	440	30.5
3. To business customers (excluding leasing)	484	27.2	457	28.6	436	29.6	366	29.8	364	25.3
4. Leasing (original cost of assets purchased for lease)	701	39.3	454	28.5	448	30.4	360	29.4	636	44.2

Note: These figures include all advances whether payable by instalment or not.
(Source: *Finance Houses Association*)

They thus become very influential in financial markets, where they have sizeable funds to invest as institutional investors. They also provide a variety of securities which are available to investors and depositors which may in fact be attractive enough to compete with the banks at times when money balances are for some reason not attractive to customers.

Unit Trusts and Investment Trusts

These two types of financial institution exist to give small investors an interest in the activities of the Stock Exchange, without the risks of losses and the relatively high charges for transactions which would apply where the sum involved is quite small. Investment trusts raise capital by issuing shares and debentures, while unit trusts raise money by selling units. The funds collected are then invested across a 'balanced portfolio' of shares, the range of shares to be purchased for a particular trust being explained in its publicity literature. Although a particular class of share (say, brewery shares) may represent only $1\frac{1}{2}$ per cent of the whole portfolio the actual shares purchased in each brewery might be £10 000. This would be an economical purchase on the Stock Exchange. The wide spread of risks is clearly advantageous; professional managers knowledgeable about the trends in business affairs are available full-time to monitor the market; their charges are low (about $\frac{3}{8}$ per cent of the value of the portfolio, levied annually, and a 5 per cent initial charge); capital gains tax problems are also simplified.

During the 1970s decreasing profitability in business generally led to a decline in investment trust and unit trust business, in real terms. The returns on many shares were very low, and better returns could be obtained by investors in other ways. Although the figures shown in Table 4.6 for unit trust total funds show an increase from 1971 to 1979, *in real terms*, when inflation is taken into account, there has in fact been a decline. The figures for investment trusts are now collected on a new basis (from 1978) and the earlier figures are not strictly comparable. In the years shown there was an actual decline in the funds employed. In 1979 there were some 300 unit trusts and some 200 investments trusts contributing statistics to the Department.

Table 4.6. Total funds available: unit and investment trusts

Year	*£ million*
	Unit trusts
1971	1991
1973	2060
1975	2512
1977	3461
1979	3937
	Investment trusts
1978	6460
1979	5752

(Source: *Financial Statistics*)

Pension Funds and Life Assurance Funds

Pension contributions and life assurance premiums are major sources of long-term savings, which bring millions of pounds every week into the investment markets. Fund managers are constantly on the look-out for investments and evaluating the portfolios which they have built up over the years. Two nationalised institutions, the Post Office and the National Coal Board, have pension funds in excess of £2 billion. In 1980 total pension funds stood at about £40 billion, a very considerable part of the UK's total capital. With such huge sums it is not surprising that difficulties can arise. We may list the following interesting points:

(*a*) A large fund with sizeable investments in a company or a class of shares finds it difficult to dispose of a security which it feels is moving adversely without depressing the market to its own disadvantage. Similarly, any attempt to buy a sizeable parcel of shares raises the price.

(*b*) Since the dealings of such institutional investors are a major part of the activity of markets they must in fact be in opposite positions on many occasions, i.e. one fund's loss is another fund's gain.

(*c*) Where a fund is advised by a broker or merchant bank which is remunerated on the basis of each transaction there is a natural tendency for the adviser to churn over the investments to increase his commission. Evidence is collecting that hyperactivity of this sort does very little for the fund, or the pensioner whose funds are being manipulated, but a great deal for the financier who is giving his advice. The trustees who permit this sort of activity are really failing in their duty to the pensioners. This is a field where new controls are desirable.

The volumes of investments in these fields for most recent years available are shown in Table 4.7

Table 4.7. Superannuation and insurance funds (£ million)

Year	*Superannuation funds*	*Insurance companies*	
		General funds	*Long-term funds*
1977	24 983	7 375	34 256
1978	31 054	8 458	38 371

(Source: *Financial Statistics*)

Investment Banks and Industrial Banks

These two classes of banks are included in the non-bank sector because, as far as the UK is concerned, they are not in general to be classified as banks under the Banking Act, 1979. Institutions with this type of function do not usually offer a full banking service and are therefore being classified as **deposit-taking institutions**. This means that they are being required to change their names under the Act, and to delete the word 'bank' from their names.

The functions of investment banks are to take funds from depositors who have funds seeking employment and find a suitable opportunity for them. Thus a great deal of 'oil-fund recycling' has been carried out in recent years as the OPEC countries have huge surpluses from the sale of oil which they have wished to invest in secure countries.

Industrial banks, frequently subsidiaries of merchant banks or commercial banks, specialise in activities (like leasing and hire purchase of capital equipment) which are of interest to the industrial sector of the economy.

Credit Unions

Credit unions under the Credit Unions Act, 1979, may be registered as organisations within the general field of the Industrial and Provident Societies Act, 1965. To be admitted to membership of a Credit Union persons must be qualified as:

(*a*) following a particular occupation;
(*b*) residing in a particular locality;
(*c*) employed by a particular employer;
(*d*) members of a *bona fide* organisation; or
(*e*) qualified by some other means approved by the Registrar of Friendly Societies.

These credit unions are small-scale credit-providing self-help organisations. The members contribute funds by contributions, often deductions from weekly pay, which may then be loaned out to other members in temporary difficulties, or for meeting expenditures. The minimum share holding is one fully paid-up share, and the maximum value that a member can be *required* to hold is £5. No member may have more than £2000 deposited with a credit union. Clearly these are relatively insignificant organisations financially, yet the service they render to members may be of great significance socially, particularly among immigrant communities, or among the less wealthy sectors of society.

4.13 Revision Test

Answers	*Questions*
—	**1.** What is a bill broker?
1. A financial specialist who takes money from those who have a surplus and makes it available to those who require it.	**2.** How is the money made available to those who want it?
2. They give the bill broker a bill of exchange for a future date, and he gives them the discounted value of the bill at once. Hence the name 'discount house'.	**3.** Where do the discount houses get their funds?
3. From banks, local authorities and anyone else who has surplus funds available.	**4.** Why are the banks prepared to lend money cheaply to the discount houses?
4. Because such loans still count as part of a bank's eligible reserve assets. If not lent to the discount house they could not be loaned out at all and consequently would earn no interest.	**5.** What is the 'lender of last resort' system?

Answers	*Questions*
5. Discount houses borrow 'short' and lend long. They must occasionally get into difficulties. When they do the Bank of England acts as lender of last resort and lends them money to balance their books.	**6.** How does this enable the Bank of England to control the short-term money market?
6. It enables the Bank to charge the discount houses a 'penal rate' if it feels they are lending too cheaply and too much. This will cause them to raise interest rates to customers.	**7.** What are 'merchant banks'?
7. Members of the London Accepting Houses Committee who specialise in providing funds for overseas trade and a wide variety of important business activities.	**8.** What are their major activities?
8. (*a*) The acceptance of bills of exchange. (*b*) New issues of shares and debentures. (*c*) Arranging acquisitions and mergers. (*d*) Portfolio and other financial advice.	**9.** What are the 'savings banks'?
9. They are the trustee savings banks and the National Savings Bank.	**10.** What is their function today?
10. To offer a wider banking service to the large section of the public with relatively small incomes.	**11.** What is the Co-operative Bank?
11. A bank developed from the Co-operative Movement which offers a full banking service to the general public, but also commands a considerable range of business because of loyalty from co-operative institutions, trade unions, labour-controlled councils, etc.	**12.** What are the functions of the building societies?
12. To offer a convenient and secure savings system to those who wish to save, and provide funds for those wishing to purchase houses for personal occupation.	**13.** What are finance houses?
13. Deposit-taking institutions who specialise in providing funds for hire purchase finance, leasing and other business activities.	**14.** What are the sources of their funds?

Answers	*Questions*
14. (*a*) Deposits from sophisticated, interest-conscious individuals and institutions. (*b*) Day-to-day balances are arranged by an overdraft facility with a merchant bank. These balances are then funded by bidding for longer-term deposits on the parallel markets.	**15.** Now try some of the questions in Appendix I.

5

MONEY MARKETS AND RATES OF INTEREST

5.1 Introduction

The previous chapters have outlined the main institutions involved with money. This chapter seeks to discover the ways in which these institutions relate to each other—how they come together in various money and financial markets. Generally 'money' markets are those dealing with short-term funds and are distinct from the medium-term or long-term 'capital' and financial markets such as the Stock Exchange. Despite these differences all markets for money, long or short, are linked to some degree by the rate of interest. To be more precise, we really should refer to *rates* of interest, since there is no such thing as a *general rate of interest*, just as there is no *general* level of prices. Instead different markets, because of different risks, etc., within them, have rates of interest peculiar to themselves, which reflect to a considerable extent conditions prevailing in that particular market. However, it is undoubtedly true that interest rates in different markets do relate to each other, and it is impossible to consider a particular rate of interest in isolation from rates in closely related markets.

5.2 Money Markets

The pattern of financial arrangements in a sophisticated mixed economy is a very intricate network of markets where financial bargains take place. An endless succession of contractual obligations is undertaken, sometimes formally and very often informally under the general principle that 'My word is my bond'. This phrase, from the Latin *Dictum meum pactum* (the motto of the London Stock Exchange), implies that an obligation undertaken by word of mouth will be as binding on the dealer who undertook it as a formal legal document that has been signed, sealed and delivered.

Some markets are highly centralised, having a recognised meeting place. Examples in the UK are the Stock Exchange (the market for existing stocks and shares) and the Baltic Exchange (the market where ships and aircraft are found for cargoes, and cargoes are found for ships and aircraft). Other markets are less centralised, deals taking place over the telephone or in the offices of individual firms where customers make bargains by 'private treaty'. Others are purely 'domestic', like the market for ordinary bank loans, where some customers are calling at the bank to make deposits and others are calling to request a loan. Such a 'market' is designated as a 'retail' market, the individual amounts dealt in being quite small. In aggregate—for example, the daily clearing at the Clearing House—these transactions are quite large, but they are still spoken of as 'retail' in character. At a higher level we have a series of markets which are called 'wholesale' markets. Here major financial institutions of all types—banks, discount houses, merchant banks, investment banks, insurance companies, major industrial companies, nationalised institutions, pension funds and local authorities—are bidding for or offering either directly or through brokers, large sums of money. There will often be a minimum contract (perhaps £10 000) but much larger sums would normally change hands.

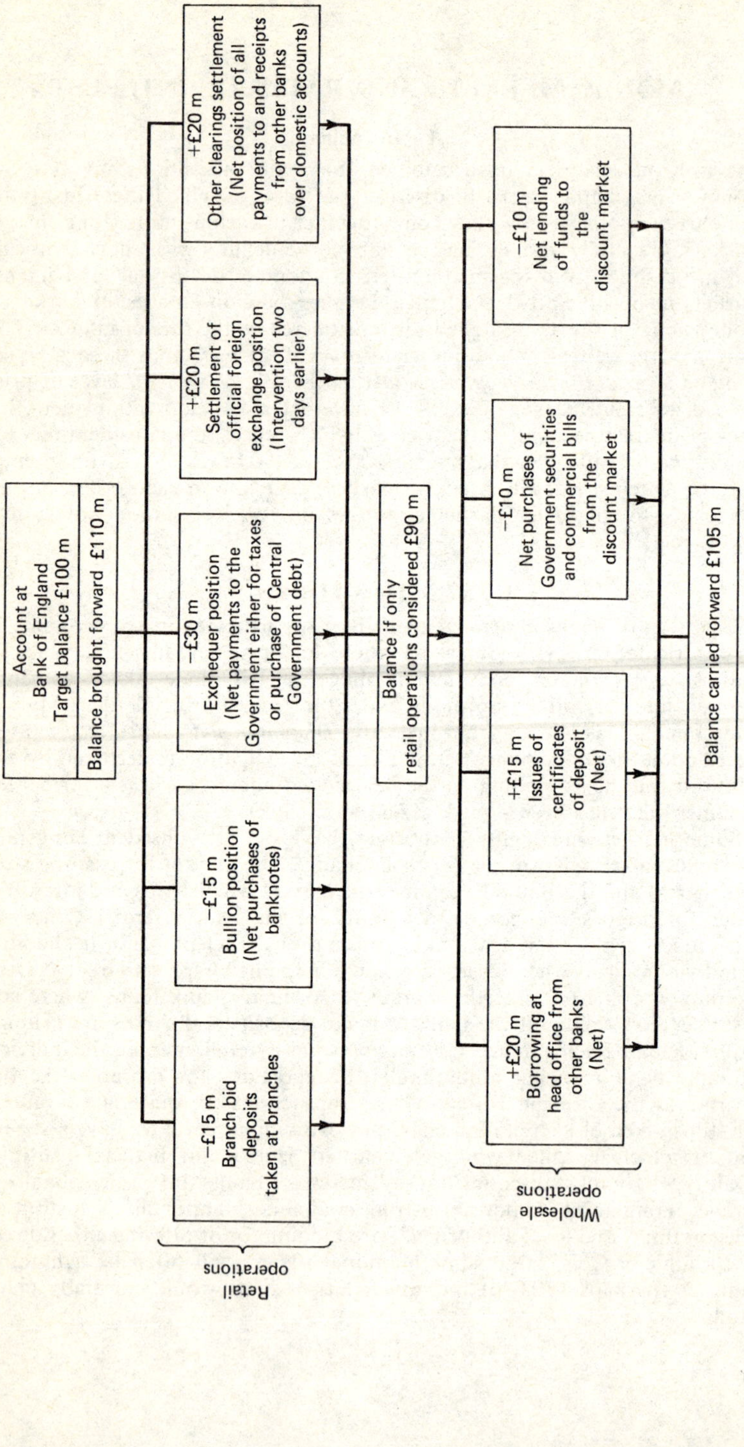
Account at
Bank of England
Target balance £100 m
Balance brought forward £110 m
−£15 m
Branch bid
deposits
taken at branches
−£15 m
Bullion position
(Net purchases of
banknotes)
−£30 m
Exchequer position
(Net payments to the
Government either for taxes
or purchase of Central
Government debt)
+£20 m
Settlement of
official foreign
exchange position
(Intervention two
days earlier)
+£20 m
Other clearings settlement
(Net position of all
payments to and receipts
from other banks
over domestic accounts)
Retail
operations
Balance if only
retail operations considered £90 m
+£20 m
Borrowing at
head office from
other banks
(Net)
+£15 m
Issues of
certificates
of deposit
(Net)
−£10 m
Net purchases of
Government securities
and commercial bills
from the
discount market
−£10 m
Net lending
of funds to
the
discount market
Wholesale
operations
Balance carried forward £105 m

Fig. 5.1. A bank and the sterling money markets.
(Reproduced by courtesy of Barclays Bank Ltd)

Notes

(i) The target balance at the Bank of England is imagined to be £100 million but on the previous day the balance was exceeded at £110 million.

(ii) The bank's day-to-day retail business was pursued. The net result of dealings at the branches was a loss of cash of £15 million. A further £15 million was spent on bank-notes from the Bank of England, while a further £30 million was paid to the Government for tax purposes, or the purchase of gilt-edged securities. To offset these losses of liquidity the daily clearing produced a surplus of £20 million and foreign exchange transactions produced a surplus of £20 million. The total effect of all these retail activities was a decline in the overnight balances to only £90 million.

(iii) Although wholesale activities in both directions are taking place during the day the bank has to regulate them so that it restores its balance at the Bank of England to the target figure of £100 million. The bank restores its position by borrowing from other banks or by withdrawing funds from the discount market, or by selling assets to the rest of the banking system. In the diagram, by borrowing from other banks, and accepting deposits against which it issues Certificates of Deposit, it achieves net inflows of £35 million. These are reduced by net outflows of £10 million for bills purchased from the Discount Market and a net lending of £10 million to the Discount Market. The final balance is above target at £105 million.

If banks as a whole are short, interest rates will rise as the banks compete for interbank funds. The extent to which the rates move depends on how much aid and in what form the Bank of England supplies the markets to alleviate the shortage.

The terms used to describe these markets vary, and it is well to sort out the pattern of terms used. First of all, these 'wholesale' money markets involve large-scale activities between specialist dealers. The primary wholesale money market is the Discount Market, which has already been described fully. All other money markets are 'secondary' markets. As these markets are operating at the same time as the Discount Market they are also spoke of as 'parallel' markets. The term has no special significance—by analogy with electrical circuits it simply means that money passing through the system from borrower to lender or lender to borrower may pass through either the 'primary' market or one of the 'secondary' markets; there are alternative, parallel routes open to it.

The commercial banks do not operate directly on the secondary markets, their direct activities are confined to the Discount Market and head office transactions with other banks. They may indirectly have dealings on the secondary markets because the network of financial links established between banks, merchant banks, finance houses, etc., is so sophisticated that mutual support and influence are exerted across the whole range of financial activities.

Operations in the Sterling Money Markets

A bank has four main aims in its dealings on the wholesale money markets. In the UK this means the sterling money markets. They are:

(*a*) To put out surplus funds which it may have available to earn market rates of interest. In some cases—for example, when it lends money to the discount houses—it will do so because it can loan the funds without any loss of liquidity, the funds being 'at call' or 'short notice'. In other cases it may lend for longer periods.

(*b*) To maintain adequate reserve assets so that it cannot be faulted with regard to the reserve ratio requirements (see Chapter 12).

(*c*) To raise the money market funds it needs to carry on the volume of business it is currently pursuing.

(*d*) To achieve its target balance with the central bank. The Bank of England requires cash deposits of ½ per cent of their **eligible liabilities** from the whole monetary sector and also extra funds from the clearing banks for clearing purposes. Just how a bank's financial position is affected by the various retail and wholesale activities it is necessarily engaged in is shown in Fig. 5.1. The notes below the caption explain the diagram.

The secondary markets may be listed as follows:

(*a*) The interbank market.
(*b*) The local authority market.
(*c*) The Eurocurrency market.
(*d*) The market in certificates of deposit.

The work of the secondary markets has grown up over the last two decades, and the institutions which deal on them do so because there is a need to make a market where buyers and sellers of money can be in touch with one another either directly or through agents. They are essentially markets where uses can be found for spare funds and where funds can be found for all sorts of purposes.

(*a*) **The Interbank Market.** The interbank market is a market in short-term money, unsecured except by the reputation of those who are dealing. A good deal of money is 'overnight' money, borrowed by banks seeking to balance their books overnight and meet their target balances at the Bank of England. Originally started by a group of brokers who quoted rates for money from 'overnight' up to a year in duration, acting as agents on a commission basis, the system has now overlapped with the primary money market in that the discount houses are active. There is also a good deal of direct negotiation between head offices of major banks, thus short-circuiting both the agents and the discount houses. The market is clearly useful in smoothing out fluctuations in receipts and payments for a particular institution, and is also used to lend credibility to transactions which otherwise would not proceed. Thus a reputable bank or finance house may borrow money on the interbank market and lend the money on to less worthy names, or even to a numerous body of petty retail customers. The rate of interest payable on the Interbank Market is called the London Interbank Offered Rate (Libor).

(*b*) **The Local Authority Market.** Prior to 1955 local authorities had access to Central Government funds, and borrowed such sums as they needed from official sources. The new system required them to borrow in their own names, against the security of the general rate fund. They borrowed chiefly by issuing relatively short-term stocks, short-term bonds, bills and temporary deposit receipts. In the early 1970s, with a great emphasis in political life on the range and quality of services local authorities should offer, the market was active. By the turn of the decade it was very subdued, and transactions were modest. There was only one issue of stock between October 1978 and June 1980, a placing of £5 million County of Cleveland Variable Rate Redeemable Stock 1984. Bonds tend to be of one-year duration.

(*c*) **The Eurocurrency Markets.** The term Eurocurrency has developed from Eurodollars, which were originally deposits of US dollars outside America, chiefly in London. The term has now been extended to cover any currency which is on deposit in a foreign country. The essential feature of these markets is that they are 'stateless', not subject to the control of any country. Although London has recently become the unofficial capital of this stateless market, because of the sophisticated network of financial expertise available, the money is essentially 'hot' money flowing into and out of countries as controls threaten or the avoidance of controls seems desirable.

The original Eurodollar deposits in the immediate post-war years may have come from the American balance of payments deficit. This balance of payments deficit was not the result of uncompetitive American industry, but was a deliberate act of the US to promote the recovery of Europe and indeed the whole world. It was an act, or a succession of acts, of generosity which made funds available in many different ways, by aid, trade and also the convertibility of the dollar—its free availability around the world. When these funds started to be used by European banks to create credit, they were of course denominated in dollars, as dollar loans. To the extent that Eurodollar loans returned as deposits to Eurobanks the banks were able to create credit and multiply up the number of dollars available in uncontrolled circulation. Slowly, over the course of 25 years, this liquidity began to affect the exchange value of the dollar, to the disgruntlement of the American authorities. True, the Vietnam War also made huge quanitities of dollars available on world markets, while the relative importance of the American economy declined as other nations recovered from the Second World War years, to the detriment of the dollar's strength.

Since many of the loans negotiated are to banks, who then lend on to other borrowers, there is a certain amount of double counting, and the actual amount of loans made to final users is only about 40 per cent of the total loans that are floated. Who are these non-bank borrowers, and what do they eventually do with the money they borrow? The answers seem to be:

(*a*) Genuine traders with the US, who want to clear dollar debts. If such dollars are paid to the US it only amounts to the return of dollars previously registered as deposits abroad, and the Eurocurrency market loses the funds and can no longer re-lend them to create credit.

(*b*) Domestic consumers who have borrowed the funds to finance domestic activities. For example, if a local authority in the UK borrows on the Eurocurrency markets to finance an education or social welfare programme, the Eurofunds will be used in the UK and will not return to the Eurobanks as deposits. The actual funds will be repatriated through the foreign exchange market. This prevents the Eurobanks from creating more credit, but it may have some inflationary effect in the domestic economy where the money is being spent—but possibly no more than if the local authority had borrowed the money in the UK.

(*c*) Third World official borrowers, who borrow in order to finance both capital projects and consumption programmes. Whether these borrowers are financially stable is an important consideration (in 1980 one Eurobank said 'If Mexico goes, we all go'—which hardly inspires confidence). If the capital projects create wealth which can finance both the debt service charges and the repayments and still leave something over for the Third World citizen then clearly this type of loan is highly desirable. Some Third World borrowers are disenchanted with the system, so it is clearly not always satisfactory.

The extent of credit creation with loans of this type depends on what happens to the funds. If the person with whom the loan is spent reinvests it on the Eurocurrency market the Eurobanks are free to create more credit with it. If the money is spent in its home country—for example, if Brazil borrows Deutschemarks to buy German goods—the Deutschemarks are repatriated and cease to be in the system.

The Eurocurrency system quickly became a complete financial system, with huge transactions taking place. With many interbank arrangements taking place a certain amount of double counting occurs, but the *Bank of England Quarterly Bulletin* in June 1981 gave the figures for the first quarter of 1981, as quoted by the Bank for International Settlements, as follows:

Total gross claims of banks	$1346.6 billion
Increase in quarter	$ 24.7 billion
Eliminating double counting we have	
Net claims of banks	$ 792.8 billion
Increase in quarter	$ 15.7 billion

The average loan in one recent month was $120 million, so clearly the Eurocurrency market is for prime-name borrowers of large-scale funds. The vast majority of dealings in the Eurocurrency market are short-term dealings with maturities of less than one year. These dealings are used by the banks and the multinational corporations to manage their short-term cash positions, with a high degree of matching between assets and liabilities.

Some monetary authorities, notably the Bundesbank and the Federal Reserve Bank, have called for control of the 'stateless currency' markets. This may reflect the fact that their currencies are under pressure. The fact remains that control is difficult to establish, and that some countries who legitimately earn foreign exchange may have good reason for not wishing to leave balances in the country of origin, for fear of expropriation. The US froze Iran's assets in 1979, for example. The Eurocurrency Market is dealt with more fully in Chapter 17.

(*d*) **The Market in Certificates of Deposit.** This market has already been referred to in the section on the discount houses (see p. 52). Sterling certificates of deposit (£CD) may only be issued with a maximum tenor of five years and a minimum tenor of three months. The word **tenor** denotes the life-time of the certificate. The minimum denomination is £50 000. For dollar certificates of deposit ($CD) the minimum denomination is $25 000, and the tenor is from five years to one day (in other words, there is no minimum tenor). The discount houses will quote prices for all maturities from one day to five years. They are dealt with on an interest-accrued basis, so that at any given moment a certificate is worth its face value plus the interest earned to date. However, the calculation of the actual value does depend upon the purchaser's estimate of what is a fair rate of interest for the days left to run to maturity, and also on his own view of the present liquidity position. The resulting calculation is somewhat complex, but a leaflet explaining the point can be obtained from discount houses in the secondary market.

Since certificates of deposit are issued in 'bearer' form, for very large sums, they must be held by an authorised depository, i.e. a bank. The function of the discount houses is to make a secondary market in the certificates: they do not issue new certificates—these are issued by most leading merchant banks.

5.3 Financial Markets

As suggested earlier, financial markets differ from money markets in that they deal in medium and long-term funds. While the primary purpose of money markets is to manage the day-to-day cash positions of businesses and banks, the longer-term markets are concerned with the provision of capital for other purposes. One common requirement is capital which can be 'fixed' as 'fixed assets' in a huge range of industries, from coalmines, steelworks, heavy and light industries down to service trades like communications and transport. The availability of capital of this sort is of crucial importance to any economy, and somewhat difficult to arrange in the present climate of industrial unrest, foreign competition and cut-throat international trade. The market for new issues of capital of this sort is the 'New Issue' market, while the Stock Exchange is the market for 'existing' stocks and shares, where those whose capital is fixed may regain liquidity by selling the stocks and shares they no longer require.

Another requirement, not quite so meritorious perhaps, is the need to obtain funds to roll over the National Debt. At times when a country is running a deficit (i.e. paying out more for social capital works and social current consumption than it is collecting in taxation) there must be borrowing to finance the deficit. There must also be funds available to service (i.e. pay the interest on) the National Debt accumulated over the years, and to repay bonds issued in earlier periods which are now falling due for repayment. At the moment of repayment investors have a choice of whether to use their money in the purchase of further Government stocks or to invest in some other area. In the UK Government bonds are called 'gilt-edged' securities, simply because they were originally recorded in a bound book with gold-leaf edges to the pages. The gilt-edged market has to be managed so as to attract the funds repaid into new bonds, and thus to roll over the National Debt.

A third market dealing with medium and long-term finance is the Eurobond market, sometimes referred to as the syndicated Eurocurrency market or the syndicated loans market. A major activity of this market since 1973 has been the recycling of oil monies from the OPEC countries to prevent a world financial crisis caused by the removal from other nations of vast sums of money paid to the OPEC nations.

A word about each of these is now desirable.

(*a*) **The Market for Existing Securities: the Stock Exchange.** A stock exchange is a highly organised financial market where bonds, stocks and shares can be bought or sold. The London Stock Exchange is situated in Throgmorton Street within a few yards of the Bank of England, and at the centre of the financial affairs of the City of London. It is a respected and valued national institution, but it is not alone. There are independent groups of stock exchanges in other large cities, while members of the Provincial Brokers' Stock Exchange also carry on business in numerous small towns. Stock-market business is world-wide, and New York, Johannesburg, Melbourne, Tokyo, Calcutta, Paris, Amsterdam and Brussels are all famous centres of stock-exchange activity.

The function of a stock exchange is to make bargains so that those who wish to sell stocks or shares and thus regain liquidity may do so, the stocks and shares being sold to those who wish to surrender liquidity in favour of investments in fixed assets. This process is fundamental to the capitalist system, which seeks to finance commerce, industry and government activity by a free-enterprise system, with a simple exchange mechanism so that investments can change hands in the quickest, cheapest and fairest manner possible.

Turning Fixed Capital into Cash—and Cash into Fixed Capital. When members of the general public invest savings by lending them to the managers of a company, they do not intend that the company shall have the use of their money for ever, for they cannot know when fate may knock on the door and present problems. The investment as far as investors are concerned is a purely temporary one, depending upon good luck to some extent. If the fates are kind the investment may last for years; if the fates are unkind they, or their heirs, may wish to withdraw the investment in cash form, just like withdrawing money from a bank.

From the point of view of the directors of the firm the matter is quite different. They regard the investment as a permanent one, for they spend the invested money on land and buildings, plant and machinery, transport and other equipment. They cannot possibly return the money, for they no longer have it. They have turned it into assets, and in the process it has been 'fixed'. Fixed capital is capital tied up in fixed assets, which have been purchased for permanent use in the business. There is no point in shareholders ringing up the secretary of the company to say that they have decided to reclaim their investment, and will call round for their money at 11 o'clock. The secretary has no way of liquefying the fixed assets and will simply point out that the only way for the shareholder to get his money back is to sell the shares for what they will fetch in the market place. This is what the Stock Exchange is: a market where those who wish to sell shares are able to sell to those who wish to buy. The company whose shares are being bought and sold has little interest in the matter, but it will register the transfer of shares in order to keep its list of shareholders up to date. The company merely pursues its lawful activities, as laid down in its Memorandum of Association, leaving the specialist dealers on the Stock Exchange to arrange matters when the public wish to buy or sell securities. A company may, however, be interested if a particular buyer is acquiring large blocks of shares, since a take-over may be under consideration.

Many dealers on the Stock Exchange deal in gilt-edged securities, and collectively make up the gilt-edged market (see below). Others specialise in industrial shares, property shares, aircraft and motor vehicle shares, etc.

Companies quoted on the UK Stock Exchange have an authorised capital which the Registrar of Companies has approved appropriate for the enterprise concerned. The directors may then issue shares up to this authorised limit as the company requires capital. Normally the issue price will be par, but shares may be issued at a premium (above par). They may not be issued at a discount, except with the approval of the courts. This situation only arises where a company has had very poor results over a number of years, and most of the original capital has already been lost. In such circumstances the Court may approve a scheme for reconstruction which includes the issue of shares at a price lower than par.

Strictly speaking we cannot talk about 'interest rates' on shares, since the sums earned are called 'dividends'. In view of the greater risks run in industrial and commercial undertakings it used to be the case that the dividends earned were much higher than the interest earned on gilt-edged securities and debentures (loans to companies). This has rarely been true in recent years, and consequently shares have been less attractive to investors. The tendency has been for companies to finance new projects out of profits ploughed back by the directors, instead of profits being distributed as dividends. This further source of dissatisfaction for ordinary shares has made shares less attractive, except to those chiefly interested in capital gains (the growth in value of shares) rather than in the income from shares. It is also unsatisfactory in principle, since capital for new inventions and developments is in short supply. If investors were paid the full dividends they might redirect the money into new projects with growth prospects, whereas the managers and directors of large companies may merely proliferate outlets in their present fields. Worse still, they frequently dissipate it in overgenerous perks, higher wage bills to ensure a quiet life and less essential projects of all types. The general return on manufacturing industry in the UK in recent years has been about 4.7 per cent on average, which is well below the rate on almost all other types of investment.

(*b*) **The Gilt-Edged Market.** The gilt-edged market is a market in Government-sponsored bonds, which enable the Treasury to borrow money at a fixed rate of interest over relatively long time scales. Thus most of the stocks issued are in the medium-term or long-term range, with medium term signifying about 5–15 years to maturity and long-term signifying 15–25 years to maturity. As maturity approaches the stocks naturally become shorter and shorter dated and there are bonds falling due for repayment all the time. Such stocks therefore become of interest eventually to institutions which only deal in short-dated stocks, with less than five years to run to maturity.

The management of the gilt-edged market is very important, since to offer huge tranches (*tranche* is the French word for slice) of stock to the market at any one time would unsettle the market, and to repay huge sums to bondholders whose bonds were due for redemption would also be unsettling. To overcome these difficulties a new stock is originally issued at a level slightly above market prices so that it is unattractive to the market and the bulk of it is taken up by the Bank of England or by official institutions which have surplus funds available. As the market itself demands more stock (often because stocks it was previously holding have now been redeemed) the Bank releases the new issue through the 'tap', which means it fixes a 'tap price' and anyone needing stock can buy it at the 'tap price'. A reverse procedure applies as the date of redemption arrives. To avoid redemption on a single day the Bank begins to buy up the stock due for redemption during the last year of its life, paying the market price for it. Naturally the market price reflects the demand for this type of short-dated stock, but it is unlikely to be above the stated redemption price because if it was the Government broker could always wait until redemption date and only pay the redemption price. By these devices the National Debt (the sum total of moneys required to be borrowed by the Government for all its many purposes) is rolled over.

A slight diversion is helpful here by looking at the statistics of the National Debt over recent years. When the Bank of England was founded in 1694 to raise money for the Government the National Debt stood at £1 200 000. Present-day figures are shown in Table 5.1.

Table 5.1. Changes in the National Debt

Year	*Amount of National Debt (£ million)*	*Increase during year (£ million)*
1694	1.2	—
1967	32 000	—
1975	46 405	—
1976	56 572	10 167
1977	67 166	10 594
1978	79 180	12 014
1979	86 885	7 705
1980	95 327	8 442

(Source: *Financial Statistics*)

Traditionally the National Debt has always been regarded as a burden the nation must carry for having participated in two world wars. However, the changes in recent peacetime years show that this is no longer true, and that in the last five years of the 1970s the National Debt rose by £48 922 million. In that five-year period the debt more than doubled, from £46 405 million to £95 327 million, yet this was in peacetime, when the Governments concerned, of both political persuasions, were reputed to be managing the economy to the best of their ability.

The gilt-edged market is something of a mystery to outsiders because there seems little rhyme or reason to the prices of stocks, the rates of interest offered on them and the yields achieved by investors. This can be illustrated by taking four different stocks on any particular day from the financial columns of any newspaper, as in Table 5.2.

Table 5.2. Four stocks on December 3, 1980

Stock	*Date*	*Years to run*	*Price for £100 stock*	*Yield to investor (%)*
2½% Consols	Undated	Infinite	£21¼	11.76
11½% Treasury	1981	1	£99⅝	11.53
5% Treasury	1986–9	6–9	£65⅛	7.68
13½% Treasury	2004–8	24–28	£104¾	12.89

Notes

(*a*) Consols were originally issued in 1745 when all outstanding Government debt was consolidated into a single undated security. Consols will not be redeemed, and their price therefore reflects the prevailing rates of interest. If current rates of interest are around 5 per cent £100 of Consols will cost £50. If current rates of interest are around 10 per cent £100 will cost £25.

(*b*) The Treasury issues stocks at rates of interest which reflect the time of issue, so that we have Treasury stocks at all sorts of rates of interest. Thus a stock issued at par at 14 per cent interest today will go above par if interest rates fall and below par if interest rates rise in the months and years ahead. Other considerations enter into investors calculations as well, such as the time to run to redemption: the 11½ per cent Treasury Stock listed above will mature at par in 1981 so that the price is unlikely to fall much below that figure—the investor would rather hold on to maturity. The low return on the 5 per cent Treasury 1986–9 perhaps reflects the reasonably short time to run to maturity. No such considerations enter into the purchase of 13½ per cent Treasury 2004–8 and its yield to the investor is the highest of those shown.

The gilt-edged market is simply a specialised facet of the Stock Exchange, and a large number of brokers deal in gilt-edged securities.

(*c*) **The Eurobond Market.** The Eurobond Market is an international capital market which floats loans (bonds) on behalf of clients anxious to raise long-term capital. The bonds are designated in a Eurocurrency, a term which implies a currency which is available outside its country of origin, as a deposit in a bank in a foreign country. Eurodollars are commonly used, but very large sums have been raised in Deutschemarks, guilders, Swiss francs, Japanese yen and Arabian currencies of various sorts. In the market's first full year of operation, 1970, $3 billion were raised in this way, but by 1978 $14 billion dollars were being raised and in the next two years growth of about 25 per cent per annum occurred. In one week alone in mid-1980, $425 million dollars of new dollar bonds were brought into the market.

In arranging these bond issues the banks bring together high-class borrowers (multinational companies, government institutions from various countries, and banks around the world) and high-class lenders (particularly the representatives of OPEC, but also banks, insurance companies and wealthy individuals). The issuing banks may also syndicate loans, grouping together a number of lenders to finance major borrowing by a single borrower for a particular project.

The Eurobond market has played an enormous part in recycling the oil incomes of the OPEC countries by taking deposits from them of the huge sums they had earned by raising oil prices, and lending them out to countries in difficulties—chiefly the less developed countries (LDCs). This is no doubt very meritorious, but a good many of these LDCs are now in severe financial difficulties, and some banks have huge loans out to very unstable countries.

As with all bonds, the rate of interest payable is a nominal rate based upon the par value at issue. Thus a bond issued in April 1980 at $15\frac{1}{4}$ per cent for the Kingdom of Sweden at par, was selling at $109 only one month later. The gain in price for a three-year stock was a record at the time, but a gain in price means a fall in yield, the interest of $15\frac{1}{4}$ per cent on the original ($100) falling to 13.99 per cent to the buyer who pays $109. He now receives $15\frac{1}{4}$ per cent on an investment of $109, which is clearly a smaller yield from the investment.

5.4 Why Rates of Interest Vary

The various rates of return on money to be found in the markets above reflect the factors which influence the operation of those markets. A vast array of influences are at work and amongst the most important it is possible to enumerate the following:

(*a*) **The structure of interest rates in primary markets.** Here the traditional influence now goes under the name of Minimum Lending Rate (MLR). The Bank of England has recently changed the arrangements so that at the time of writing the market-determining role of MLR has largely been abolished and operators in primary markets have been left to arrange the spread of interest rates more independently and, as has been the hope of recent governments, with more regard to competitive forces. (See Section 12.4 for the new arrangements.)

(*b*) **The structure of interest rates in secondary markets.** One of the major ways in which the secondary markets have differed from the traditional ones is that they have had only tenuous links with Bank Rate/MLR. The secondary markets have always been more susceptible to variations in supply and demand and have generally proved more volatile and ready to adapt to emergency needs. This is not to say that MLR had no significance for secondary markets. Because these markets are in competition with the primary ones where MLR played a more significant role, the influence of MLR did filter through.

Factors which affect the structure of interest rates in all markets, though sometimes in vastly differing degrees, are:

(*a*) Changes in rates in international markets, especially as reflected through Eurocurrency rates.

(*b*) Currency crises, such as those surrounding sterling in the 1960s and the dollar in the 1970s.

(*c*) The monetary policy operated by the US, and to a lesser degree other major trading partners.

(*d*) Political disturbances, such as those in Iran in 1979, and localised conflicts, such as in Afghanistan in 1980.

The main reasons why rates should respond differently in the various markets are:

(*a*) Although there are some overlaps and in some areas a great deal of competition, the various markets are not generally offering the same product. In particular, the period of time involved is a crucial differentiating factor. Usually the higher rates are paid on longer-term money, which is as one would expect. The longer the period of time the greater the degree of uncertainty, and the greater likelihood that unforeseen events can intervene. There are situations, though, where short-term loans earn more than long ones—for example, on occasions competition for overnight money pushes the *annual* rate on it over 30 per cent.

(*b*) Although economists can invoke *ceteris paribus* (all other things being held equal) in their theoretical arguments, the real world cannot avail itself of this luxury. Consequently not all loans carry the same risk. Some, such as those made to the UK Government, bear hardly any risk at all, since the Government can call upon its immense power of taxation (and further borrowing) to back them. Other loans—for example, the lending of development capital to shaky Third World governments, or the provision of hire purchase finance—carry much more risk, and in commercial markets the rates charged will to a large degree reflect this risk, the 'safer' borrowers being able to borrow at lower rates.

(*c*) It might be supposed that the movement of money, which hardly involves physical transportation at all, could be achieved at close to zero cost. This, however, is not the case. Dealing in money requires the services of money specialists and also involves documentation, probably a great deal of documentation in those markets subject to the greatest degree of government control and supervision. In such circumstances due regard will be given to economies of scale. It probably costs as much to arrange and document a loan of £10 000 as it does one of £10 000 million and therefore borrowers of very large amounts are likely to receive more favourable terms than those who are seeking less. There are some types of lending—for example, hire purchase—where the administrative costs are very high for what are relatively trivial sums.

(*d*) From the end of the 1960s the commercial banks in particular became worried, and still are worried, about competition from building societies. There is a significant link between the rates which these banks give for deposits and those on offer from building societies. Amongst the reasons quoted for the growth of building societies one in particular is significant for interest rate differentials—convenience. Some forms of lending (and borrowing) offer much greater convenience than others. Both the commercial banks and the building societies occupy sites in common with stores, public houses, etc. They therefore find it easy to attract customers who are familiar with 'retail' outlets. In this respect the building societies probably offer marginally more convenience, being open on Saturdays and into early evening most days. The building societies also offer one other facility which depositors find convenient and that is the provision of a 'tax paid' return.

5.5 Revision Test

Answers	*Questions*
—	**1.** What is a 'wholesale' money market?
1. A market in which large-scale financial transactions take place between parties of undoubted creditworthiness.	**2.** Which is the primary money market?
2. The market run by the discount houses who are members of the London Discount Market Association.	**3.** What is a 'secondary' or parallel market?
3. A market in short-term money run by other institutions who wish to achieve an optimum position in their financial affairs.	**4.** What are the aims of those who deal in short-term money markets?
4. (*a*) To put out surplus funds at market rates of interest. (*b*) To raise the funds they require for the volume of business they are doing. (*c*) To preserve adequate reserve ratios to conform with any official requirements about the conduct of their affairs. (*d*) To achieve any target balance at the Bank of England as required.	**5.** What are the chief secondary markets?
5. (*a*) The interbank market; (*b*) the local authority market; (*c*) the Eurocurrency market; (*d*) the certificate of deposit market.	**6.** What is LIBOR?
6. The London Interbank Offered Rate.	**7.** What are the long-term money markets?
7. (*a*) The New Issue market; (*b*) the Stock Exchange (or capital market); (*c*) the gilt-edged market (an element in the Stock Exchange); (*d*) the Eurobond market.	**8.** Why do rates of interest vary from market to market?
8. (*a*) Because of differing degrees of risk. (*b*) Because of different time periods. (*c*) Because of differing costs of documentation, record-keeping, etc. (*d*) Because of different degrees of service to the borrower, convenience of withdrawal, etc.	**9.** Go over the list again until you are sure of the answers. Then try some of the written questions in Appendix 1.

Part 2

THE THEORY OF MONEY

6

THE CREATION OF MONEY

6.1 Introduction

Chapter 1 pointed out the way in which banking in the UK developed from the activity of goldsmiths. It also showed how, as organised society developed, first 'commodity money' and then 'fiduciary money' began to circulate as a medium of exchange. The appeal of commodity money is obvious: it has an intrinsic value in which the holder can place his faith. It also has a number of drawbacks, the chief amongst them being that any commodity is subject to normal market forces, those of supply and demand. These can render the exchange value of any commodity used extremely volatile and may even leave it virtually useless as money. Even the favourite commodity money of modern man—gold—does not escape from this disadvantage, a point recognised by the splitting of the gold market into two parts: the official (monetary) market and the commercial market (see Section 15.4).

In the past, when paper money started to circulate in an economy it only did so to the extent that it was backed with a popular 'commodity', usually gold or silver. In the UK during the whole of the nineteenth century and until 1914 gold was used as the 'backing' for paper money. In order to give the public faith in the paper money issued almost all the notes were backed by an equivalent amount of gold held by the Bank of England Issue Department. There was also a small 'fiduciary issue' of notes. Today the fiduciary issue is one which instead of being fully backed by some commodity such as gold, is backed by government debt. This means that it is backed by a written undertaking, by paper promises from the government to pay a specified sum to the holder of the paper at some time in the future. Gradually, as the Bank of England came to hold less gold, and as the amount of gold available in the world failed to expand at a rate necessary to finance international trade, all the note issue in the United Kingdom became fiduciary. (See the Bank Return on p. 12).

6.2 Banks and the Creation of Credit

The definitions of 'money supply' given in Chapter 1 have already suggested that money in a modern economy is not confined to notes and coin alone. In particular, the banking sector in most economies is able to create its own money: bank credit, commonly known as 'advances'. Banks are able to make advances by creating deposits. Thus if a banker agrees to make A an advance of £500 he credits the amount in A's current account as if A has deposited that sum. Of course he also opens a loan account for the same amount in A's name, which will be repaid in some agreed manner in due course, with interest. This does not affect the fact that A is able to use a cheque book to purchase whatever he requires up to the figure of £500 and it is a sign of the general faith in the banking system in the UK that those who take A's cheques in settlement of his debts are quite happy to deposit them in their own bank accounts. The deposits therefore continue to exist after their initial creation, instead of being exchanged for some preferable alternative, such

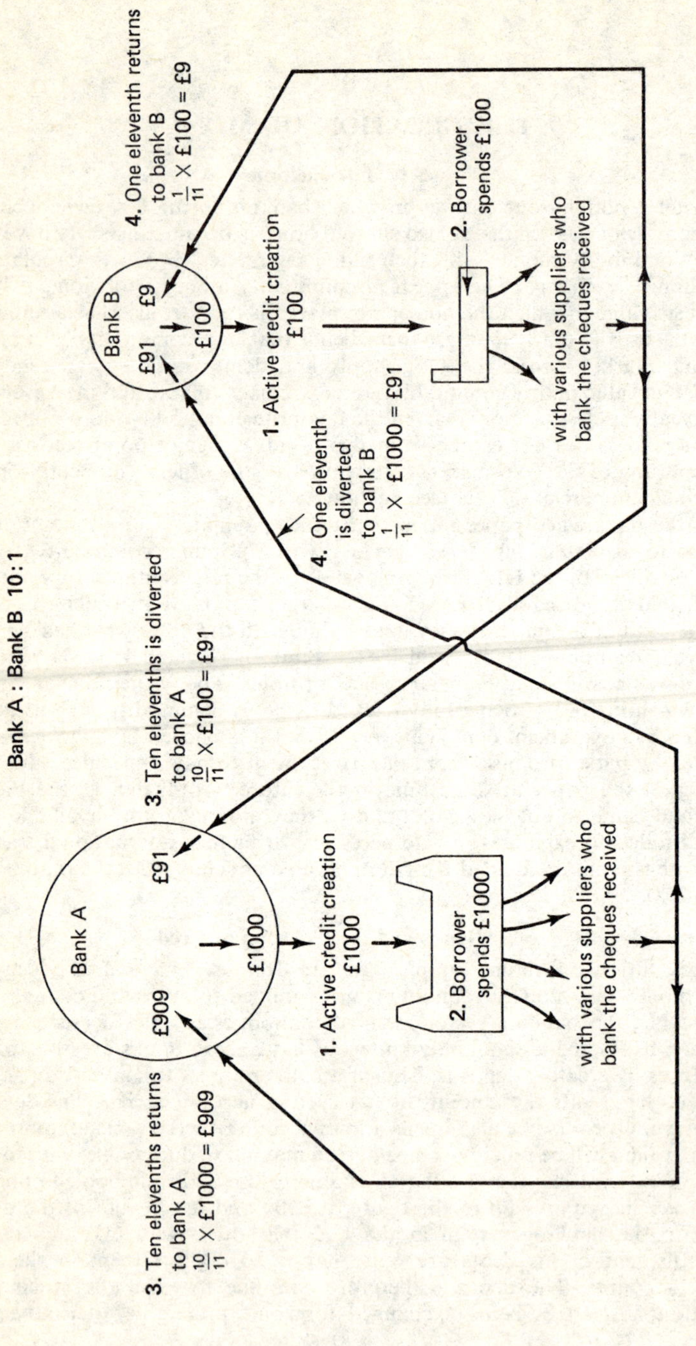
Bank A : Bank B 10:1
Bank A
£909
£1000
£91
3. Ten elevenths returns to bank A 10/11 × £1000 = £909
1. Active credit creation £1000
2. Borrower spends £1000
with various suppliers who bank the cheques received
3. Ten elevenths is diverted to bank A 10/11 × £100 = £91
Bank B
£91
£9
£100
4. One eleventh returns to bank B 1/11 × £100 = £9
1. Active credit creation £100
2. Borrower spends £100
4. One eleventh is diverted to bank B 1/11 × £1000 = £91
with various suppliers who bank the cheques received

Fig. 6.1. 'Keeping in step' when creating credit.

Notes

(i) We are imagining there are only two banks in the system and that Bank A is ten times as big as Bank B. The ratio of the business they do is 10:1.

(ii) Any loan made by either bank (any *active* creation of credit) will be spent by the borrowers with firms $\frac{10}{11}$ths of whom bank with Bank A and $\frac{1}{11}$th with Bank B. The money received by these suppliers will therefore return as *passive* deposits in this ratio to the two banks.

(iii) So long as the banks keep their loans in the same ratio as the business they do, each will receive back as passive deposits as much as it pays out in active loans. Neither will lose liquidity to the other.

(iv) The reader should now repeat the calculations with Bank A lending £100 and Bank B lending £500. Which bank loses liquidity to the other? This bank will be forced to restrict its lending until it is in step with its size.

(*Bank B loses £446 to Bank A*)

as cash. That holders of deposits do not attempt to turn them into cash indicates that businessmen and the public in general are prepared to accept the settlement of debts by the transfer of deposits—by the use of cheques. There is therefore no need to make a mass movement from deposits to cash.

Bank deposits become 'credit' balances which a banker owes to his customers. Deposits will be owed because the banker has taken something from the depositor—currency, another bank deposit, securities (e.g. Treasury bills) or a claim upon the customer.

Where a banker builds up deposits in exchange for cash or other deposits the deposit creation is said to be **passive** since there is no net effect upon the supply of money. Where the deposits are created as a result of advances made against securities or a claim upon the customer, these creations are termed **active**, since there will be a net addition to the money supply.

Needless to say the process can work in reverse; what the banks have created they can also destroy. The total amount of money in circulation can be reduced by the destruction of actively created bank deposits (banks might have to do this if, for example, they are squeezed by governments). The destruction of credit cannot be achieved quite as rapidly as credit can be created, for the customer to whom an advance has been made has a contractual arrangement which the bank cannot break at once. Any 'squeeze' applied to the banking system therefore operates to prevent the creation of any extra credit except for the most justifiable reasons. As repayments are being made day by day by all sorts of customers in the course of meeting their loan arrangements, this money will be withdrawn from circulation and the general money supply will be reduced as a result.

The ability of banks to engage in active deposit creation rests upon public confidence in bank transfers as a method of payment. Because the public has confidence in the banking system only a small proportion of the claims upon banks are ever requested in the form of cash (on average about 5 per cent today). This means that, providing banks can continue to attract a small proportion of their deposits in cash form, they can theoretically create massive active deposits.

To repeat the historical example given in Chapter 1, but with the more modern cash ratio of 5 per cent, suppose a customer deposits £100 in cash (of which he is only likely to request £5 back); this £100 is 5 per cent of £2000. The bank could therefore in theory create £1900 of credit, by making advances to borrowers of that amount. This £1900 would be paid out by borrowers using cheques, and these cheques would return as deposits to the banking system by the traders who received them. Since these traders will only have a 5 per cent cash ratio, they are unlikely to ask for more than 5 per cent of £1900 = £95, which is precisely the amount of cash available.

Where the banking system is composed of only one bank the cheques obviously will return to the creating bank and there will be no cash loss. Where there are a number of banks, though, it is theoretically possible for one bank to lose cash to the others. In fact this does occur but providing that the cash drain is not large and/or continuous banks make provision for it in the way they structure their assets (see Chapter 6). Also banks do their best to avoid the problem by following, as far as possible, a system known as **'keeping in step'** (see Fig. 6.1).

Keeping in step involves banks in creating active deposits (credit) in proportion with the amount of business they do (the volume of passive deposits they take). Suppose that there are two banks. Bank A and Bank B. Bank A is approximately 10 times as large as Bank B; it has passive deposits 10 times as great. Suppose also that Bank A lends £1000 by way of an advance, creating an active deposit. The probability is that it will receive back approximately £909 worth of the cheques paid out by the borrower of the £1000. (There are 11 'parts' of business available; Bank A has 10 of these, Bank B only one.) Bank B will receive the remaining 11th (approx.)—£91. In order to keep in step Bank B now needs to create active deposits of £100 (one 10th of Bank A's £1000). The probability is that £9 of this will return in the normal course of business to Bank B; the other £91 will be paid, by traders into Bank A. Bank A thus creates £1000 of credit and receives £1000 back; Bank B creates £100 and receives that amount in return.

In the real world, of course, there are many more banks, but the process is basically the same. The liquid asset ratios which banks have imposed, or have had imposed, upon them greatly help them to create credit 'in step' and thus reduce the likelihood of one bank losing significant amounts of passive deposits, particularly cash, to the rest. Keeping in step also has implications for competition amongst banks (see Chapter 11).

Readers might have noticed that expanding deposits in step not only protects banks' cash, but also expands their passive deposits. One bank actively creates credit. Some of this credit is deposited in another bank, where it is treated as a passive deposit—a base upon which to create active credit! This facility for supposed limitless credit creation has been of concern to those involved with the banking system for many years. The various restrictions applied to the banking system in the UK by successive governments are in part the result of a desire to prevent an 'explosion of credit', and a runaway money supply. In fact, there are a number of considerations which limit the ability of banks to create deposits ad infinitum.

6.3 Factors Limiting the Creation of Bank Deposits

One of the problems facing the banking system is that of finding 'eligible borrowers'. It is not merely a question of banks advancing money, but of advancing money to borrowers who are regarded as a safe risk. There is bound to be a limit to these eligible borrowers and it is also likely that competing financial institutions, such as building societies and insurance companies, will find themselves pursuing broadly the same group, in an effort to conduct 'safe' business.

Obviously, the level of economic activity will have a significant effect upon the level of borrowing. Generally, the more buoyant and active an economy, the greater will be the borrowing requirement in order to take advantage of the greater opportunities. Prospects of profitability are poor in a stagnant economy, and this is likely to discourage entrepreneurs. To a limited extent the creation of bank credit will stimulate the level of economic activity and hence the future level of demand for further bank advances, but even then there is a limit to the amount of advances which can safely be made—a limit to the demand from eligible borrowers.

THE COMMERCIAL BANK LTD.
Balance sheet (simplified and annotated) as at Dec. 31, 19 . .

	£ millions	£ millions
Current liabilities		
Dividends due	24	
Creditors	1582	
Amounts owing to depositors and other classes of customer	26300	
		27906
Provision		
For taxation		169
Long term liabilities		
Borrowings of foreign subsidiaries		153
Debentures issued		262
Minority shareholders' interest		86
Ordinary shareholders' interest in the bank		
Capital contributed	233	
Reserves ploughed back in past years	1523	
		1756
	£	30332

	Comments	% of total assets	Likely profit margin	£ millions
Liquid assets				
Till money and items in course of collection		5.7	0%	1730
Balances at Bank of England.	$\frac{1}{2}$% of ELs compulsory	1.3	0%	403
Money at call and short notice (loaned to discount houses).	} Must be 6% of ELs on average	11.6	Average $1\frac{1}{2}$ below base rate	3514
Local authority and other first-class bills of exchange.	All liquid assets part of prudential reserve ratio	1.2	Up to $2\frac{1}{2}$% above base rate	356
Other trade bills of exchange.		1.1		329
	Total liquid assets →			6332
Investments (nearly all in gilt-edged securities)	Held to earn income, but could be sold on the Stock Exchange	5.1	A little above base rate	1536
Illiquid assets				
Advances to customers	Loans made to earn income, repayments coming in regularly of course	70.5	2–5% above base rate	21384
Frozen assets				
Special deposits	By order of Central Bank	0.5	About base rate	164
Fixed assets				
Premises and equipment	Never likely to be realized in cash form	3.0	0%	916
		100	£	30332

Fig. 6.2. Balance sheet of a typical commercial bank.

Notes

(i) Banks publish their balance sheets in the order of liquidity, with the most liquid items first.

(ii) Since July 1981 the Bank of England has required all institutions to provide $\frac{1}{2}$ per cent of their eligible liabilities (roughly speaking a bank's sterling deposits) as non-operational, non-interest-bearing deposits with the Bank. In addition the clearing banks provide an agreed amount of funds for clearing purposes.

(iii) In addition each bank is required to keep an average of 6 per cent of its ELs with members of the London Discount Market Association, or with gilt-edged jobbers. This will be 'call' money or 'short notice' money. Most banks will in fact have more than this available on call or at short notice. Now that the minimum reserve ratio has been abolished banks have returned to operating their own 'prudential reserve ratio' which will be monitored by the Bank of England as part of its control procedures.

(iv) In general, money at call or short notice earns less than base rate, but its liquidity is the chief reason for lending it so cheaply to the discount houses.

(v) Local authority and other first-class bills of exchange are readily saleable to other market institutions or to the Bank of England and hence form part of the prudential reserve ratio.

(vi) Trade bills of exchange are less reliable than (v) above but are more profitable, and will be liquidated in a matter of months as the trading ventures they were issued to finance come to fruition.

(vii) Investments (gilt-edged securities) are readily saleable if required, but at some possible loss if the market is falling.

(viii) The huge range of advances to customers shows the vulnerability of the banking system in any general economic disruption (such as war conditions). Although illiquid, some debts are being repaid every day and security, particularly for longer-term debts, will have been taken.

(ix) Special deposits are a means used by the Central Bank to reduce bank lending, by removing cash from the banks into 'frozen' accounts at the Bank of England.

(x) Premises and equipment are necessary assets, but do not yield income directly.

(xi) On the liabilities side we have:

(xii) The vast majority of current liabilities are owed to depositors for deposits, which may have been 'passive' or 'active' at the time they were created. It is the threat of withdrawal of these deposits which represents the danger to the banking system, since the 'cash available' (see assets side) only represents 5.7 per cent of the total liabilities (and about 6.5 per cent of these deposits).

(xiii) Note that the original capital contributed represents less than 1 per cent of the total balance sheet value, and even with the reserves of profits ploughed back over the years it represents less than 6 per cent. The Companies Acts state that the creditors of a company must look to the capital of a limited company for satisfaction, but clearly this is not much help in a bank bankruptcy, and this explains the need for 'rescue operations' in any banking collapse.

One way to get these borrowers to take more is to offer them advances at reduced interest rates and hence make potential schemes more attractive to them or to lure them away from competing sources of finance. Eventually though, the process of interest rate reduction runs into problems. Presumably the rates *offered to depositors* for time deposits cannot be reduced (unless competitors obligingly reduce their own rates) and there is every likelihood that the administration of increasing volumes of bank lending will run into rising costs and bad debts. A point is reached where the creation of further advances becomes unsafe because those who can only borrow if borrowing is cheap are less creditworthy than other borrowers.

A closely related problem for banks hoping to increase their lending is whether or not customers are prepared to hold increased quantities of deposits. This problem revolves around the substitutability of money for other assets. In the past economists have tended to regard money as unique—and therefore as having no close substitutes. More recently though, the economists' view of money has changed and the general feeling is that there is a fair degree of substitutability of money for other assets and vice versa. It is now felt that individuals (and organisations) have an idea of the way in which they would like to hold their wealth. In other words they have *a preferred portfolio of assets*. One of these assets, but only one, will be money. The question is, what determines the composition of the portfolio?

The answer is to be found in diminishing marginal returns. Each of the financial assets which individuals or organisations can hold will have attributes which make them attractive—stability of yield, stability of profit, expected appreciation in value, convenience, etc. At various times one or more of these attributes might be regarded more highly than the rest: this will bring a shift in the distribution of assets within the portfolio. But the original spread of assets and subsequent changes depend upon the marginal satisfaction to be gained from extra units of each type of asset. In the same way that consumers try to maximise total utility by equating the (net) marginal returns from each type of good or service consumed, so those involved with finance will try to achieve an 'equi-marginal balance'. (Readers who have not studied Economics might like to read a companion volume, *Business Economics Made Simple*, on marginal utility at this point.)

In this respect money is no different from other assets. The greater the quantity held, the less highly units are valued. Only by making the holding of money more attractive, by lowering the rate at which it is offered (relative to other assets), can people be induced to take money into their portfolios. This brings us back to the point made earlier: that eventually the cost of lending relative to the return will make the operation unattractive to the bank. If people can only be attracted into taking advances by reducing the rate of interest, the lending of money becomes less attractive to the banker.

It is worth mentioning in passing that the way in which individuals and organisations come to decisions about the spread of their portfolios is mirrored by the way in which banks determine the composition of the assets they hold. The advantages and the costs of various types of assets, including advances, must be weighed against each other.

It has been suggested above that even if banks are given a free rein they will reach a stage where their credit-creating capacity will cease. In the real world they never have this free rein. Quite apart from the banks' own practice of keeping a reserve of cash and near-cash investments to accommodate their customers (a practice built up over centuries of trading), the Government has its own requirements. These are designed to assist the Government in its attempts to control the total supply of money. They therefore act as a further brake upon unlimited bank lending. Government liquidity requirements are dealt with in much greater detail in Chapter 12, but obviously having to set aside a fixed proportion of assets in a specified form limits the way in which one bank's 'active' deposit creation can lead to other banks' 'passive deposit' growth being used for yet further 'active deposit' advancing. Not only this, but the need to obtain other 'reserve' assets to maintain a proper reserve ratio against lending bids up the price of these 'near cash' assets and pushes up the marginal cost of lending throughout the money market.

We may conclude that without doubt money is a special class of asset. Whilst there is confidence in it, money is the ultimate form of liquidity and has exceptional convenience. In this respect the banks when they create money are creating an asset of particular significance in an exchange economy. However, the long established feeling that banks, providing they operate 'in step', can create money ad infinitum is unfounded. Banks have three main forces operating upon them which limit their credit-creating capacity:

(*a*) The cost and risk of further lending.

(*b*) The willingness of individuals and organisations to take further money balances into their portfolios.

(*c*) Reserve requirements, both bank imposed and Government imposed.

6.4 The Balance Sheet of a Commercial Bank

Some idea of the range of assets and liabilities held by a typical commercial bank is given in Fig. 6.2. and described in the notes below it.

6.5 Revision Test

Answers	*Questions*
—	**1.** What is commodity money?
1. Any commodity used as a medium of exchange.	**2.** What is fiduciary money?
2. An issue of money not backed by a commodity but issued 'as a matter of trust'.	**3.** How do banks create money?
3. By creating deposits for customers.	**4.** What kind of deposits?
4. Active ones. Passive deposit creation does not increase the supply of money.	**5.** Can banks individually create as much credit as they choose?
5. No, they must keep in step.	**6.** Can banks taken as a group endlessly create credit?

Answers	*Questions*
6. No, there are factors which limit their ability to create credit.	**7.** What are these factors?
7. (*a*) The costs and risk involved in lending. (*b*) The necessity to find 'eligible borrowers'. (*c*) Government reserve requirements.	**8.** Go over the page again until you are sure of it. Then try some of the written questions in Appendix 1.

7

THE RATE OF INTEREST

7.1 Introduction

When a borrower takes a sum of money over a period of time it is customary for a payment to be made—this payment is termed **interest**. Viewed in this way interest is a reward to the owners of capital for allowing it to be used as a factor of production. Capital is money which can command a share of the consumer goods and services created in the previous period. If the owners of capital forgo current consumption and allow the capital to be used by another, they are entitled to some reward for doing so.

The payment is necessary because capital, in common with other resources, can be put to alternative uses. Interest, then, tends to perform two tasks. It induces those who own capital to part with it, and it allocates the capital amongst competing uses—that is, it allocates capital to those who have the strongest demand for it.

Interest rates can therefore be thought of as prices; prices given for money. Like any other price an interest rate is determined by the interaction of supply and demand. It might be thought, therefore, that consideration of interest rates would simply be a matter of balancing supply and demand. Whilst it is obviously true that balances between demand and supply forces will be struck, the subject of interest rates is much more complicated than cursory consideration might suggest. Over the years a great deal of dispute has arisen over what the interest rate does—what is involved in the demand for, and supply of, money. Several theories have been developed to account for the rate of interest and explain the job it is doing. We may reduce the common strands of the many presentations to two basic approaches. These are the 'real' and 'monetary' theories of the rate of interest.

7.2 'Real' Theories of the Rate of Interest

A great deal of the economic theory relevant to today was developed by a group of economists termed by Keynes 'the classical economists'. This large group drew its inspiration from Adam Smith and his *Wealth of Nations* (1776), and became renowned for their belief in, amongst other things, freedom of action for the individual. A word of warning is perhaps necessary here. Although loosely referred to as a 'group' of economists they in no way constitute a tightly knit band with identical ideas. There has always been a fair degree of dispute among prominent members. This is not surprising when one realises that the classical tradition spans from 1776 to the present day (if the neoclassical economists are included).

The 'classical economists' believed in the money 'veil'. They thought that money was merely a medium of exchange which in part 'hid' the 'real' transactions which it facilitated. Without money the same transactions would take place, but with more difficulty. The effect of an increase in the supply of money would be a rise in the price level; the effect of a shortage of money would be a reduction in the price level; and the complete abolition of money would mean the return to barter. Money itself had no real effect on the exchange of goods and services except that it made exchange much more simple.

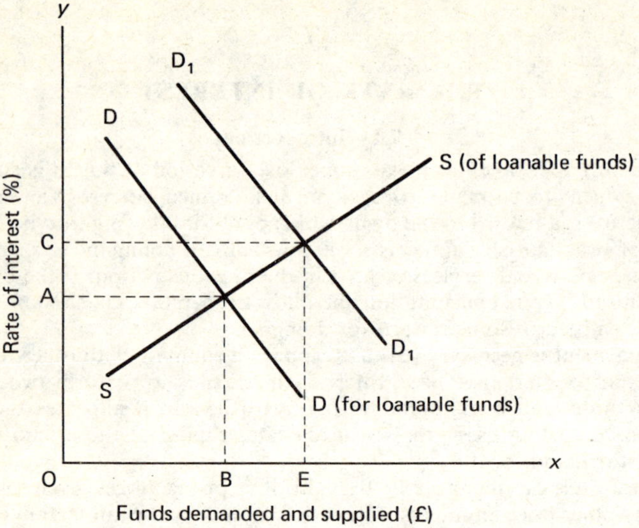

Fig. 7.1. Loanable funds and the rate of interest.

Notes

(i) Imagine a situation where the demand for loanable funds is shown by curve DD and the supply of loanable funds by the curve SS. The equilibrium rate of interest is therefore A per cent.

(ii) Should the demand for loanable funds rise—shown by the new demand curve D_1D_1—this will force up the rate of interest to C and bring forward extra lending in pursuit of the higher rate of interest.

(iii) The rate of interest always adjusts to settle at that level where those who wish to lend funds are lending the quantity they wish to lend **at the going rate**, and those who wish to borrow are borrowing just the quantity they wish to borrow **at the going rate**.

According to classical economists the rate of interest had a simple, but vital, role to play. If the total of earnings were all to be spent, savings must be made to equal investments and this was the task of the rate of interest. It was suggested that savings took place for reward, that savers abstained from consumption in order to take advantage of a return—the rate of interest paid. If the rate of interest rose, then more abstention from consumption took place as savers responded to the increased rewards. Borrowers, on the other hand, adjusted downwards their demand for loanable funds when interest rates rose. The rate of interest was therefore seen as a sensitive mechanism for regulating both the demand for and supply of loanable funds—it was responsible for bringing about an equilibrium between savings and investment. Fig. 7.1 illustrates this process.

The classical economists' view of the role of money was one which reinforced their attitude to the rate of interest. The feeling was that money was a medium of exchange—it was required because it gave command over goods and services but had no value in itself. Those who hoarded (stored but did not use) funds were regarded as irrational, especially when a reward for non-consumption in the form of the rates of interest was being offered.

The rate of interest was thus seen as determined by the 'real' forces of thrift and the return to be derived from making investments. The greater the range of investment opportunities and the returns to be derived from these, the more investors would be prepared to pay to borrow funds. Demand for funds therefore depended upon the 'buoyancy' of the economy and the effect this had upon investment opportunities. The supply of funds depended upon the thrift of the population; the more willing persons were to forgo consumption the greater the supply of funds. The two forces demand and supply met, and together set the price for money—the rate of interest.

7.3 Monetary Theories of the Rate of Interest

Monetary approaches to the rate of interest really commence with John Maynard Keynes, whose work revolutionised economics. Keynes' view of money was quite different from that held by classical economists. He agreed with classical economists that the stock of money held by the community at any one point in time would depend upon their everyday trading needs (**the transactions motive**) and on provision for occurrences which could not be foreseen (**the precautionary motive**). But Keynes suggested one further reason why money might be held, even where this meant that a return (the rate of interest) would have to be sacrificed. This reason he termed **the speculative motive** for holding money, and its existence was due to the possibility of making future gains (or avoiding future losses) through the simple expedient of holding cash. The point depended upon the inverse relationship between interest rates and the value of paper assets. The following example should convey the essentials of Keynes' reasoning.

Suppose that a 7 per cent Consol (a negotiable perpetual bond) has been issued at par value of £100. This means that the interest rate on the bond is 7 per cent. Subsequently the rate of interest rises to 14 per cent on *new* debt of similar quality. This now means that the holder of the bond, if he were to part with his asset, would suffer a loss of 50 per cent of his capital outlay. No rational person would pay £100 for a 7 per cent bond when £50 on a 14 per cent bond gives the same actual return—£7 per annum. On this basis it became *rational* rather than irrational to hoard in circumstances when interest rates were low and expected to rise.

People therefore had good reason to hold money as an asset **in itself** instead of merely as a medium of exchange. According to Keynes, then, the rate of interest was not determined by the supply of and demand for loanable funds. How then did he explain interest rate determination?

He did this by extending his interpretation of money outlined above. This commences with the view that money is desired for speculative as well as transactions and precautionary reasons. The rate of interest then becomes a **reward for not hoarding** rather than a reward for not consuming, and it is determined by the interaction of the supply of and demand for money—as opposed to the supply of and demand for loanable funds. The supply of money (currency and bank credit) is largely in the control of the Government, but it is the public at large who determine what the demand for money will be. At any one time all the money in existence will be held by someone, but the important question is: do they wish to continue holding it? It might be that a proportion of those holding money would, in the near future, like to exchange their money for income yielding assets. What is it, therefore, which will determine the public's demand for money, i.e. what can influence the community to exchange money for income-yielding assets?

Keynes felt that the public's demand for money depended upon two factors: (*a*) the level of aggregate income and (*b*) the rate of interest. He maintained that as the community's income rose so would its need to hold more money for transactions and precautionary reasons. He also maintained that the speculative motive for holding money would depend primarily upon the rate of interest *and the view the community took of the future movement of the rate of interest*.

If the community expected future rates of interest to rise they were likely to hoard as a hedge against capital loss; if they expected future rates to fall then dis-hoarding would be logical, in order to take advantage of capital gains. We have already seen that a 7 per cent bond valued at £100 falls to £50 if the rate of interest rises to 14 per cent. Clearly, if the rate of interest falls to $3\frac{1}{2}$ per cent it will be worth £200. Therefore when interest rates were low, hoarding would be much more likely than when they were high (on the basis that low rates can be expected to rise). This rather startling conclusion was directly the opposite of what the classical economists would have forecast—since at low rates more people would, they believed, carry on consuming.

Keynes termed the tendency of the community to hold hoarded funds when interest rates were low the **'liquidity trap'**. He felt that the 'trap' would apply to institutions as well as private individuals. Banks are in the business of borrowing from the public but they normally do not hold large idle balances (hoarding); they lend to those who wish to borrow. When the economy is depressed though they may find their lending potential diminished by a lack of eligible borrowers. There is one way out, however: lend to the Government at a secure rate of return. This seemingly attractive solution to the banks' problem of idle balances becomes much less attractive when the possibility of significant capital losses arise: banks, like individuals, may hoard for speculative purposes.

The essence of the mechanics of the Keynesian interpretation can be conveyed with an example. Imagine an increase in the supply of money (perhaps by Government buying back securities). How can an equilibrium between the (increased) supply of money and the demand for money be arrived at? Assuming that there is no change in the size of national income there is no reason to suppose that the public will extend their transactions and precautionary balances. Those who received the extra cash balances (in exchange for securities) will have amongst their number some who would prefer to hold income-generating assets. As demand for these assets increases their price is likely to be bid upwards—a movement which will bring a reduction in the rate of interest. As the rate of interest falls, members of society are less unwilling to hold extra money balances. In this way, the rate of interest and the supply of money interact to bring about a new equilibrium which will allow the extra money to be absorbed into the system, partly as idle balances. This was a complete reversal of the 'loanable funds' approach of the classical economists, which stressed the importance of thrift and the productivity of capital without even considering the view that money could be held for speculative purposes.

7.4 The Two Approaches Compared

'Real' theories of the rate of interest seek to show that real factors—thrift and the productivity to be derived from investment—are the main determinants of any interest rate. The amount of money in circulation, though important for the general level of prices, will not affect the 'real' basis upon which interest rates rest.

Monetary theories—sometimes known as **liquidity preference theories**—revolve around the idea that the rate of interest reflects the demand for money and the supply of money. Since the monetary authorities are assumed to have control of money supply, the greatest attention is devoted to the demand for money. This is seen as being very different from the straightforward demand for loanable funds (which would depend upon the productivity of business investment). In particular the community might choose to hold large amounts of apparently 'idle' money—to protect against the fall in value of capital assets or to take advantage of expected falls. 'Real' theories saw no logic in the maintenance of idle balances when they could be put to work to earn interest.

Stated in a different fashion, those supporting the 'real' approach believe that a **flow** of funds and demands for funds, over a period of time, come together to determine an equilibrium interest rate. The liquidity preference approach recognises the importance of the existence of stocks of money (and other financial assets) and therefore regards the process of interest rate determination as much more volatile.

It might be thought that the two approaches have no common ground but the outlines given above tend to represent the most extreme attitudes of 'real' and 'monetary' views. In truth, the majority of economists support the idea that determination of the rate of interest (more realistically a *range* of rates) depends on a middle view. In support of this they point out that whilst at first sight the two approaches seem incompatible, in reality this is not the case. For instance, classical economists soon adapted their theory of loanable funds so that it took account of hoarding and dis-hoarding—took account, that is, of money stocks. Keynesians in their turn recognised that the rate of interest required to balance the demand for and supply of money was not likely to diverge for long from the rate required to equate saving with investment (the supply of funds and the demand for funds). An increase in the quantity of money might reduce the rate of interest—as money became less attractive than other financial assets—but it was also, through the lower rate of interest, likely to stimulate the level of business investment. As business investment pushed ahead of saving, money incomes would rise, prices rise, and the level of money balances required would also rise. The rate of interest would return to its former level (or something close to it).

In fact, in the theoretical state of complete equilibrium—that is, equilibrium in commodity, factor and money markets—the rate of interest which gives equality between the demand for and supply of money (monetary approach) will also be that rate which gives equilibrium between savings and investment (real approach). This must be the case otherwise there could be no complete equilibrium: there would still be movement in one of the markets which would lead to further variation in national income. Since there can only be one equilibrium rate of interest for each level of income theoretically possible within an economy, adjustment would take place in all markets until a single, equilibrium, rate of interest is reached.

We may therefore conclude as follows:

(i) The rate of interest is the price for money—the rate which governs the demand for and supply of money.

(ii) It is possible to use two distinct and seemingly conflicting approaches to the determination of interest rates. One of these, the 'real' theory of interest rates, stresses the importance of real factors—thrift and the productivity of investment. The other 'monetary' theory of the rate of interest stresses the importance of the desire to hold money as a good in its own right.

(iii) In reality, the two approaches are not as incompatible as they first appear. In the final analysis there can only be one equilibrium rate of interest—that which balances all markets.

(iv) In fact, as we have already seen in Chapter 5, there is not one rate of interest but many rates of interest. After reading this chapter the reader might like to turn back to that chapter and review his understanding of the range of interest rates in the light of these theories of interest.

7.5 Revision Test

Answers	*Questions*
—	**1.** What is interest?
1. A payment made by a borrower of funds—the price of money.	**2.** In a simple sense, what determines the rate of interest?
2. The supply of, and the demand for, funds.	**3.** Is there general agreement about the factors determining the rate of interest?
3. No. There are two main approaches to the rate of interest.	**4.** What are they?
4. The 'real' approach and the monetary approach.	**5.** Briefly define the 'real' approach to interest rates.
5. Money is a veil; it has no direct effect upon relative prices which are set by 'real' factors, as also is the rate of interest.	**6.** In relation to interest rates what are these 'real' factors?
6. Thrift, and the productivity of business investment.	**7.** This view of interest was taken by which group of economists?
7. The 'classical economists'—the group which developed around the writings of Adam Smith.	**8.** Briefly define the monetary approach to interest rates.
8. Besides being a medium of exchange money can be desired for its own sake. It is therefore not the demand for and supply of 'loanable funds' which sets interest rates but the supply of and demand for money.	**9.** Whose work is this approach built upon?
9. That of J. M. Keynes. It is part of his re-statement of the theory of money.	**10.** Go over the page until you are quite sure of the answer to each question. Then try some of the written questions in Appendix 1.

8

THE SIGNIFICANCE OF MONEY IN THE ECONOMY

8.1 Introduction

In the simplest of terms, money functions as a medium of exchange, and in this respect it is of great significance to an economy, which without money would have to revert to some form of barter. However, in more recent times money has been credited with much greater significance than that of a mere agent of exchange. In particular the way in which the amount of money in circulation affects the level of economic activity has attracted a great deal of attention. By the level of economic activity we mean the size of the national income, its distribution amongst the population, and the movement of the price level by which it is valued.

The two previous chapters have suggested that monetary theory is an area where significant disputes exist. Such a suggestion is continued in this chapter where attitudes polarise around three approaches, two of which are still fiercely contested. The other is discussed today only as a foundation for the other two. In chronological order these approaches are (*a*) the classical quantity theory of money, (*b*) Keynesian theory and (*c*) modern monetarism.

8.2 The Classical Quantity Theory

Classical economists were impressed by the way in which 'real' factors influenced relative prices. These factors—the tastes of households, factor supplies and technology—were thought to operate regardless of the quantity of money. In this respect money only facilitated exchange, it was neutral. For example, it might take twice the quantity of resources to construct a mobile steam engine in relation to a stationary one: the price of the mobile engine relative to that of the stationary engine would be 2:1—whatever the price level.

However, though the classical economists denied any role for money in the determination of relative prices, they did believe that money was important in the determination of the general price level. One of the best known expressions of this belief has come to be termed the 'Fisher Equation of Exchange', after its originator, the American economist Irving Fisher.

The Fisher equation states:

$$MV = PT$$

where M is the quantity of money, V is the velocity of money, P is the general price level, and T is the number of transactions within the economy.

The Fisher equation therefore states that the amount of money in circulation, times the frequency with which it circulates within a given period, equals the average value of transactions times the number of transactions which take place within the defined period. Viewed in this way the so-called Fisher equation is not an equation at all, it is merely an identity—it only states what must be the case. The money we have, multiplied by the number of times we spend it, must be the same as the number of things we spend it on multiplied by their price.

The significance of the Fisher equation though, and a source of many criticisms levelled at it, lies in the way in which it is possible to isolate the variables within it and then suggest a pattern of behaviour for them. In particular, classical economists assumed that V and T could conveniently be regarded as constants. In the case of V it was felt that a society would only hold money in order to make exchanges. The amount they needed to hold would depend upon institutional factors—for example, were they paid daily, weekly or monthly. Obviously the weekly paid would need a bigger stock of money than the daily paid, etc. Since it could be safely assumed that such institutions as salaried or non-salaried employment would change only slowly within a society V, in the short run, would remain constant.

Classical economists regarded T as constant because of their belief in full employment equilibrium. If a society was producing at its maximum then real output could not change in the short period, but only over longer time periods as a result of new technology, etc.

The equation was therefore reduced to a direct relationship between M and P, though most classical economists did not claim an exactly proportional change in prices when the money supply varied, as the modified formula below seems to suggest.

$$M\not{V} = P\not{T} \text{ (eliminating the constants } V \text{ and } T\text{)}$$
$$\therefore \quad M = P$$

An alternative expression of the classical quantity theory, and one which readers are likely to encounter elsewhere, is known as the 'Cambridge Equation', because it was developed over the years by economists at that University—particularly Marshall and Pigou.

The Cambridge Equation is often expressed as

$$M = KPR$$

For convenience, in order to maintain as close a link as possible with the Fisher Equation of Exchange, we shall use the formula

$$M = KPT$$

where M is the quantity of money, T is the volume of output (called R in the first equation), P is the price level, and K is the community's demand for liquid balances expressed as a fraction of the total income it (the community) receives.

Since the community's income is the same as the value of its outputs, i.e. PT (or PR), then by way of illustration, if $PT = £100\,000$ and $K = \frac{1}{2}$, £50 000 is demanded in liquid balances; if PT rises to £300 000 then £150 000 would be required in liquid balances. Therefore with T and K constant, P once more depends on changes in M.

There were many problems surrounding the Quantity Theory of Money. Some of these were:

(*a*) In order for V to remain constant it was necessary for the population to have constant expectations, particularly as regards future price changes. Expectations of increases in prices might lead to accelerated spending and an increased V. Expectations of decreases in prices might lead to deceleration in spending and a decreased V. Once V is on the move, changes in M can be absorbed by V and not transmitted to P. (An illustration of this occurred in the late 1960s, when persistent attempts to control inflation by reducing the money supply were defeated by an increased velocity of money as factor owners pursued the higher standard of living they deemed they were entitled to enjoy.)

(*b*) Full employment of all resources depends upon the flexibility of wages and prices, both in an upwards and downwards direction. Without such flexibility the volume of real output, *T*, will be subject to change, as the economy passes through varying levels of unemployment. *T* also could be capable of absorbing the effects of *M* and therefore forestall a potential change in *P*.

As suggested in the introduction, the classical quantity theory is no longer regarded as a serious explanation of how an economy functions. It is primarily of interest because of the way in which it was used as a point from which to develop more modern explanations.

8.3 The Keynesian System

The first of these approaches was the one developed by Keynes and further modified by other writers after his death. It is known under the title of the 'Keynesian System'. It has already been demonstrated (see Chapter 7) that Keynes rejected the classical interpretation of money and the rate of interest. This was of the greatest importance for by destroying the classical approach to the rate of interest Keynes made the level of income a burning issue. If there was no guarantee that all income would be spent (and with speculative balances and the liquidity trap there wasn't) then the level of national income could fluctuate quite widely over time *and* could become stuck at an under-employment equilibrium, producing *less* than the maximum possible output.

It was Keynes' belief that the level of income was the major influence upon saving. He firmly rejected the idea that people save in order to earn interest, and instead suggested that most saving was a residual, comprising what was left after consumption to ensure an acceptable level of consumption. If this utilised all of their current income then no saving took place (indeed, it is not unusual for consumption to outstrip current income and for dis-saving to occur, or the pledging of future income). Only where income was large enough to allow acceptable consumption and some residual for saving, would saving take place. Further, he believed that as a society became more affluent its propensity to consume (see appendix to this chapter) would diminish, and consequently its propensity to save would rise. Such a development has profound implications for the level of investment required in an economy. If income levels are to be maintained in situations where consumption expenditure becomes a smaller *proportion* of total income, the expenditure gap needs to be filled by investment expenditure.

In part Keynes rehabilitated the rate of interest when dealing with the determinants of investment. He believed that businessmen would compare the expected rate of return from the life of a project with its cost. One of the important elements in the cost calculation was the rate of interest—the price of borrowed money (or the alternative return on accumulated funds of the business). However, it is important to note that stress is laid upon *expected* returns. One of Keynes' major innovations was the introduction of the role of expectations into economic theory. Crudely put, when businessmen in aggregate are optimistic they will tend to make new investment; when they are pessimistic they will not (or they will make less of it). The important question then is to ascertain what it is that generates business optimism or pessimism. Keynes himself linked the matter of business confidence to the level of income. When incomes rose more consumption took place and, stimulated by a consumer boom, businessmen became optimistic about profit potential and were eager to make new investment. Similarly, if income and consumption fell this made the business community pessimistic and less likely to make new investment.

One implication of far-reaching importance to arise from this interpretation of investment related to the necessity for increasing absolute amounts of investment as incomes rose. Because affluent societies spend a smaller *proportion* of their rising incomes on the almost automatic consumption items, a significantly *increasing proportion* of their incomes must be devoted to investment expenditure. This is necessary even to *maintain* the higher levels of income. To push incomes even higher in future periods still greater quantities of investment must be made. Keynes doubted the capacity of businessmen's expectations to provide the impetus for the required amounts of new investment—he felt that the business community were often likely to sink into pessimism. When this pessimism became prolonged then a situation of underemployment equilibrium such as that from 1922 to 1938 in the UK was likely to occur. His prescription for the defeat of pessimism and the regeneration of levels of output and income was to have the central government make expenditures to compensate for the lack of private investment. He suggested that when economies were very depressed the schemes upon which expenditure took place were less important than the expenditure itself. Money pumped into the economy would increase the circular flow of income and generate optimism amongst investors. These investors would then be moved to make investment decisions themselves, which would have the effect of further increasing the level of income. Eventually, it was hoped, the new equilibrium level of income which the economy arrived at would be that at which output, income and employment were maximised.

For an equilibrium level of income to exist it is required that all income generated is expended. If this is not the case the level of income begins to alter. If less is spent than is generated (net saving), then the level of income will fall as some groups within the economy find their personal incomes reduced. If more is spent than is generated by current incomes (net investment) then personal incomes rise and so does aggregate income. Only when the total of savings are equal to the total of investment will income neither rise nor fall—it will be in equilibrium.

One of the processes by which income was expected to grow was first introduced by a contemporary of Keynes. The process was known as the 'multiplier' and its origination is credited to R. F. Kahn. It had a very important role in the Keynesian system since it was the multplier which described by how much aggregate income would have to rise in order to generate enough saving so that the total amount saved once more equalled the total amount invested.

The multiplier is explained in greater detail in the appendix to this chapter (Section 8.7) but the essentials of it can be conveyed by a simple example. Suppose that the economy is in equilibrium, i.e. the total of savings equals the total being invested. Then investors decide to increase the amounts which they have previously invested. Obviously the level of income of those employed in the capital goods industries will rise—extra investment expenditure will make sure of this. However, other groups within the economy will also benefit from the investment; those who work in the capital goods industries, and those who provide capital and material resources for them, will pass on a proportion of their increased incomes in the form of increased expenditure. The extra expenditure then becomes extra income for those who provide the extra goods and services supplied to those working in the capital goods industries. They in turn pass on a part of their extra incomes in the form of extra expenditure, and so the income-creating process goes on. The process only stops when the aggregate level of income has risen sufficiently to allow the population a large enough residual after consumption once more to equate the level of savings with the new (higher) level of investment. This would then be a new equilibrium point where income would neither grow nor shrink, providing that savings and investment levels did not change. The concept of the multiplier gives a precise indication of the extent to which income must grow before the new equilibrium level of income is reached. If the new injection (investment) amounted to £100 000 and the community was accustomed to withdrawing (saving) one quarter of its incremental income, then total income would have to rise by £400 000 before enough saving had taken place to offset the original investment. Obviously this is a much simplified example and in reality the total of withdrawals are likely to be greater than savings alone (for example, leakages in purchases abroad). Further, the period over which the level of income will grow may be such that there is a significant lag between the initial investment and the total income generation. Such factors tend to result in the necessity for the generation of a larger increase in income than would be the case in a simple theoretical model.

It is also of critical importance to consider which groups within the economy receive the incremental income. The marginal propensity to save of affluent groups is likely to be much greater than that of poor groups. Should the former group receive the bulk of the extra income the multiplier effect will be less than had most income gone to the latter.

Keynes, then, supplied an explanation of how an economy works which rested upon the level of aggregate income, and the manner in which it grew and shrank. He was the first to consider the movement of income in this manner, because he was the first to believe that there could be serious long-term departures from the maximum income possible: his predecessors simply did not think it worthwhile to analyse a variable which they felt did not vary!

Using variations in income he attempted to demonstrate that the total of withdrawals from the circular flow of income was capable of equalling the total of injections at almost any level of economic activity, i.e. at almost any level of income and employment. When withdrawals are equal to injections there can be no 'multiplier' effect, and the economy will be stable at the existing level of national income.

The significant question which Keynes now felt able to answer was why the economy would become stuck in underemployment equilibrium. The key rested in the income-generating role of investment. If businessmen were pessimistic and would not increase the net levels of investment, income would not rise. If the feelings of the business community were such that 'replacement only' investment was entered into, a relatively low level of income could be maintained for a considerable period of time. Without the stimulus of new investment there was little that could be done to push the economy to full employment (maximum output) equilibrium.

This brief outline of the Keynesian system highlights the importance attached to investment: it is changes in the level of investment which are responsible for bringing variations in income. It was felt by Keynes that the primary role of money would be played here—in the area surrounding investment. Money was viewed as an asset, desirable to hold for its own sake. Like any other asset it had a range of substitutes, some close, some distant. Probably the closest substitute was to be found amongst short-term financial assets. When the supply of money increased, the money balances of the community (relative to the prevailing national income) became excessive. Substitutes were sought for these excess money holdings—say bonds. As the price of bonds were bid up so the yield on them fell; effectively the rate of interest was reduced. A reduced rate of interest should stimulate the business community to undertake increased investment, since it meant that those schemes with a relatively low marginal efficiency of capital became more viable.

To summarise, a change in the quantity of money would affect:

(*a*) The rate of interest, and then, through the level of investment.
(*b*) The level of income.

In general Keynesians had little faith in the ability of money supply to affect interest rates (a view echoed by the Radcliffe Report) and therefore advocated fiscal rather than monetary measures as a means of controlling the economy.

8.4 Modern Monetarism

During the 1950s and 1960s it seemed that Keynesianism, and the fiscal measures which it promoted, were adequate to deal with all problems presented by an economic system. However, during the 1970s this confidence waned and opened the way for a group of economists, led by Milton Friedman, to re-establish the validity of monetarism, a task which they had been attempting since the 1950s.

The basic contention of monetarists is that money does not have a limited range of very close substitutes, but that it is instead unique. They feel that money is merely a temporary resting place for purchasing power, and when money is being demanded there is, in effect, a demand for a certain volume of purchasing power to be held. Because monetarists do not believe in the 'few close substitutes for money' argument they feel that there is no reason why those who hold money balances should choose to place any excess money into securities, bonds, etc., instead of, say, goods and services. They go on from this point to re-establish the rate of interest, except that their rate of interest has a much broader base than that dealt with by the old classical economists. The claim is that the various methods of holding wealth—money, bonds, equities, physical goods and human wealth—all give a yield which can be termed 'interest', i.e. some benefit derived from the holding of wealth. In the case of money this benefit is the convenience which holders of cash experience; in the case of 'human wealth', the acquisition of skills or the possession of physical power implies the holding of a flow of future income.

In the construction of portfolios of wealth individuals attempt to balance the benefit derived from the holding of a particular form of wealth against the 'cost'—which is the benefit forgone by not holding some alternative asset. In this way an equi-marginal balance is struck.

Unfortunately for monetarists, the calculation of the various 'interest' rates on the whole range of assets which might be held is impossible and they are therefore prevented from building in the rate of interest as an important element of their theories. However, the idea that money is one element of a wide 'portfolio' of assets and that if communities build up excess balances they can easily attempt to remove them by purchasing goods and services, is an important one. It allows monetarists to claim that increases in the money supply are apt to be reflected in increases in the level of prices, because for every level of income there is a 'correct' quantity of money. Monetarists in fact are claiming a stable relationship between the quantity of money and the value of income. Further, they suggest that the relationship between money supply and income is more stable than relationships between expenditure and income. In essence this is a belief that the monetarist approach is superior in a technical sense to the Keynesian approach.

Such claims are based not only on reasoning but also on a vast amount of empirical testing which purports to show how changes in the supply of money are the main cause of economic fluctuations. However, the statistical evidence amassed has not gone unchallenged. Keynesians have countered that oversimplified expenditure/income models have been used and this is why they have performed badly. Keynesians have also attacked the idea of 'time lags'. Monetarists are unable to say exactly how long after a change in money supply occurs, the effects of such a change are felt in the economy. Keynesians have suggested that if time lags do not exist the relationship between money supply and economic activity could well be one of economic activity bringing about changes in the money supply.

The result of statistical tests certainly vary according to the complexity of the model tested, the time period taken, and what one means by 'money'. They are in a sense, inconclusive.

The basic monetarist position, though by no means followed by all monetarists, is that money can be destabilising. Whatever objectives a government seeks to achieve in the economy can be upset by the monetary effects arising from what they try to do. The fine-tuning of an economy (using injections of money to influence aggregate national income) is uncertain in its results because of unpredictable time lags, and therefore a steady expansion of the supply of money (preferably in line with productive capacity) is all that should be attempted.

8.5 Conclusion

In the 1950s and 1960s the general feeling was that Keynesianism could tackle successfully the problems of advanced economies, and that fiscal policy was more direct and more reliable than monetary policy.

In the 1970s and 1980s, however, despite much dispute over tests and results, the feeling has arisen that monetary policy, whilst perhaps not a complete answer in itself definitely has an important role to play, particularly in the control of inflation.

8.6 Revision Test

Answers	*Questions*
—	**1.** Why is the concept of money as a mere medium of exchange somewhat out of date today?
1. Because all schools of thought agree that the amount of money in circulation affects the level of economic activity.	**2.** What is 'the level of economic activity'?
2. It is the level of wealth the nation creates which constitutes the national income, its distribution among the population and the movement of the price level by which the nation's wealth is valued.	**3.** What is 'the classical theory of money'?
3. Irving Fisher's equation of exchange, $MV = PT$.	**4.** What did the classicals believe about V (velocity of money) and T (the number of transactions made possible by the output of goods and services)?
4. That they were both constants, leaving $M = P$.	**5.** Where did the theory break down?
5. Velocity proved to be variable if expectations changed, and T proved to be variable, since economies did not work at full employment levels as the 'classicals' thought.	**6.** What theories about money replaced the classical theory?
6. (*a*) Keynesianism; (*b*) the 'new monetarism'.	**7.** What was the Keynesian system?
7. A system that held that an economy could get stuck in an 'underemployment' equilibrium, and that the more prosperous an economy the greater the need to increase investment income year by year. In both situations business confidence in the prospects of profitability was crucial.	**8.** What was Keynes' solution to the 'underemployment' problem.
8. Direct government action to increase the money supply and generate confidence—fiscal measures, not monetary measures.	**9.** Explain the 'multiplier' in a Keynesian economy?
9. (Here the reader will need to read the text in the appendix to this chapter (Section 8.7) and work out a concise explanation.)	**10.** What is the approach of 'new monetarism'?

Answers	*Questions*
10. It revives the role of 'interest' in a broader way than ever before. Every form of wealth yields a benefit which constitutes an 'interest' payment. People strike an equi-marginal balance between these benefits in deciding what 'basket of wealth' to hold for their families.	**11.** What is their conclusion about this?
11. That for every level of income there is a 'current' quantity of money to hold, and if incomes rise too fast they must force prices of goods and services up because the marginal utility of money falls relative to goods and services, and in competing for these desirable items the people will bid up the prices.	**12.** What are the problems of monetarism?
12. (*a*) The 'time lags'—we do not know how long it will be before action on the money supply is reflected in the economy. (*b*) People take evasive action to neutralise bad effects of monetary policies on them, and since the system is based on indirect action rather than direct action controls to compel compliance are less effective, if not impossible.	**13.** Go over the page again until you are sure of all the points.

8.7 Appendix to Chapter 8

Propensities to Consume and Propensities to Save

It has already been suggested that as the aggregate level of income within the community rises, the proportion of income spent upon consumption is likely to decline; Fig. 8.1 helps to illustrate this process more precisely.

The Multiplier

The multiplier is the mechanism which is responsible for bringing equilibrium between changed levels of investment and saving. It does this by altering the size of aggregate income. Should investment exceed saving (a net injection), the multiplier shows to what extent any given injection will be expanded (multiplied) before the savings process removes it from circulation and once again equates total savings with total investment. Obviously, the size of increment in income required will depend upon how much of an increase in income the society in question is likely to retain in the form of savings, i.e. the propensity to save. If all of the increase in income is saved by those who receive it, there will be no necessity for a multiplier process at all—extra savings will almost immediately equal extra investment and income in total will rise by an amount

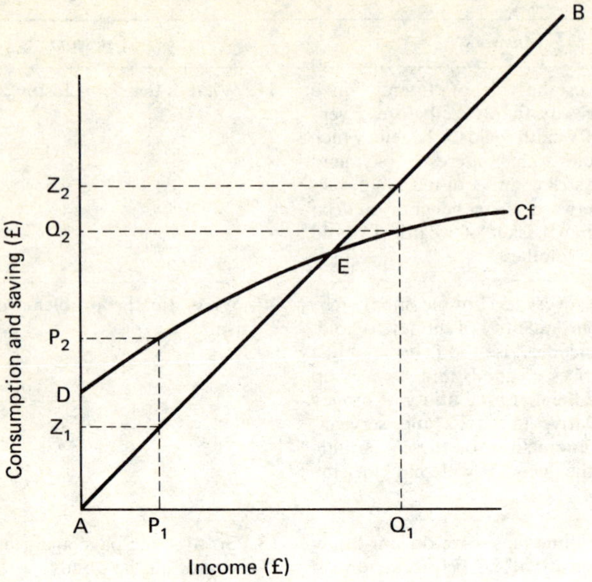

Fig. 8.1. Propensities to consume and save.

Notes

(i) The line AB is the equilibrium line where income equals expenditure. (In mathematics it is the locus of points where income and expenditure are equal.)

(ii) If all income within a community were consumed the path of consumption as income increased would be described by the line AB. However, experience shows that as aggregate incomes rise, and the more basic needs of a society are met, the level of saving will rise. This causes the consumption function (Cf), which plots the path of actual consumption, to depart from the total hypothetical consumption line AB.

(iii) The lower part of the Cf curve, DE, recognises the fact that at very low levels of income societies are forced to dis-save in order to help maintain consumption levels. Thus at an income of £P_1 consumption would be £P_2 and dis-saving of £P_2Z_1 would have occurred. By contrast, at higher levels, such as £Q_1, consumption of £Q_2 will take place and savings of £Q_2Z_2 will occur.

(iv) The relationship between the level of consumption and the level of aggregate income (Y) is known as the average propensity to consume (APC). It is usual to express this as a fraction, e.g. if income is £80 million and consumption £60 million

$$\text{APC} = \frac{C}{Y} = \frac{60}{80} = \frac{3}{4}$$

That income which is not spent upon consumption is savings. The average propensity to save (APS) is also expressed as a fraction, e.g. if income is £80 million and saving £20 million

$$\text{APS} = \frac{S}{Y} = \frac{20}{80} = \frac{1}{4}$$

The APC and APS, when added together are, of course, 1.

(v) Of greater significance than the average propensities are the marginal propensities to consume and save. The marginal propensity to consume (MPC) describes the degree of consumption which takes place out of extra income, e.g. if income rises by £10 millions and extra consumption is £7 million, then

$$\text{MPC} = \frac{\Delta C}{\Delta Y}$$

$$= \frac{7}{10}$$

(N.B. The symbol delta (Δ) merely means 'change in'. ΔC means 'change in level of consumption expenditure' and ΔY means 'change in level of aggregate income'.)

Similarly, if out of the extra income of £10 million there is extra saving of £3 million

$$\text{MPS} = \frac{\Delta S}{\Delta Y}$$

$$= \frac{3}{10}$$

The reason why marginal propensities are more significant than average propensities is that they tell us the likely proportion of any extra income that will be consumed, or saved. In economics it is often what consumers do with any extra income that has implications for the entrepreneur proposing to produce a new product, or expand output of an existing product.

(vi) The slope of the consumption function (Cf) in Fig. 8.1 gradually moves further away from the total consumption line (in relative terms) and this indicates that as incomes rise the marginal propensity to consume is declining and the marginal propensity to save rising. This will not be unusual in an affluent society. There are, however, a number of other influences upon the propensities to consume and save, besides the level of income. These include the distribution of income, the structure of institutions and consumers' expectations of future behaviour of prices.

equal to the extra investment only. However, in normal circunstances (the 1920s and 30s being exceptions) societies are not likely to save the total of extra incomes—the MPC is likely to be greater than 0, since consumers will respond to extra income by spending some of it. Once consumption spending takes place out of extra income, it in turn helps to generate further income.

For example, suppose a small builder is engaged to construct a storeroom for a local butcher. He is paid £10 000 for the job. From this he may obtain a personal income of £2500 (the other factors of production—labour, supplies of materials, capital, etc.—receiving the remaining £7500). Out of this he may spend £2000 on personal consumption—food, heating, drink, holidays, etc. This means that his MPC is $\frac{4}{5}$, i.e. $\frac{2\,000}{2\,500}$. If the MPC of the factors he employs (and of the groups he and they spend $\frac{4}{5}$ of the £10 000 with) is also $\frac{4}{5}$, then the calculation of spending in the next round becomes

Original investment £10 000

$$\text{MPC} = \frac{4}{5} = £8000$$

Generated income is therefore £8000. With an MPC of $\frac{4}{5}$, only part of this £8000 (£6400) is likely to be passed on in the form of consumer spending.

In this way consumers will continue to generate income for others until the effect of the initial injection has worked itself out (the figure eventually being passed on is reduced to almost nothing).

A shorthand way to arrive at a figure for the size of the effect of the multiplier is to use a formula. The easiest is one which relates the size of the multiplier—denoted *k*—to the size of the reciprocal of the MPS; in other words, the MPS turned on its head. This formula clearly indicates that the expansion effect produced in total income depends upon the size of MPS.

$k = \frac{1}{\text{MPS}}$ (really the MPS in its normal form is $\frac{\text{MPS}}{1}$; its reciprocal is found by turning it upside down)

Where MPC is $\frac{4}{5}$, the MPS must be $\frac{1}{5}$ (the two together making 1), and therefore

$$\begin{aligned} k &= \frac{1}{\frac{1}{5}} \\ &= \frac{1}{1} \div \frac{1}{5} \\ &= \frac{1}{1} \times \frac{5}{1} \\ &= 5 \end{aligned}$$

This indicates that the total rise in income necessary to generate enough saving to equal the new investment of £10 000 is £50 000. This will be composed of the original investment of £10 000, plus the secondary or generated increment £40 000.

Obviously, the process does not in practice operate as smoothly as suggested. Time lags occur and there are leakages (such as spending abroad).

Part 3

FISCAL AND MONETARY POLICY

9

FISCAL POLICY AND THE NATIONAL DEBT

9.1 Introduction

Since the Second World War UK governments have accepted overall responsibility for the regulation of the economy. They have done this in order to further their main policy objectives, which have been as follows:

(*a*) To maintain a high level of employment;
(*b*) To secure continuous economic growth;
(*c*) To keep inflation to a low level;
(*d*) To maintain a healthy 'balance of payments' and, in the days before exchange rates were floated,
(*e*) To keep a fixed external value for the pound.

It is worth mentioning that in the pursuit of these main objectives governments have an almost impossible task, for they are to some extent irreconcilable. For example, to solve a balance of payments deficit the government might have to reduce the aggregate level of demand in the economy—a policy which can be expected to *increase* the amount of unemployment. What does tend to occur is that one, or perhaps two, of the main objectives are pursued with more vigour than the rest—in recent years a much reduced level of inflation has been the primary target. Concentration upon a reduced range of aims (though not necessarily always the same ones) is a tacit admission that measures taken to help achieve one aim might be damaging to the attainment of one or more of the 'competing' aims.

Despite this, as Keynes pointed out, there is a theoretical position where the major policy goals could be simultaneously achieved—he called this the 'equilibrium level' of income. It could only occur at full employment level. Governments still try to get somewhere near this 'equilibrium level', even though they recognise that today 'full employment' is not quite the same as in Keynes' days.

Generally in its efforts at regulating the economy the Government is attempting to ensure that this imperfection is minimised and it normally does so by affecting, where possible, the size of aggregate income. In its efforts to secure its main aims the government can bring to bear **three types of policy: fiscal; monetary and direct**. Every enterprise, and indeed every individual, is likely to be aware of the workings of at least some portion of these policies. In a modern advanced economy, such as the UK economy, the biggest single influence in the environment of firms is Government policy. The Government has huge incomes to spend, and these can easily influence the aggregate demand in the economy, because the revenue is obtained from the ordinary public.

The Government has three main sources of revenue: taxation, borrowing and trading revenues.

9.2 Fiscal Policy

Fiscal policy comes from the Latin *fiscus*, the Roman Emperor's purse, which was filled by taxation. Although governments have been raising revenue through taxation for centuries, fiscal measures as a means of economic control are a comparatively recent phenomenon. Only when the ideas of John Maynard Keynes were accepted by the UK Government did fiscal policy assume a significant role. During the period when governments felt that Keynesianism had *every* answer to economic problems, fiscal policy became dominant, and there can be no doubt that UK Governments still rely very heavily upon changes in taxation to achieve their economic objectives.

Fiscal policy concerns the raising of revenue by taxation; in particular the amounts to be raised in this way relative to the expenditures envisaged—which involves perhaps a budget surplus or deficit—and the timing of variations.

Taxation

During the early part of the twentieth century taxation was a relatively straightforward matter. The Government had certain expenditures to make; it therefore needed certain revenues to 'balance the budget'. Taxation was the prime source of income. There is, though, much more to modern taxation than a simple attempt at keeping Government books in balance.

Taxes are now frequently varied in order to influence the level of aggregate demand. A rise in direct taxes, e.g. income tax, reduces the population's disposable income and hence aggregate demand (assuming that the Government does not itself spend all of the tax take). A reduction in direct taxes has the opposite effect. In theory direct taxes can be changed easily, but the mechanics of actually doing so with a hard-pressed revenue service effectively means that only infrequent changes occur (usually in the spring budget).

The brunt of tax variation falls upon indirect, particularly expenditure, taxes. This is because any administration costs involved in a change are borne by traders and distributors, and not by the Government service. There tends, therefore, to be an absence of administrative bottlenecks. Variations in indirect taxation affect the level of aggregate demand in a similar way to changes in direct taxation. When indirect rates rise the population has less income to spend on other items once it has purchased those which have been taxed. When rates fall it has more income left to spend on other items once it has purchased those taxed. There is, of course, always the argument that consumers need not buy goods which have indirect taxes upon them. Whilst this is true, the Chancellor does tend to choose goods with a high level of price inelasticity of demand, consumers on the whole still buying the good despite its tax (price) increase.

One development towards flexibility in tax changes is the introduction of the 'regulator'. First used in 1961, this technique allows the Chancellor to change the main expenditure tax rates by up to 10 per cent either side of existing rates, without recourse to Parliament. Many argue that such a small change in tax rates (price) would only have effect when applied to goods with a high price elasticity of demand. However, the regulator concentrates upon goods with inelastic demand in relation to price and draws disposable income *away* from expenditure upon other goods (assuming of course that consumers do not seek to maintain their real purchasing positions through higher wage and salary claims).

The reaction of the population to tax rates is an important and topical

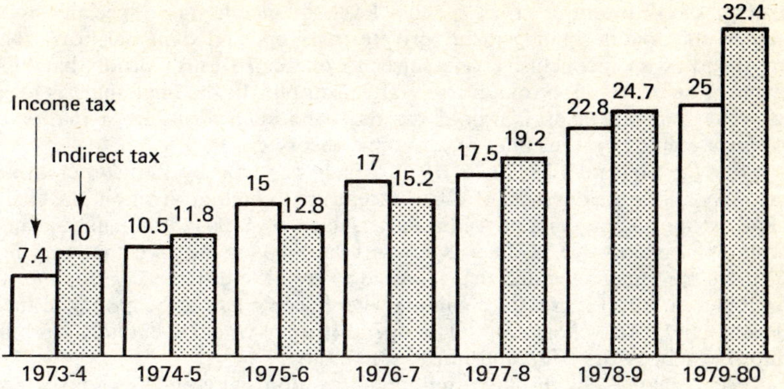

Fig. 9.1. Direct and indirect taxes in recent years (£1000m).

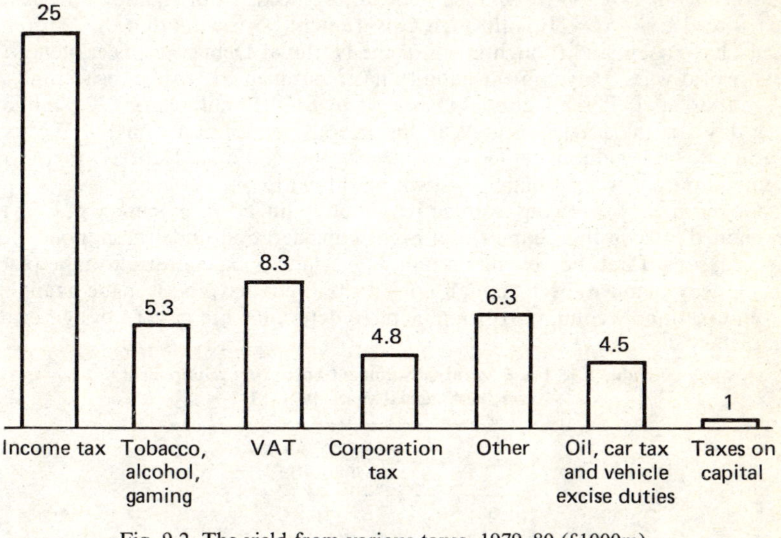

Fig. 9.2. The yield from various taxes, 1979–80 (£1000m).

consideration. Whilst almost everyone who pays tax would like to pay less (presumably whilst enjoying the same level of services!) debates over tax rates concentrate less upon a *reduction* of tax than they do on the distribution of the tax burden between direct taxes (such as income tax) or indirect taxes (such as value added tax, VAT). On the one hand those of Socialist leaning claim that direct taxes are preferable since they take a higher proportion of a rich man's income than they do of a poor man's income. The rich, having more to spend, presumably find the indirect tax burden easier to bear than the poor. On the other hand are those (usually of free-enterprise leanings) who argue for higher indirect and lower direct taxation. This argument centres around the disincentive effect of high levels of income tax, especially upon higher and middle management, private investors and dynamic firms. The argument is an inconclusive one since no one can furnish proof that high levels of direct taxation do adversely affect output. In the final analysis ideas of what is regarded as fair hold the day, and such ideas are a matter of political ideology rather than of economic theory.

After the General Election of 1979, which was won by the Conservatives precisely about the question of tax disincentives to high production, the chairman of one major company earning a salary of £106 000 per annum and other emoluments of £30 000 was left with £61 000 (against previous earnings of £32 000). He commented that it would make little difference to the output he achieved, but if it created a climate where people had more money in their pockets and a free choice of how to spend it there would eventually be some improvement in the effort put into the economy.

Recent changes in the distribution of taxation between direct taxes and indirect taxes are shown in Figs. 9.1 and 9.2.

9.3 Central Government Borrowing

Governments rarely meet all their expenditure needs from taxation and hence are forced to borrow. It is through Government borrowing that the National Debt has arisen, and though much of the National Debt owes its existence to two world wars, Government liability has continued to grow in peacetime.

In the year 1978 the National Debt rose by £12 014 million, or £32.9 million per day. In the First World War the average expenditure on the Western Front was £1 million per day, so clearly the National Debt is no longer something that we can blame on two 'world wars'.

Government borrowing is an activity closely linked to monetary policy (as explained later in this chapter) but needs consideration under fiscal policy for two reasons. First, borrowing permits Government expenditure to take place in the way planned, even though not all the funds have been made available from taxation. Second, borrowing helps to determine the pattern of aggregate monetary demand.

Table 9.1. UK Central Government borrowing requirement for the financial years 1971–81

Year	*Borrowing requirement* (£ million)
1970–1	21
1971–2	584
1972–3	1 981
1973–4	2 164
1974–5	5 082
1975–6	8 803
1976–7	5 944
1977–8	4 431
1978–9	8 084
1979–80	8 227
1980–81	13 500

There are two figures frequently referred to in the press, the Central Government Borrowing Requirement (**CGBR**) and the Public Sector Borrowing Requirement (**PSBR**). Figures for the former are published regularly in the Bank of England *Quarterly Bulletin*, and make interesting reading. The figures for the 1970s are given in Table 9.1.

The PSBR includes the local government borrowing and is therefore larger than the CGBR. Critics argue that with a very high PSBR (around £10 000 million per annum in the UK) funds which otherwise would be available for private investment are being diverted into Government activities. With private industry starved of funds the level of aggregate income, it is argued, is adversely affected. The Conservative Government of 1979 were so convinced of the accuracy of this interpretation that they immediately slashed £1000 million off the PSBR in order to make more funds available for private industry.

9.4 Trading Incomes

In a consideration of Government finance it should not be forgotten that both central and local governments receive trading revenues. One example relating to Central Government trading income is the charges made by the Agricultural Advisory Service.

9.5 Government Expenditure

When it is recognised that UK central and local government is responsible for disposing of over 50 per cent of the total National Income, it can be appreciated that Government expenditure forms a very important component of aggregate demand. Since the Government has direct control over public expenditure, and public expenditure involves such vast sums, it might be thought that regular adjustments, of sufficient magnitude, to public expenditure would constitute all the control which the economy required. However, in practice this is not the case. Historically adjustment has tended to be made to Government revenue rather than Government expenditure, and this is because of the inflexibility of Government expenditure plans. Since the Plowden Report in 1961 the Government has tended to plan its expenditure on a five-year roll-over basis—each year the four remaining years' expenditure being updated (in part to take account of higher prices) and the fifth year's expenditure is added. The first three years of this five-year period normally represent plans which are regarded as finalised. Only in crisis situations are significant changes (usually cuts in expenditure) made. Such 'last-minute' cuts normally involve losses. The most recent set of Public Expenditure Statistics available at present is shown in Table 9.2.

When public expenditure is reduced this reduces the level of aggregate demand; when it is increased then the level of aggregate demand rises. This is something of an oversimplification though because much depends on whether the private sector takes up 'released' income when public expenditure is cut or is squeezed of income when public expenditure rises.

There is often concern that high levels of public expenditure 'starve' the private sector of resources. The first Conservative budget of 1979 was an atypical one in that it cut about £1600 million from public expenditure in an attempt to release resources into private enterprise. Subsequent attempts to make further cuts were rather unsuccessful—indeed, forecast expenditure of

Table 9.2. Planning for the 1981 budget, for 1981–2

	1981–82	*1978–79*	*Outturns* *1979–80*	*1980–81 estimated*	*1981–82*	*Plans* *1982–83*	*1983–84*
	£ billion projected cash spend			*£ million at 1980 survey prices*			
Public expenditure programmes							
1. Central government (including Government finance for nationalised industries)	76.5	54 737	56 109	58 435	58 655		
2. Local authorities	25.5	21 426	21 762	20 250	19 200	76 900	75 200
3. Certain public corporations' capital expenditure	1.5	1 251	1 225	1 190	1 130		
Adjustments							
4. Nationalised industries' net overseas and market borrowing	−0.8	537	−322	−500	−585	−400	−550
5. Special sales of assets (net)	−0.2	—	−999	−325	−175	−125	−125
6. Contingency reserve	2.0	—	—	193	1 500	2 000	2 000
7. General allowance for shortfall	−0.7	—	—	—	−500	−500	−500
8. Planning total	104.0	77 951	77 776	79,245	79 225	77 900	76 000
9. Percentage change on previous year		+4.8	−0.2	+1.9	—	−1.6	−2.4
Memorandum items							
A. Debt interest—gross	13.7	9 767	10 439	10 820	10 400	10 300	10 100
—net	6.1	2 853	3 834	4 290	4 600	4 600	4 600
(Not included above)							
B. Nationalised industries' total net borrowing (Included in lines 1 and 4)	1.0	1 349	1 535	1 550	815	−50	−700

(Reproduced by courtesy of H. M. Stationery Office)
(Source: Public Expenditure White Paper)

1981 was £2000 million higher than in 1979 despite strenuous efforts to reduce public expenditure.

9.6 The Budget

The budget in the UK has ceased to be presented solely to raise revenue to meet Government expenditure. Instead it is primarily an instrument of economic management. In its management role the budget aims at keeping aggregate demand in line with aggregate supply. When forecasts for the months ahead indicate that aggregate demand is likely to exceed the economy's capacity to meet that demand, then this indicates that too much spending power is being injected into the economy. Some of this excess spending power must be withdrawn by taxing it away.

If there is an excess of injections over withdrawals then a budget which makes net withdrawals will be introduced, one which reduces a deficit or even goes into surplus. A deficit occurs where the Government proposes to spend more on its budget than it is raising; a surplus occurs where revenue raised by way of the budget exceeds proposed spending. If forecasts indicate that aggregate demand is likely to fall below aggregate supply then indications are that withdrawals will exceed injections and a budget making net injections is required, i.e. one with a reduced surplus or a deficit, or even an *increased* deficit. A neutral budget is one which does not embody net withdrawals or net injections. Thus the Chancellor might raise some taxes and lower others but the final result would be neutral, and there would be no change in aggregate demand as a result of the budget changes.

In order that the Government can make reasoned policy decisions in the budget it is necessary for them to have reliable information on the likely movements of consumers' demand, investment demand, private saving, the balance of payments surplus or deficit, etc. Such forecasts are prepared by the Treasury. Forecasts are made on the basis of a number of assumptions—e.g. investment expenditure remaining the same, investment expenditure rising 2.5 per cent, etc. Generally a 'middle' forecast is taken, though even in published statistics alternative forecasts are often given, or some margin of error is shown.

Because the budget emanates from Parliament, where financial proposals are subject to the (slow) legislative process, budgets used to have a once-for-all air about them (at least, that is until the following year's budget!). However, the needs of a modern economy have required a less rigid approach to fiscal policy. Consequently where estimates are seen to be significantly incorrect, as the year progresses, a 'mini-budget' may be introduced. This is a package of measures designed to take account of events differing from the estimates—it might even change the order of priority of the policy objectives outlined in the main budget, at least temporarily. In addition, in recent years the Government has had the power to make changes in taxation (e.g. the 'regulator') and expenditure between budgets without recourse to full parliamentary procedures. Such flexibility is essential if 'fine tuning' of the economy is to have a chance of success.

Most budgets have tended to concentrate upon bringing about changes in consumers' demand as a way of affecting the level of aggregate demand. This is because the level of consumers' demand is relatively easy to manipulate, since a majority of consumers do not have long-term, rigid expenditure plans.

On the other hand, Government expenditure plans might have been calculated years in advance and are generally regarded as difficult to change. In this respect the June Budget of 1979 was a departure from the norm in its emphasis upon cuts in public expenditure. The Government in this budget stated that 'Previously public spending has tended to determine the raising of finance, in future the reverse will be the case'.

9.7 The National Debt

One of the obvious reasons for the existence of a National Debt is the need to provide Governments with funds when taxation fails to cover expenditure, but the National Debt can be a much more subtle instrument of Government than this. In particular, it is important for Governments pursuing policies of aggregate demand expansion or contraction to ensure that the private sector holding of debt is of such a level that it complements their efforts. They must therefore make certain that the demand for and supply of Government debt are such that private sector spending decisions do not move out of line with the rest of Government policy; in effect that private holders of Government debt should not be induced to liquidate it (and therefore possibly spend more) when Government is attempting to reduce spending and vice versa. The way in which Governments deal with this problem has a significant effect upon the general operation of monetary policy.

It is of course possible for Governments to raise revenue by selling non-marketable debt—National Savings Certificates, Premium Savings Bonds, etc.—or they can effectively create money for Government use by increasing the quantity of notes and coins in circulation. However, Governments have not so far chosen to use the former method as a means of exerting short-term influences on monetary policy and are wary of the latter lest it prove inflationary. It is therefore in the area of marketable Government debt that debt management impinges upon monetary policy.

Marketable debt is of two types: long-term debt (the gilt-edged or long-term bond) and short-term debt (Treasury bills). Basic borrowing is in the form of longer-term bonds with weekly and daily adjustments being made through the use of Treasury bills. Governments tend to issue long-term bonds in blocks of large proportions—hundreds of millions of pounds at a time. Such an increase in the supply of bonds though is likely to have a disturbing effect upon the bond market, and so initially 'official' holders—the Bank of England, the National Debt Commissioners, etc.—take up the issue. The bonds then become available to other potential holders 'through the tap'. Here the Bank of England fixes a price (known as the tap price) at which it will release bonds from the new issue. In this way bonds become available when demand is sufficient to maintain stable prices.

Redemption of bonds follows a similar pattern: once they are within a year of maturity the Bank of England gradually buys up the issue. The impact of sudden increases or decreases in the supply of bonds is therefore avoided.

Obviously the Government has an interest in a stable market for bonds (and for bills) and it is in order to protect this interest that great efforts are taken to 'smooth' the effects of issues and redemptions. Without doubt a stable market simplifies the process of *future* borrowing—a point which no Government can afford to ignore. This objective of stability, though, is by no means the one which Governments pursue when '*Managing the National Debt*'.

The Government is interested in borrowing on terms which are as favourable as possible to itself; it seeks to control the supply of money and it tries to influence interest rates, in line with whatever other policies it is pursuing. Often these objectives conflict!

One of the problems encountered by Governments is that whilst they may require a set amount of borrowed funds each day of the year, it is not practicable to set a daily target for sales of bonds. Governments which did set targets would be at the mercy of the forces of demand and would have to accept wide variations in the price of bonds (and therefore of the rate of interest). Because market conditions do not necessarily reflect the borrowing requirements of Governments there is a danger that temporarily a Government may run short of funds. To overcome this problem Treasury bills (with a maturity of three months) are used. These bills do a great deal to fill in the 'gaps' left by the irregular sale of bonds.

Treasury bills find their way onto the market in two ways

(*a*) Through a weekly tender—this always occurs on a Friday.
(*b*) Through a 'tap' process.

Those who tender for Treasury bills and are successful are allowed to take their bills on a specified day the following week—a day which they, the purchasers, are allowed to nominate. This causes a slight problem that the daily flow of funds might not meet the Government's daily borrowing requirements. This is overcome by making bills available through the 'tap'. Here treasury bills are created and made available through the Bank of England—they can be sold at any time and have no single period of maturity.

9.8 The Effects of Debt Management

The Bank of England can influence the rates of interest paid on bonds and bills fairly easily. This does not mean, though, that the amounts lent, spent or borrowed can be as easily affected. Governments tend to borrow regardless of the rate of interest so changes in bond and bill rates do not necessarily have a direct affect upon borrowing and expenditure. However, Government debt such as bonds and bills tends to be dealt with alongside other debt instruments for which they may or may not be good substitutes. This question of substitutability is an important one because the rates of interest charged on very close substitutes cannot vary by much. This means that if other forms of debt can easily be substituted by Government bonds and bills any movement in the rates paid on bonds and bills will be reflected in the rest of the market.

Because the majority of Treasury bills are held by the discount houses, changes in their rate of discount have little direct effect upon the banks and the *non-financial* sector. There is, however, an indirect rate—and that is through the discount houses themselves. If the quantity of treasury bills offered rises then the price tendered is likely to be lower—and the rate of interest earned higher. But to get extra funds necessary to purchase a larger block of Treasury bills the discount houses need to offer banks more for their call money, and this call money is a substitute for other short-term liquid assets. The question of substitutability is complicated in the case of Treasury bills because they are reserve assets for banks and discount houses. This latter point is not a problem with Government bonds and they are therefore a better substitute for non-Government long-term debt. If anything, Government long-term debt is preferred because of its greater security.

In addition, manipulation of the National Debt through open-market operations affects decisions to lend and spend (see Chapter 11.3).

9.9 Revision Test

Answers	*Questions*
—	**1.** What is the purpose of the Budget?
1. To regulate the economy.	**2.** What are the policy objectives?
2. (*a*) To maintain high employment. (*b*) To secure economic growth. (*c*) To keep inflation down. (*d*) To maintain a balance of payments.	**3.** Can all these policies be pursued at once?
3. No; to some extent they are mutually irreconcilable.	**4.** What is fiscal policy?
4. Policy which is concerned with the public purse; the raising of revenues and the expenditure of the public sector.	**5.** How may taxation regulate the economy?
5. By influencing aggregate monetary demand. The aim is to ensure that 'demand' in the economy is in line with the ability and inclination of industry to supply, the Government either injecting demand or withdrawing it by the policies it pursues.	**6.** How may the Government withdraw demand?
6. By taxing away incomes and then not spending the revenues collected—budgeting for a surplus.	**7.** How may the Government inject demand?
7. (*a*) By reducing taxation, leaving spending power 'fructifying in the pockets of the people'. (*b*) By public spending, despite its lower revenues, the balance being borrowed—budgeting for a deficit.	**8.** What is a 'neutral budget'?
8. A budget where injections and withdrawals cancel out, and do not affect demand in aggregate—only rearranging it between products or services.	**9.** What is the National Debt?
9. The accumulated debt of the nation, since 1694 when the Bank of England was founded to lend money to the Government.	**10.** What are the various elements in the National Debt?
10 (*a*) Long-term marketable debt, in the form of 'gilt-edged' bonds. (*b*) Short-term marketable debt (Treasury bills). (*c*) Non-marketable debt (savings certificates, premium bonds, etc.)	**11.** Go over the page again until you are sure of the answers. Then try some of the questions in Appendix 1.

10

A CONSIDERATION OF MONETARY POLICY

10.1. The Development of Monetary Policy

Chapter 9 referred to the main objectives of Government policy in the UK. To reiterate, these are:

(*a*) To maintain a high (and stable) level of employment.
(*b*) To secure continuous economic growth.
(*c*) To keep inflation to a low level.
(*d*) To maintain a healthy balance of payments and manage the pound sterling on the international exchange markets. Before the system of 'floating' currencies this meant keeping a stable value of the pound at a fixed exchange rate. Today it means managing the pound within the International Monetary Fund's guidelines.

In the 1960s governments (and not only in the UK) felt that they had, in fiscal policy, the means to tackle all of these objectives. This is not to say that they felt confident of attaining full satisfaction of their main objectives simultaneously. There was always recognition that to a degree the main policy objectives were conflicting, but this still left governments with the chance of stressing some aspects at the expense of others; given correct governmental choice the main problems could be tackled.

Today governments are much less confident about their abilities to control economic events. The managed Western economies of the 1960s appear to have slipped out of control largely, but not solely, as a result of high and persistent levels of inflation. Consequently fiscal policy has had to give way to monetary policy. Monetary policy emerged from the doldrums as a result of the inability of fiscal policy to act as the expected panacea for every economic ill. Now fiscal policy and monetary policy are operated shoulder to shoulder as governments pursue their main economic objectives. In some economies it would even be correct to say that monetary policy has assumed the dominant role. The remainder of this part of the book is devoted to a brief consideration of the *policy mix* required to achieve the UK Government's economic objectives. How much monetarism, and what sorts of fiscal policy, will best achieve the objectives listed above?

10.2 The Relationship between Objectives and Policies

A closer examination of each of the objectives listed in Section 10.1 and of the alternative viewpoints about each is now necessary.

The Level of Employment

There is a degree of dispute as to what constitutes full employment. Some might suggest that full employment only occurs when every person registered as unemployed has been found work. Others feel that a low percentage of unemployed (say 3 per cent) constitutes effective 'full' employment. By this latter measurement the UK economy had full employment for the first 25 years after the Second World War. Either way it is clear that the current levels of unemployment (in the early 1980s over 11 per cent, representing nearly three million persons) is well above that which can be classified as 'a full employment level'.

Readers fortunate enough to have spent their adult lives in secure employment might wonder why governments and trades unionists make such a fuss over unemployment. The main reasons are:

(i) That most of those unemployed do not want to be out of work. They feel that they are society's rejects if their periods of unemployment persist for any length of time. They resent the significant financial consequences following from long periods of unemployment.

(ii) Governments particularly stress that unemployed resources are wasted resources. At one level this is obviously true of labour. Man-hours lost today can never be made up; they are lost forever. Governments are also alarmed at the prospect of large numbers of people turning to petty crime or political agitation if they are persistently unemployed and therefore have time on their hands.

For these reasons since 1944 avoidance of unemployment has been a major Government objective, and the gradual increase to a (1981) total of nearly three million has been viewed with general alarm. Three million unemployed is an emotive number, and raises visions of the 'Great Depression' of the 1930s when there were three million unemployed in the UK and 12 million in the US. Some critics of the current statistics maintain that these figures by no means indicate a failure of successive Government policies, and do not merit comparison with the 1930s. They remind us that in the 1930s married women were not regarded as 'unemployed' at all. Many companies and nationalised institutions required female staff to resign their posts on marriage, a requirement which led many women to keep their marriages a secret. These critics argue that before making comparisons we should delete from the statistics that half of the present-day unemployed who are married women. They further claim that the balance should be reduced still more to allow for a wider concept of frictional unemployment. The plain truth is that redundancy payments and earnings-related benefits have allowed most unemployed to take a longer holiday 'between jobs'. There are vacancies they could fill if they were penniless, but we have arranged that they are not penniless. These are powerful arguments, and seem to be borne out by the fact that malnutrition, rickets and other poverty-related diseases are not yet in evidence. At this point it is worth detailing the main causes of unemployment.

A great deal of unemployment is what is termed **'frictional unemployment'**, principally that of people moving between jobs. Such unemployed people are not long-term sufferers and policy-makers usually ignore frictional unemployment. There is though, a special form of frictional unemployment known as **'structural unemployment'** and this is a cause for concern. Structural unemployment occurs when industries which have entered a long period of decline shed labour which possesses a high degree of very specific skills. The decline might be caused by a change in the pattern of demand, the advance of technology, overseas competition, etc. Irrespective of the cause those displaced often face prolonged periods of unemployment.

The chances of those structurally unemployed will be especially slim if yet another form of unemployment exists within the economy: **cyclical un-**

employment. This form of unemployment follows upon what used to be termed the 'trade cycle' and is the result of insufficient aggregate demand.

The question must then be 'How can monetary policy help governments overcome structural and cyclical unemployment?' There is not much that governments can do in the short term to overcome structural unemployment, measures such as retraining, relocation and regional policy having longer-term effects. One exception is where structural unemployment is caused by import penetration. There may be several reasons for import penetration but to the extent that it is the result of an overvalued currency brought about by high interest rates the remedy is simple. A reduction in interest rates can cause 'hot' money to move out of the economy and the currency to reduce in value.

More usually governments expect to have significant short-term influence upon cyclical unemployment. They do this by affecting the level of aggregate demand. Until recently only fiscal policy was thought to be of value here, but now some economists are prepared to give the major role to monetary policy. They would argue that a tight monetary policy would lead to deflation and perhaps more unemployment, whilst a relaxed monetary policy should reflate and reduce the level of unemployment.

Economic Growth

Economic growth is measured by the amount of goods and services which become available to an economy, usually in *per capita* terms. The fact that the average person in the UK in the 1980s is better off in a material and 'services available' sense than his predecessor in 1900 can be taken as evidence that economic growth has occurred in the intervening 80 years. Economic growth is vitally important to all of us because it is through growth that we can expect a richer material life, and a working life reduced in toil, with greater leisure to enjoy our material riches.

Unfortunately for planners, economic growth is not only one of the most vital of objectives, but it is also one for which legislation is difficult. Very little seems to be understood of the underlying causes of economic growth. Most growth models give great stress to investment levels. Improved education, acceptance of new technology, improved health, etc., figure prominently in others. In short, the area is one of much confusion.

Given these circumstances it is difficult for economists to recommend with confidence and vigour positive policies aimed at growth. A number of advisers suggest that governments should avoid driving the economy into depression since this obviously reduces the rate of growth. In the long term this need not be the case; the 'lost' growth might be made up when the depression ends. Others suggest that anything which stimulates investment should stimulate growth. Thus low interest rates and a generally 'slack' monetary policy ought to help growth. A 'slack' monetary policy implies that the money supply will be allowed to grow, interest rates will be reasonably low so that entrepreneurs are encouraged to proceed with projects that they feel will be profitable, and there will be no direction of lending. These attitudes should result in increased business activity and the growth of the economy providing, of course, that any extra borrowing/spending is going towards domestic investment and not towards an import-fed consumer boom.

Control of Inflation

Inflation occurs when the general level of prices moves upwards. Most governments are unconcerned with low rates of inflation—say, 2 to 3 per cent—and only become alarmed when annual rates are relatively high—say, 10 to 15 per cent. The key word of course is relative: most South American countries would regard 15 per cent inflation as stagnation of prices.

Governments become alarmed with high rates of inflation because:

(i) Certain members of society may lose through inflation, generally those not in a position to defend themselves from the effects of attack by inflation. Examples are the old and the unrepresented. Others of course gain at the expense of the losers. Every heavily mortgaged householder hopes to see the mortgage eroded by inflation, providing that their income can keep ahead of the rate of inflation.

(ii) Nations rarely have inflation rates which are exactly in line with their trading partners; sometimes they race ahead of the rest. This may not be important if the foreign trade sector is relatively small or if it is felt that the exchange rate can adjust to compensate for this. As the UK enters the 1980s neither of these conditions applies.

Unfortunately for governments it is difficult to explain why particular inflations occur, although there are a *number* of causes which might be present. One of these is demand inflation, i.e. inflation caused by excess demand in the economy, the so called 'inflationary gap'. Generally demand inflation is thought of as occurring when the economy is at or close to full employment. In such a situation, should the level of aggregate demand continue to rise, an increased output to meet this demand will not be possible since all the factors of production are fully employed. The result will be a gap between production and desired consumption and the inevitable consequence will be rising prices.

An alternative explanation is one which depends upon structural rigidities within the economy. This argues that whilst wages and prices frequently move upwards, they do not often move downwards—even when the sector under consideration is a declining one. This not only prevents the effect of falls upon the general level of prices (which, if they occurred, would offset rises elsewhere) but actually helps the general level of prices to rise, since rigid wages and prices keep resources static for longer periods, discouraging them from moving to those parts of the economy eager to expand. The expanding sectors are thus forced to bid higher for the resources they require.

Yet another standard explanation is known as 'cost-push'. It explains inflation as a situation where the costs of manufacture are pushed up by monopoly suppliers of factors. Thus the price of skilled or unskilled labour is frequently pushed up by trade unions, and the price of oil has been raised by OPEC countries. Some economists ask, though, 'Why should trade union power vary from period to period?' In the UK why should trade union power have been almost dormant in the full employment 1960s and burst out in the 1970s when the level of unemployment was growing? Such questions are as yet unresolved.

One group which feels it has the answer to inflation is the monetarists. The group sets aside other explanations and argues that all significant periods of inflation have been accompanied by a rapidly expanding supply of money. With the uncontrolled inflations of the 1970s the monetarists increased their influence. Most economists would agree that monetarism goes at least some way to accounting for inflation. Hyperinflation seems to be associated with indiscriminate increases in the supply of money. If an inflationary period starts, for whatever reason, it will not be able to sustain itself without an accommodating increase in the money supply.

Unfortunately monetarists are much better at explaining past inflations than curing present inflations, because of 'lag' problems. (These are explained later.) Monetarists are unable to offer policies designed to adjust inflation rates finely. Instead they believe that governments should not try to tamper with the money supply in an attempt to 'fine-tune' but should set a target of monetary expansion somewhere around the level of increase in real income and hold to it. A tight money policy is thought to be proof against inflation!

Balance of payments

In an accounting sense the balance of payments always balances; in a real sense it rarely does. Imbalance need not worry a government unless it affects a fixed rate of exchange (a system now abandoned by most governments) or persists for a long period of time in the same direction. Of course whilst governments are committed in principle to working towards an exact balance, their efforts to correct a surplus are much less energetic than those to correct a deficit.

Generally there are two groups of internal factors which cause changes in the balance of payments:

(i) The pattern of consumption might change as a result of innovation (more or less being bought from abroad).

(ii) Domestic inflation might price a country's goods out of its own and other markets.

In addition, problems can be caused for the balance of payments by movements in capital account items (investment and/or speculative funds).

In theory in a country with a floating exchange rate, such as the UK, the balance of payments should not be a problem—it ought to be self-adjusting. Domestic inflation rates *ought* to be compensated for by the float in the currency. Of course, as is usually the case with such simple and attractive explanations, in practice there are complicating factors. These are:

(i) The UK possesses North Sea oil, a considerable asset and one which engenders foreign confidence in the economy, even though its manufacturing base may be in decline. The UK is regarded as a good, safe place to put money.

(ii) The UK is an especially good place to invest money since its interest rates have been raised to deal with inflation.

From a monetarist point of view a balance of payments deficit can be tackled in the following ways:

(i) In the short run by increasing rates of interest in order to attract foreign money on capital account. This inflow of funds will restore the balance and win a breathing space. Of course the opposite effect might be experienced if this strengthens the currency, making exports dearer, with a consequent effect upon the volume of exports and the ability of industry to meet foreign competition.

(ii) In the long run the high rate of interest combined with a tightly controlled money supply ought to dampen domestic demand and cause the domestic economy to buy fewer imported goods (as well as fewer domestically-produced goods). Should the problem be a balance of payments surplus the most likely thing is that no action will be taken at all until it becomes manifest that a constant 'creditor nation' position is embarrassing other countries. It was many years before West Germany could be persuaded to take steps to 'cure' her balance of payments surplus, her politicians claiming that it was 'for the sick to take the medicine'. To reduce a surplus on the balance of payments the monetarists would suggest the opposite policy, i.e. a reduction in interest rates and modest domestic expansion—principally through relaxing control on the supply of money. Any relaxation would presumably be slight, in line with monetarists' views that it is harmful to tamper too much with the money supply.

The Conflict between Objectives

It has been pointed out that attempts to achieve a number of policy objectives lead to conflicting actions on the part of governments. To help cure unemployment there should be a policy of easy credit availability and low interest rates. This is exactly the opposite of the prescription for tackling inflation. Such policies were possible if the two situations never coincided, but in the 1970s they did occur together. Moreover, easy money and low interest rates (for the benefit of employment) are also likely to lead to an increase in imports as aggregate demand grows, leading in turn to balance of payments difficulties.

These are only two of many policy conflicts and the policy-makers' role consists to a great degree in 'trading off' the effects of policies on the various objectives. The term 'trade-off' implies that the benefits of a particular policy in achieving one objective must be weighed against its adverse effects on other objectives. The problem is to arrive at the best 'mix' of policies to achieve the maximum favourable impact with the minimum unfavourable side-effects.

10.3 The Terminology of Policy-Making

When considering economic policy in general and monetary policy in particular, readers might be helped by a brief explanation of the terms used by governments and economists. They include:

(*a*) **Targets.** Policy-makers have objectives towards which they are, presumably, working. These are their targets: such variables as the level of unemployment and of economic growth. These variables are not capable of being directly influenced by policy makers in democratic economies. They can only be influenced through the medium of other variables. For example, governments attempting to reduce the level of unemployment cannot act upon the level of unemployment directly—they cannot decree it out of existence. Instead they attempt to encourage more spending (increase the level of aggregate demand) in the hope that this extra spending will cause unemployment to diminish. The preceding section has outlined one of the main problems of targets: they tend to conflict with each other.

(*b*) **Instruments.** Whereas targets are those variables which governments wish to act upon, there are other variables which governments use merely as a way of influencing their targets. Such variables are known as policy instruments. Hence a central bank might enter major markets to sell government stock (open-market operations) not because the government wishes to sell stock for its own sake, but because by selling stock the supply of money will be reduced. The reduction of this **intermediate variable** (a sort of transmission mechanism) in turn should influence the selected target or targets.

In an ideal world there would be one policy instrument for each target and the application of a policy would be a simple matter. In reality the use of an instrument to achieve a target 'A' might render the possibility of achieving target 'B' *more*, not *less*, remote. Policy-makers must therefore mix their instruments so that *overall* they have a package which is capable of affecting their various targets in the manners intended.

(*c*) **Indicators.** Monetary authorities need some indication of the effect their policies are having upon their targets. They might get this by designating certain variables as indicators, providing of course that the variables are reliable as indicators. In the realm of monetary policy the problem of indicators is a serious one. The monetary authorities appear incapable of arriving at a reliable statement of the effect their action is having. This really stems from other problems associated with monetary policy—that no one is really sure how monetary policy works or will work upon a range of variables.

It has been suggested that variables such as the rate of interest or the stock of money could be used to indicate the effectiveness of monetary policy. In some way slow expansion of the money supply and/or high interest rates might be regarded as representing 'tight' monetary policy and a rapid expansion of money supply and/or low rates 'slack' monetary policy. However, all rates are relevant only to the particular economic circumstances in which they were introduced. Interest rates at 10 per cent in the UK would have been very 'tight' in 1952 but 'slack' in 1980. Also there is the problem of just what the Government is measuring when it attempts to measure the supply of money. Even leading bankers are not convinced of the accuracy of the 'money supply' figures, and it is difficult to see how figures for 'Domestic Credit Expansion' in particular can be accurate since the abolition of exchange control, as changes in loans to and from the overseas sector are a vital part of the calculation of DCE.

(*d*) **Lags**. Earlier we referred to the preference of monetarists for a policy which did not induce frequent charges in the expansion of the money supply, and which did not attempt to 'fine-tune' the economy. Apart from the problem referred to above of knowing just how large the money supply is, the main reason for this preference is to be found in the existence of 'lags'. A lag, as the name suggests, is a delay—in this case a delay between one event, perhaps engineered by the monetary authorities, and the desired response on the part of the rest of the community. Also the monetary authorities themselves may not respond to events as quickly as they might had they perfect information. The following are amongst the 'best-researched' lags at present:

(i) *The Interest Rate Lag*. Earlier, in Chapter 7, it was suggested that the money supply will respond to changes in interest rates. The change though is not immediate: a period of time elapses before the full effect of interest rate changes is felt. Because of this lag it is easy to 'overdo' interest rate changes because at first they are not having the desired effect.

(ii) *Information Lags*. Policy-makers can only act if they receive information that action is necessary. It is highly likely that such information will only be received after a period of delay and that its accuracy will be marred by random factors.

(iii) *Implementation Lags*. Policy-makers do not spring into action as soon as information is at their fingertips. A period of time must elapse before alternative policies can be considered and introduced.

(iv) *Variable Lags*. In order to achieve action a number of variables—instruments, intermediates and targets—all have to react to policies applied by the monetary authorities. Each stage in the process implies the possibility of a time lag occurring.

10.4 Conclusion About Monetary Policy

It has already been suggested that monetary policy as a tool of government owes its revival to the failure of fiscal policy to act as a panacea for all economic ills. Consequently, it would be unreasonable to expect monetary policy to adopt the mantle cast off by a discredited fiscal policy. This chapter has, hopefully, suggested that monetary policy is surrounded by sufficient controversy to prevent it being viewed as an economic panacea. The following two chapters should reinforce this view.

10.5 Revision Test

Answers	*Questions*
—	**1.** Why did monetary policy go through a period of disfavour?
1. Because of the great stress given to fiscal policy.	**2.** What are the Government's main economic objectives?
2. (*a*) Full employment; (*b*) stable prices; (*c*) economic growth; (*d*) a Balance on external payments.	**3.** What brought about the revival of monetary policy?
3. The failure of fiscal policy to tackle inflation.	**4.** Can monetary policy tackle inflation?
4. Probably more effectively than fiscal policy.	**5.** At what cost?
5. If pursued vigorously enough, at the cost of conflicting objectives such as full employment and economic growth.	**6.** Are there any drawbacks to monetary policy?
6. Yes, particularly time-lags, i.e. results from a change in policy taking some time to have effect.	**7.** How do monetarists propose to overcome these drawbacks?
7. By restraint in the operation of monetary policy lest it prove destabilising—in effect, an admission that the difficulties cannot be overcome.	**8.** Now try some of the questions in Appendix 1.

11

MONETARY POLICY TECHNIQUES

11.1 Introduction

In Chapter 10 it was suggested that monetary policy sought to influence economic variables through increases or decreases in the quantity of money circulating within an economy. However, it was also suggested that the monetary authorities in the UK do not have direct control over the quantity of money in circulation. This depends to a great extent upon the actions of financial institutions not directly controlled by the authorities *and* the reactions of their customers. In such circumstances monetary authorities are forced to adopt measures which operate in a roundabout way; they take direct measures which are used, not for their initial impact, but because of the indirect effect which this impact has upon those areas where influence is really desired. This point can be illustrated by considering the main techniques of monetary control favoured by the UK monetary authorities. These controls tend to fall into two groups:

(*a*) Those affecting specific institutions or groups of institutions and the way in which they deal in assets and liabilities.
(*b*) Those of a general market nature designed to have a wide impact.

11.2 Specific Techniques

Of those options of a specific nature open to monetary authorities, persuasion might appear to be a technique lacking in bite. In fact, in many countries persuasion works particularly well. What does persuasion amount to? It is where the monetary authorities, usually through the use of the central bank, seek to influence the activity of commercial financial organisations, without recourse to compulsion.

The reasons why central banks prefer persuasion to other options available are as follows:

(*a*) Persuasion is a very flexible way of achieving their aims. It does not involve legislation, imposition of rules, policing, etc. Any change in the situation which led to the operation of the agreed policy can quickly be met with an appropriate response; the agreed policy can be modified or scrapped altogether.
(*b*) Often, the public interest and the best market deal for particular institutions are in conflict. Persuasion is, in such circumstances, an attempt to modify the market mechanism in such a way as to improve the nation's position. It is also an appeal to institutions to yield a little of the private benefit which they might otherwise derive. In the UK since the Second World War there have been many occasions when clearing banks have been persuaded to divert funds to exporters at the expense of private (personal consumption) borrowers despite the fact that higher rates might have been had from this latter group.

If the financial institutions are giving up potential commercial benefit what are they getting in return? Amongst their rewards are the following:

(i) Modern economies depend heavily upon a workable monetary system, and central banks first arose to safeguard such systems. They still have this role. Not surprisingly, commercial financial institutions are also interested in the health of the monetary system. They know that whilst in the immediate term they might have to surrender commercial advantage at the request of the central bank, in the longer term the central bank can be relied upon to repay the debt by doing everything possible to maintain public confidence in the monetary system.

(ii) Cooperation with the central monetary authorities can result in greater familiarity between those who run commercial enterprises and those who formulate official policy. In such circumstances the ideas and interests of the commercial organisations are likely to be known and favourably considered when monetary controls are being introduced.

(iii) Most institutions like to project the image of being not only efficient but also reasonable and helpful. This is particularly true of financial institutions which earn very large profits. Cooperation with the authorities allows them to publicise their 'helpful' role in the national interest! It also makes it easier for them with some justification to blame the authorities for the size of the profits they make.

(iv) Compulsory measures are avoided, since if commercial financial institutions did not cooperate they might be ordered to comply with the wishes of the monetary authorities.

A consideration of compulsion brings us to a method of control which is similar to persuasion but which is carried through by force, i.e. direction or, as it is known in the UK, the use of **directives.**

In 1946 the Bank of England was nationalised. Clause 4 of the Nationalisation Act gave it the statutory power to issue directives to the clearing banks. In reality the Bank of England has preferred to issue a series of 'requests', though it is of course recognised that should the 'requests' be ignored further action could be taken. In the event, requests have always been complied with. Requests have taken many forms—the favourable treatment of one industry or group of industries, the variations of charges for certain types of business, the limiting of lending in total—but can be classified under two main headings:

(*a*) **Quantitative Controls.** A request (directive) made to commercial banks requiring them to limit their total lending. Such a lending ceiling was imposed, for example, in April 1975.

(*b*) **Qualitative Controls.** Requests which are more selective in that they seek to regulate advances made for particular purposes. For example, in December 1964 banks were asked to encourage lending which would lead to investment in manufacturing industry and increased exports, whilst reducing the amounts available for personal consumption.

In the period since 1959 when the monetary authorities were trying to work with imperfect cash and liquidity bases, the temptation to use quantitative 'ceilings' backed up with qualitative 'advice' was too great to resist. Since the introduction of 'Competition and Credit Control' in 1971 there has been a much reduced use of the directive request, though, of course, the Bank of England's power has not been diminished in this respect.

It seems from the above that the UK experience is one where direction is not required, though requests are always reinforced by the hidden threat of direction. This is largely true; the UK financial sector is fairly closely knit, and has relatively few members. In such circumstances cooperation is not difficult to foster. With large numbers of institutions in only partial contact, it is much more difficult to pursue a policy of cooperation. Compulsion must therefore be used, such as Regulation Q in the US, which sets a legal limit on the rates which banks may pay for deposits.

Even the UK has not escaped some forms of direct monetary control. Not until the Autumn of 1979 was the country freed from foreign exchange controls introduced in 1939. (These are explained in greater detail in Chapter 16.) Generally though, attempts to influence the activity of important financial institutions have centred upon what are known as 'reserve requirements'.

Reserve Requirements

A reserve is something which is set aside to meet a contingency. In the context of commercial financial institutions, particularly banks, a reserve is a sum set aside to meet customers' potential demands for cash. Such a reserve is sound banking practice; the banking system depends upon confidence and nothing is likely to undermine confidence more than the inability of depositors to draw upon 'their' cash when they wish to do so. In all reputable banking communities the banks therefore impose upon themselves the holding of a sufficient cash reserve, or ratio, to meet normal (or even abnormal) customer demands.

Eventually governments found it possible to influence the amount of bank lending by *imposing* minimum reserve requirements. These were *cash* or *liquidity ratios*, i.e. a minimum proportion of assets had to be in cash or near cash form. Such reserves assist governments in the following way. Suppose a bank has assets of £10,000, 4 per cent of which (£400) it is required to keep as a reserve to meet customers' demands. The remaining £9600 of its assets are in the form of debtors, who owe back advances they have received—created credit. The government now has two possible ways of influencing the level of *advances:*

(*a*) By withdrawing from the bank some of the reserve assets—in our example cash. Should the government succeed in winning £200 cash, then bank advances will have to be reduced to £4800 to retain a 4 per cent ratio.

(*b*) By varying the ratio required. Suppose the government requires banks to keep not 4 per cent but, say, 8 per cent of their total assets in the form of cash. This means that the bank has to find another £400 in order to maintain its level of advances at approximately £9600, or it has to reduce its advances to £4600. Its assets will then be £5000 (£4600 + £400) and the cash ratio will be 8 per cent.

In fact, banks have a much wider range of assets than cash, and do not seek to create credit to the fullest extent. This means that the scope for dramatic government control is greatly reduced. However, governments rarely seek dramatic movements in the amount of credit available by variations of cash and liquid-asset ratios. More generally they are hoping to bring about marginal adjustments only and reserve requirements may greatly assist here.

In an effort to temper the optimism of the preceding paragraph it should be pointed out that governments will only be able to bring about the adjustment they require in bank advances through reserve requirements, providing they have control over the content of the reserve. If the government does not have tight control over the way in which banks get their cash (or their liquid assets which can easily be converted into cash) then banks will be able to thwart government intentions and in all likelihood maintain the level of their advances.

Another specific technique which has been employed intermittently is the system known as 'Special Deposits'.

The Special Deposits Scheme

This is essentially a modified version of the system used in the US and known as the 'variable liquid assets ratio'. The purpose of Special Deposits is to give extra control over liquidity. This is achieved by the Bank of England taking a proportion of cash from each bank's normal account (from the Bankers Deposits) and placing it in a special account. Whilst in the special account the assets do not form part of the clearing banks' cash or liquid assets base—they are effectively 'frozen'. At the start they earned only a nominal interest of 1 per cent; later they were allowed to earn interest at about the same rate as that available on Treasury bills. The Bank of England, in fact, lends the 'confiscated' money to the Government, which means that less needs to be borrowed on Treasury bills.

The amounts called for by way of Special Deposits vary according to the Bank of England's view of the monetary situation. When it calls for Special Deposits it requires the surrender of a certain percentage of the banks' own deposits. The first call was for 1 per cent of deposits in April 1960; in November 1970 3½ per cent of clearing banks' own deposits had been called for. With the introduction of Competition and Credit Control in 1971 Special Deposits were repaid. The scheme was reintroduced in 1977 and for most of 1977–9 some 3 per cent of the banks' funds were confiscated in this way. The current figures may be found in the Bank of England *Quarterly Bulletin*.

11.3 General Techniques

Open-Market Operations

The specific effect of reserve requirements depended to a great extent upon the use of a general technique known as 'open-market operations'. These were used extensively to bring about desired changes in the cash base of the clearing banks. They still figure prominently in present-day controls. The following illustrates how this system works.

Should the Government wish to decrease the commercial banks' cash base it will instruct its broker to sell extra Government bonds on the stock exchange. Those who purchase them (businesses, banks, or even individuals) will pay with a draft on their own bank and this effectively means that the commercial banks owe cash to the Bank of England. The Bank of England will subtract this from the commercial banks 'Bankers Deposits' which it holds. Since 'Bankers Deposits' form part of the cash base, any reduction means that other assets (such as loans to customers) have to be trimmed to maintain an appropriate reserve ratio. Similarly, an increase in the cash base can be brought about by a marginal increase in purchases by the Government broker on the Exchange. This will encourage the banks to lend to customers.

In the nineteenth century, when open-market operations were merely a supplement to 'Bank Rate' policy (see below), the system worked quite well. However, in the 1950s commercial banks were carrying sufficient liquid assets (commercial as well as Treasury bills being amongst these) to enable them to maintain their cash positions without difficulty—only a marginal switch out of liquid assets being required. Lending could then proceed undisturbed.

This excess of liquid assets made control of the banks ineffective. The Report of the Radcliffe Committee in 1959 recognised this ineffectiveness and successfully recommended the operation of a 'liquid assets' base instead. Eventually a 'liquidity ratio' of 28 per cent of total assets was arrived at in October 1963. Liquid assets were defined as cash in the till and at the Bank of England, money at call and short notice, and discounted bills close to maturity (these were predominantly Treasury bills).

With the advent of the liquid assets base (in addition to a cash one) a modified form of market operation came more prominently into use. This was known as 'funding of the national debt'.

Even before the 1959 Radcliffe Report the banks had held about one third of their assets in cash and liquid form. The single most important liquid asset was the Treasury Bill, and in the 1950s the Government attempted to induce the commercial banks to limit their lending by 'starving' them of Treasury bills. The National Debt is Government borrowing, very largely from domestic sources. It consists, broadly, of two types of debt: (*a*) **floating, or short-term, debt** and (*b*) **funded, or long-term debt.** Treasury bills, which are offered for sale every Friday and are repayable in three months' time are obviously short-term debt and by moving Government borrowing away from this short-term debt towards longer-term (funded) debt, the Bank of England can cause a 'shortage' of Treasury bills. Since Treasury bills have a short life they could be regarded as 'liquid' assets, part of the Banks' liquidity ratio. Forcing the banks to buy long-term funds reduced their liquidity and encouraged them to restrict credit to customers.

When Treasury bills represented over two thirds of all the bills discounted with the clearing banks, some marginal adjustment of their supply had a reasonable chance of interfering with the bank's liquidity ratio. However, during the 1960s the importance of treasury bills in commercial banks' liquid assets holdings diminished significantly, so that funding became an ineffectual operation. Its effectiveness increased during the 1970s as the public sector borrowing requirement grew positively enormous, so that once again Government borrowing became a substantial part of the banks' assets.

Funding is not without its disadvantages; lengthening the average maturity of the National Debt has both cost and flexibility considerations.

Bank Rate and Minimum Lending rate

Bank Rate has been defined by the Radcliffe Committee as 'the minimum rate at which the Bank of England stands ready to lend at last resort to a discount house . . . either by re-discounting of bills, or of short-dated Government securities'.

The narrow official definition, though, tended to understate the role of the Bank Rate. Whilst the Bank of England was undoubtedly lender of last resort to the discount houses, Bank Rate as a policy instrument had far wider significance than a simple 'rescue' operation.

In the nineteenth century and early part of the twentieth century, the Bank Rate was the main means of monetary control. Even when open-market operations were used it was usually to reinforce a change in the Bank Rate, e.g. to soak up surplus funds from the money market and prevent market rates from falling below Bank Rate. Bank Rate became so important that all other interest rates were tied to it, including clearing bank cartel rates. A change in Bank Rate then had repercussions throughout the whole economy: theoretically when Bank Rate rose lending and therefore aggregate demand would fall; when Bank Rate fell, lending and aggregate demand would rise. Experiences in the early 1930s showed that practice did not finely follow theory: though Bank Rate fell to 2 per cent in 1931 (and stayed there until 1952, war excepted) Keynes' liquidity trap prevented any stimulation of lending.

One of the purposes of Bank Rate was to keep down the cost of Government borrowing but in the 1950s and 1960s Bank Rate was becoming more significant as a means of attracting (or discouraging) the flow of foreign funds into London. By 1971 many rates were diverging from Bank Rate, e.g. building society rates, and when changes in Bank Rate were announced they tended to be supported by other official measures.

Competition and Credit Control changed the position of Bank Rate altogether. Prior to 1971 Bank Rate had been a market leading force, other rates tending to be pulled along by it (especially clearing bank rates). When the clearing bank cartel came to an end and an era of competition began the idea of Bank Rate setting market rates became anomalous. Hence Bank Rate *followed* market rates. By 1972 Bank Rate was so far out of line with market rates that a new *market-determined* Minimum Lending Rate (MLR) was established.

MLR was established using a formula (in order that it would be arrived at by market forces rather than political ones). The formula worked by taking the average rate on Treasury bills at the weekly Friday tender, adding $\frac{1}{2}$ per cent and rounding up to the nearest $\frac{1}{4}$ per cent.

Initially MLR did follow market rates. However, some attempts at influencing rates did occur, initially indirectly (e.g. forcing discount houses to borrow at penal rates in order to keep rates up), but eventually by forgetting about the formula when calculating MLR.

Finally, in May 1978, the pretence of MLR being determined by the market ceased when the formula was dropped and the authorities once more stated that interest rates were a major part of monetary policy. MLR was once more like old-style Bank Rate. Its main object was to fix the price of money; only indirectly did it affect money supply.

For the next two years MLR was used in a very similar way to the old Bank Rate; as a market-leading and market-determining device.

In one sense the return to 'old style' Bank Rate was an admission that the banking sector, and particularly the clearing banks, can compete only to a limited degree; they must 'keep in step'. Because of the way that the banking system works no bank can get out of step with other banks; they must all keep their interest rates more or less in line or they will be caught by the liquidity controls. Suppose Bank A decides to be competitive and lend on an increasing scale at less than the other banks are charging. Bank A's loans will surge ahead and those granted loans will spend the money. But as most of the cheques paid out will be paid into other members of the banking community, each day on the daily clearing at the Clearing House Bank A will be in debt to the other banks. It will have to pay cash to these banks, so that reserve assets decline but eligible liabilities will be rising. They will soon get out of their prudential reserve ratio and hence they must reduce loans and cease their 'competitive' activity. It is just impossible for one bank to be 'competitive', and the cartel simply recognised an inescapable fact.

The developments in 1981, and the Monetary Control Provisions introduced on August 20, 1981, are described in Chapter 12, Section 12.4.

11.4 Conclusion

This chapter has concentrated upon the ways in which the monetary authorities (usually through the central bank) attempt to control the activities of commercial financial institutions—particularly in the UK. It would be very easy to convey the impression that control is precisely and regularly achieved. This would be incorrect. Control of commercial financial institutions takes place largely in order that there can be control of the money supply. However, it has to be admitted that the willingness of commercial financial institutions to lend and of customers to borrow are major determinants of money supply. They may come partially within the control of the monetary authorities (using the techniques outlined above) but not completely.

11.5 Revision Test

Answers	*Questions*
—	**1.** What specific techniques are available to the monetary authorities to control the money supply?
1. (*a*) Persuasion; (*b*) directives; (*c*) reserve requirements; (*d*) special deposits.	**2.** Why is persuasion an effective technique?
2. (*a*) Because the institutions need a well-organised monetary system and therefore cooperate in their own interest. (*b*) The institutions find it beneficial to cooperate because their points of view are fully explained and taken into account. (*c*) Cooperation is essential if nationalisation pressures are to be resisted.	**3.** What was the reserve ratio requirement, in the decade of Competition and Credit Control?
3. Institutions had to keep their eligible reserve assets (as designated by the Bank of England) at 12½ per cent (later 10 per cent) of their eligible liabilities (as designated by the Bank of England).	**4.** What are open-market operations, and how do they affect the money supply?

Answers	*Questions*
4. They are open-market activities by the Government broker to buy or sell securities. If securities are sold to the general public the sums paid for them reduce the banks' available cash and cause the banks to lose liquidity. This causes them to reduce loans to customers and cut the money supply. Purchases of securities by the official broker increase bank liquidity and encourage the banks to lend money to customers.	**5.** Define Minimum Lending Rate.
5. Minimum Lending Rate is the minimum rate at which the Bank of England will lend money to the discount houses as lender of last resort.	**6.** How is MLR decided?
6. The formula method has been abandoned, and it is now announced by the Bank of England whenever it feels a strong statement of interest rate policy is needed. The decision to raise or lower MLR reflects Government policies in the light of current economic conditions.	**7.** Go over the page again until you are quite sure of all the answers. Then try the exercises in Appendix 1.

12

THE OPERATION OF MONETARY POLICY IN THE UK SINCE 1945

12.1 Introduction

Until the 1930s those responsible for Government economic policy (and Governments intervened only to a limited extent) believed in the workings of some form of 'quantity theory' of money. It was felt that economic fluctuation reflected changes in the amount of, or the availability of, money. Obviously this meant that monetary policy was pre-eminent amongst the instruments which Governments used in their limited attempts to control the economy. In the main monetary policy was put into effect through Central Bank operations in the open market and through changes in the Bank Rate.

The experiences of the 1930s undermined faith in the ability of monetary policy to 'nudge' the economy back into balance when it had strayed into disequilibrium. Between the wars (1918–39) Governments in the UK did not accept overall responsibility for the operation of the economy; they merely felt obliged to tinker here and there in order to allow the self-equilibrating mechanism to perform its task. Towards this end a policy of 'cheap money' was adopted, in the belief that this would stimulate the level of investment and eventually employment and output. There were dissenters from this view, among them John Maynard Keynes, who believed that monetary policy was inadequate to deal with depression. His ideas were so different from prevailing economic orthodoxy that it took a world war and the immense State involvement with the economy which it brought to convince Governments of their value. Keynes was at the Treasury during the war; this must have helped. Eventually they were convinced and by 1945 had accepted full responsibility for the orderly working of the economy. They proposed to ward off depression and pursue their regulatory role principally through the use of fiscal policy—Keynes' main weapon in the fight with depression. It was widely believed that a return to depression would be the over-riding problem of the post-war years.

Such an outlook meant that there was little contribution expected from monetary policy. Keynesian economists had little faith in the impact of interest rates in the short run, but felt that low rates might help to encourage investment. Therefore the pre-war cheap money policy was continued. Cheap money had one other great advantage from the Government's point of view. A cheap money policy reduced the cost of Government borrowing and a Government pursuing expansionary fiscal policies could be expected to borrow significantly. It also meant that the massive debt built up during the war years could be serviced cheaply.

The Bank of England found it easy to keep short-term rates of interest low since its involvement in the bill market gave it a dominant role. In 1945 short-term rates actually fell below 1 per cent. Longer-term rates, though, proved to be more difficult to operate upon. Potential holders of longer-term stock did not expect interest rates to remain as low as the $2\frac{1}{2}$ per cent which the Government favoured—a reasonable enough assumption in view of the inflationary pressure building up in the immediate post-war economy. Because of this general expectation of a rise in long-term interest rates the Government met with a disappointing response when it tried to dispose of $2\frac{1}{2}$ per cent undated stock in 1947 (October). The cheap money policy was allowed quietly to expire. This did not mean an immediate return to an active monetary policy. Such a turn-around had to wait until the election of a Conservative Government in 1951—a Government less dedicated to direct intervention in the economy.

One of the problems to be tackled by the new Government was the inflationary boom caused by the Korean War, a boom which expressed itself also in the balance of payments. It was in order to effect short-term correction in the balance of payments that the Bank Rate was revived as a policy instrument from 1951 onwards. Control of the money supply also found favour primarily through the informal operation upon banks' asset holdings. (Eventually, in 1963, a liquidity ratio was formally imposed at 28 per cent of bank liabilities.) The funding of the National Debt was responsible for a gradual rise in long-term interest rates, since such a rise was necessary to induce the holding of greater quantities of long-term debt.

The period after 1951 should in no way be regarded as one when monetary policy played a predominant role; fiscal policy was still the biggest gun in the Government battery. At the end of 1955 monetary policy lapsed into disfavour as a result of its ineffectiveness in helping to control the boom of that year. The fall from grace was finalised by the Report of the Radcliffe Committee in 1959.

12.2 The Radcliffe Report, 1959

The Radcliffe Report successfully disposed of the supply of money as a meaningful policy variable for a decade or more. One of its findings was that variations in the supply of money had virtually no effect upon spending, principally because there were so many near-money substitutes. As the supply of money fell those who 'wanted' money were easily driven out of the market for it when interest rates rose, and into markets for alternatives. Hence interest rates would not rise by much if the Government did nothing but reduce the supply of money. This view reflected the belief prominent in the Radcliffe approach that the main impact of monetary policy upon the economy could be expected to make itself felt through interest rates—particularly in the way interest rates affected credit. Taking this a stage further, more direct controls upon credit could be expected to be even more effective.

Policy-makers were quick to adopt the ideas of the Radcliffe Report. The money supply was set aside as a target; the wider 'liquidity' was almost impossible to define and thus could not be operated upon; but control of credit received a new lease of life. Control of credit available to consumers was found to be particularly effective—since a significant quantity of consumer durables—cars, washing machines, televisions, furniture, etc.—were purchased using hire purchase or personal loans. Hence hire purchase came under control. The controls were of two main types. These were:

(*a*) **Imposition of a minimum deposit.** For example, if 20 per cent of the purchase price of the good has to be paid at once, some consumers will be unable to buy as they do not have the necessary deposit. If a minimum deposit is already payable the percentage may be increased.

(*b*) **Imposition of a maximum period for completion of the purchase.** The consumer must pay a larger sum each week or month if the repayment period is short. This may make it impossible for buyers to budget for the purchase, and they will withdraw from the market and reduce the demand for credit.

Personal loans also came under control, particularly those offered by commercial banks. During the difficult times of the late 1960s direct controls on the banking sector grew significantly. The picture as regards monetary policy towards the end of the 1960s was as follows:

(*a*) The rate of interest was used predominantly as a tool to influence the inflow and outflow of funds from abroad; its effects were therefore primarily upon the balance of payments.

(*b*) The rate of interest was released for the balance of payments role because of the direct controls which were brought to bear upon banks. These were both *quantitative* (lending ceilings being regularly specified by the Bank of England) and *qualitative* (specification of where lending should be increased, held or curtailed). For example, in December 1964 banks were asked to limit lending to the building industry.

(*c*) Hire purchase controls, as outlined above, were widely used.

Throughout the 1960s both commercial banks and the monetary authorities expressed themselves dissatisfied with direct controls. The use of special deposits from 1961 was an ineffective attempt to escape from direct controls. The authorities, although dissatisfied, were constrained by short-term considerations such as the exchange rate and the effect upon it of a persistently adverse balance of payments. One of the biggest causes of concern for those within the financial sector was that direct controls distorted the efficient working of the monetary system—in other words, the loss of a free market impaired efficiency in the financial sector.

There were other complaints voiced too. One indication of dissatisfaction with pre-1971 methods of monetary control is to be found in the **Cash Deposits Scheme.** In the 1960s the rapid rise in lending by banks other than clearing and Scottish banks suggested to the monetary authorities that some form of control over these institutions was necessary. Under the Cash Deposits Scheme the Bank of England could require these other banks to deposit cash with it in proportion to the size of their business. As was the case with Special Deposits, interest at current Treasury bill rate was to be paid. The scheme never operated: before it could be put into practice the new 1971 regulations came into force. The importance of the Cash Deposits Scheme was that it signalled the determination of the authorities to control all major financial institutions, not just the clearing banks. This process is still being developed. It commenced in 1971 with the issue of a consultative document known as Competition and Credit Control 1971.

12.3 Competition and Credit Control, 1971

As suggested above, the system of monetary control operating before 1971 had many weaknesses, in particular:

(*a*) Competition between clearing banks was limited by the controls used by Government. It was also limited by a cartel (price-fixing) arrangement between the Scottish and clearing banks which tied the rates of interest they paid and charged to the Bank Rate.

(*b*) Control was chiefly upon Scottish and clearing banks. This had the effect of limiting the rate of expansion of their business during stringent periods of control, but allowing merchant banks, finance houses, insurance and hire-purchase companies to step in and fill the gap.

(*c*) Largely as a consequence of (*b*) above, monetary policy was concerned with levels of bank lending and not with the money supply as a whole.

(*d*) Because of their large holding of liquid assets, it was difficult to be sure that control of the clearing banks was proving as effective as required.

It was therefore no surprise that in May 1971 the Bank of England issued a consultative document entitled *Competition and Credit Control*. The main points were agreed and in September 1971 a new system of control was introduced. Most of this system applied until August 20, 1981, although the rate of eligible reserve assets was cut from 12½ per cent to 10 per cent in 1981. The most important aspects of *Competition and Credit Control* were:

(*a*) The clearing banks were no longer required to keep the 28 per cent liquid assets ratio. Instead they, and all other banks, had to maintain a ratio of **eligible reserve assets** which amount to 12½ per cent of **eligible liabilities.**

At first sight this seems to be a significant change in the quantity of reserve assets maintained, but in fact 12½ per cent was chosen because it would support the same level of deposits as the old 28 per cent ratio. This is because the eligible liabilities, of which allowable assets represent 12½ per cent, were defined more widely than previously, whilst the allowable assets themselves were defined more narrowly. The assets which qualified as allowable were:

(i) Bankers' balances at the Bank of England.
(ii) Money at call or short notice.
(iii) UK Treasury bills.
(iv) Company tax reserve certificates.
(v) Local Authority bills eligible for re-discount at the Bank of England.
(vi) Government stock with less than one year to maturity.
(vii) Commercial bills eligible for re-discount at the Bank of England, providing that these did not exceed 2 per cent of the total of eligible liabilities.

From the point of view of the clearing banks one significant omission from this list was **till money.** Clearing banks are the retail end of the business and need to keep cash in the till for the convenience of customers. Previously this had always counted towards the reserve ratio; now that it no longer did so the clearing banks felt that they were being unfairly penalised.

Eligible liabilities were defined as:

(i) Deposits of those institutions listed as banks.
(ii) Deposits of UK and overseas residents with an original maturity of two years or less.
(iii) Liability (net) to overseas offices.
(iv) Suspense accounts.
(v) Credits in the course of transmission (60 per cent of the value of these) between listed banks and own branches.
(vi) Certificates of deposit issued.
(vii) In addition to these eligible *sterling* items, banks are allowed to include

as eligible liabilities the net total of sterling which *could* be obtained if foreign currencies were converted.

(*b*) The clearing banks maintain 1.5 per cent of eligible liabilities, in cash, at the Bank of England.

(*c*) Special Deposits apply to all banks.

(*d*) The discount houses and money trading departments of non-clearing banks had to maintain at least 50 per cent of their borrowings in public sector debt, e.g. Treasury bills. In 1973 this requirement was modified so that these institutions could only hold 20 times their *capital and reserves* in other than public sector debt.

(*e*) Finance houses which held eligible liabilities of more than £5 million had to hold reserve assets of only 10 per cent of eligible liabilities.

Competition and Credit Control largely answered criticisms relating to divergent controls for different sectors of the banking system (with most control falling on the clearing banks). However, some commentators felt that the structure of allowable reserve assets under the new system was far from ideal. Their main concern related to the way in which the supply of reserve assets to the banking system was not fully under the control of the Bank of England. Also they were uneasy over the way in which reserve assets were held widely outside the banking system and could with relative ease be brought in as allowable assets (perhaps one reason why the 'corset' (see below) was considered necessary, since it penalised banks for 'excessive' growth of eligible liabilities). At a time when great stress is given to monetarism and changes in the supply of money (special scrutiny being given to the liabilities of the banking system) some critics feel that a 'monetary base' system would be preferable since they believed that this would be more easily controlled by the Central Bank (see Section 12.4).

The final aspect of *Competition and Credit Control* related to the Scottish and clearing banks cartel on interest rates. They agreed to abandon it and to set their own base rates but in fact it is not easy for banks to compete with one another. (This has been explained in Section 6.2.)

Measures of Money Supply

Before the period of Competition and Credit Control there were four methods of measuring money supply, designated M1, M2, M3 and Sterling M3.

M1 is the narrowest definition, and includes only notes and coin in circulation and the private sector current account balances at the banks. **M3** is a very wide definition, which includes even foreign currency deposits held by both the public and the private sector. **Sterling M3** is a slightly narrower definition. **M2**, another definition, was abandoned in 1971 when changes in the banking system made it rather misleading. However, in late 1976 the UK government was forced to turn to the International Monetary Fund for assistance in controlling its balance of payments deficit, and the IMF insisted, as part of a package of measures designed to improve the situation, that monetary targets should be based not on M1 or M3 but on the IMF's favourite measure, **DCE** (Domestic Credit Expansion).

The DCE mechanism measures not the money supply itself, but changes in the money supply, and is therefore a particularly sensitive measure for a

Table 12.1. Measures of money supply

Name of measure	*M1*	*Sterling M3*	*M3*	*DCE*
Purpose of measure	Measures stock of money on a narrow definition	Measures stock of money on a broader definition which relates only to the UK domestic money supply	Measures stock of money on a very broad definition	Measures *changes* in domestic credit (the IMF's favourite)
Items included:				
(*a*) Notes and coins in circulation	Yes	Yes	Yes	The *change* in this
(*b*) Bank current accounts of private sector (less adjustment for items in transit)	Yes	Yes	Yes	No
(*c*) Bank deposit accounts, in sterling, including certificates of deposit, both private sector and public sector	No	Yes	Yes	No
(*d*) Bank deposit accounts as in (*c*) but designated in foreign currencies	No	No	Yes	No
(*e*) Loans in sterling by UK banks to private, public and overseas sector during period	No	No	No	Yes
(*f*) Overseas lending to public sector and bank lending to public sector in foreign currencies during period	No	No	No	Yes
Some seasonally adjusted figures for each measure:				
1975	£17 344m	£37 205m	£40 189m	+£4 468m
1976	£19 140m	£40 580m	£44 550m	+£7 248m
1977	£23 330m	£44 660m	£48 760m	+£1 181m
1978	£27 190m	£53 061m	£56 931m	+£8 014m
1979	£27 660m	£55 750m	£61 030m	+£10 275m
1980	£30 123m	£66 769m	£73 561m	+£13 978m
1981	£35 710m	£85 870m	£94 400m	+£13 890m
Advantages	Easy to understand as 'money'; it is cash and cheques	The best measure of purely domestic money supply	Includes all 'money', including some fairly illiquid items	The IMF prefers it because a target can only be achieved if the domestic money supply is controlled
Disadvantages	Does not include deposits, and these are so easily moved into current accounts that they are virtually current items	—	Not best definition for a country with balance of payments problems	Aimed at correcting balance of payments imbalance rather than at other targets

In the late 1970s it was realised that these statistics took no account of private sector assets held in other places than banks—for example, building societies, the National Savings Bank, etc. Since the public could readily turn to these sources for additional funds it became important, when trying to control the money supply, to know how such funds were being used. This led to two further measures, PSL1 and PSL2. PSL stands for *private sector liquidity*. The figures are collected (or in some cases estimated) in four main blocks: (A) 'money'; (B) other money market instruments; (C) savings deposits and securities; and (D) certificates of tax deposit. Only liquid assets held by the UK private sector (except banks) are included. Public sector holdings are omitted.

PLS1, the narrower definition, is made up of (A), (B) and (D) above. PSL2, the broader definition, includes the savings of 'retail' funds in building societies, etc., by the broad mass of ordinary citizens (C above).

These figures are shown in Table (2.2. To avoid a mass of statistics the items included in each main group have been listed, but only the totals for each group have been shown.

Table 12.2. Components of private sector liquidity

£ millions	*1978*	*1979*	*1980*	*1981*
A 'Money'				
Notes and coin in circulation				
Sterling bank deposits:				
Sight				
Time				
Certificates of deposit				
Total	49 288	55 574	66 128	83 181
Total (seasonally adjusted)				
B Other money-market instruments				
Treasury bills				
Banks bills				
Deposits with local authorities				
Deposits with finance houses				
Total (gross)				
less:				
Finance houses' holdings of 'money'				
Finance houses' holdings of other money-market instruments				
Total (net)	3 677	5 969	5 155	3 744
C Savings deposits and securities				
Shares and deposits with building societies				
Shares and deposits with building societies (seasonally adjusted)				
Deposits with trustee savings banks				
Deposits with the National Savings Bank				
National savings securities				
Total (gross)				
less:				
Savings institutions' holdings of 'money'				
Savings institutions' holdings of other money-market instruments				
Buildings societies' deposits with other savings institutions				
Total (net)				
Total (net; seasonally adjusted)	40 979	45 236	49 557	49 161
D Certificates of tax deposit				
Certificates of tax deposit				
less:				
Holdings by building societies				
Total (net)	731	701	1 069	699
PSL1 (A + B + D)	53 696	62 244	72 352	87 624
PSL2 (A + B + C + D)	94 675	107 480	121 909	136 785

(Seasonally adjusted. Source: Bank of England *Quarterly Bulletin*)

country which has balance of payments problems and is trying to reduce home demand by reducing credit to the general public.

The best source of money supply statistics is the Bank of England *Quarterly*

Bulletin. Originally issued free of charge, it is now sold on annual subscription, but most reference libraries are subscribers. Students should consult a copy at their local library.

The various types of money included in each definition are shown in Table 12.1.

Considering the few innovations in monetary policy before the 1950s one might expect that with *Competition and Credit Control* change would come to an end. This is not so, however, and developments in the field of monetary policy continue to be one of the most dynamic areas of government activity. The major post 1971 innovations are outlined below.

12.4 Developments Since 1971

Having in *Competition and Credit Control* in 1971 largely abandoned control of the money supply through interest rates and ceilings, the Government became alarmed in 1973 at the runaway expansion of the money supply. It therefore had either to reinstate the rate of interest as a measure to control borrowing or attempt more stringent control of 'monetary aggregates' (the supply of money). It chose the latter. Consequently in 1973 an additional type of Special Deposit, known as the Supplementary Special Deposit or '**corset**' was introduced. The term is appropriate because it attempted to 'squeeze' a financial institution more and more tightly as it put on 'fat'. 'Fat' meant that it had been so generous in its credit policies that its deposits (and therefore eligible liabilities) had increased.

Supplementary deposits under the corset system were called for in relation to the expansion of each institution's interest-bearing resources. (These interest-bearing resources were the interest-bearing element of each institution's eligible liabilities and were known as Ibels.) The supplementary deposits did not earn any interest—a serious penalty.

Describing the corset in June 1979, the Bank of England *Quarterly Bulletin* stated:

'Under the arrangement announced on June 8, 1978, deposits became payable if an institution's average interest-bearing eligible liabilities for the three months August/October 1978 grew by more than the specified rate of 4 per cent over the average for the six months November 1977/April 1978. On August 17, 1978, it was announced that further growth of 1 per cent per month would be permitted for the following eight months, and on April 3 the operation of the scheme was extended for another three months, again with permitted monthly growth of 1 per cent. The rate of deposits is progressive, according to growth in excess of the guideline, at 5 per cent (up to 3 per cent excess), 25 per cent (over 3 per cent up to 5 per cent) and 50 per cent (over 5 per cent) of interest-bearing eligible liabilities. The same institution can therefore be penalised in one, two or all three tranches in any one month.'

The figures for Special Deposits and Corset Deposits to June 1980 were as shown in Table 12.3.

The corset was a scheme which tended to be used intermittently—on in 1973, off in 1975, used a little in 1976 and back on again in 1978. Though it proved effective in limiting the creation of credit whilst it was on, some commentators felt that it led to a scramble for Ibels in the period when it was

Table 12.3. Special and Supplementary Deposits

£ million: number of institutions in italics

	Special Deposits			*Supplementary Special Deposits*							
	Rate of call (per cent)	*Banks*	*Finance houses*	*Total*		*1st tranche*		*2nd tranche*		*3rd tranche*	
1979											
Aug. 15	1½	504	6	10	*14*	6	*14*	3	*5*	2	*3*
Sep. 19	2	760	8	4	*10*	3	*10*	—	*2*	—	*1*
Oct. 17	2	770	8	1	*11*	1	*11*	—	*2*	—	—
Nov. 21	2	794	8	3	*8*	—	*8*	—	*4*	3	*3*
Dec. 12	2	794	8	3	*8*	—	*8*	—	*4*	3	*3*
Dec. 17	2	822	9	19	*20*	10	*20*	8	*7*	2	*2*
1980											
Jan. 16	—	—	—	28	*14*	9	*14*	9	*5*	10	*2*
Feb. 20	—	—	—	104	*22*	15	*22*	31	*15*	58	*7*
Mar. 19	—	—	—	132	*23*	12	*23*	31	*16*	89	*7*
Ap. 16	—	—	—	216	*27*	14	*27*	31	*21*	171	*8*
May 21	—	—	—	219	*28*	13	*28*	31	*18*	174	*8*
Jun. 18	—	—	—	242	*30*	19	*30*	37	*18*	187	*7*
Jul. 16	—	—	—	456	*47*	27	*47*	63	*28*	366	*11*

(Source: Bank of England *Quarterly Bulletin*)

relaxed, as banks sought to capture a larger share of the market. More serious effects led to its disuse in August 1980.

The Problem of Disintermediation

In normal financial affairs the banks act as intermediaries between those who wish to borrow money and those who have money to lend. If we wish to control the money supply all we have to do is control the banks by some sort of credit control system. Unfortunately, in the sophisticated affairs of an advanced economy, any attempt to control the banking system with increased severity may lead to 'disintermediation'. The normal intermediaries will be by-passed, and borrowers will borrow outside the banking system. For example, companies might borrow from one another directly without the use of a bank as intermediary, or they might borrow from the local authorities, or from abroad. These borrowings would not be subject to control, and in late 1980 it became clear that despite the most stringent controls over some aspects of the money supply there were areas where controls were ineffective. It was this that led to the removal of the corset, enabling the banks to resume their role as intermediaries.

The Reserve Assets Ratio and 'Prudential' Controls

Since the banking system developed in the eighteenth century the banks have always exercised 'prudential' controls over their liquidity. As a matter of prudence a reasonable cash ratio was always preserved, as well as a much larger 'liquidity ratio' of near cash items which could be realised quickly in the event of any run on the bank. Official controls such as the reserve assets ratio

(1971–81) were only therefore an official recognition of the banks' traditional prudential controls.

The point that monetary controls were different from, and should be separated from, prudential controls was recognised in the late 1970s. This sentiment was reinforced after entry to the EEC by the need to harmonise with European practices—where official prudential controls are well established—and by the secondary banking crisis of 1973–4.

The Green Paper—Monetary Control

In March 1980 a Green Paper ('Monetary Control') was published as a discussion document to air the problems of improving short-term monetary control. The chief features of the document were as follows:

(*a*) **Sterling M3 and Monetary Targets.** There was a commitment by the Government to continue to express its monetary targets in terms of sterling M3. This is the most restrictive definition of money supply (apart from the IMF's favourite, Domestic Credit Expansion, which is most valuable in crisis circumstances). This clear support for the tightest of the three definitions of money supply was a gesture of determination to keep as tight a grip as possible on the supply of money.

(*b*) **Medium-Term Controls**. The medium-term monetary objectives of a Government do not give too much cause for anxiety since they are susceptible to control through fiscal policy and interest rates. The proposals to reduce the public sector borrowing requirement as a percentage of national income should ease the medium and long-term position in the years ahead.

(*c*) **Short-Term Controls: Special Deposits and the 'Corset'.** The more difficult area is control of the money supply in the shorter period. The corset (the supplementary special deposits scheme) had ceased to be a useful instrument for the reasons listed above, and was accordingly discontinued in 1980. The Special Deposits Scheme will continue to be used to guard against possible adverse effects of excess liquidity in the banking system but it is in fact at present (January 1982) not in use. Figures for 'special deposits' are published in the Bank of England *Quarterly Bulletin*, and readers are urged to check the current position from time to time.

(*d*) **A 'Monetary Base' Method.** In seeking to find adequate controls over the short-term money supply the Bank had considered schemes operating elsewhere. One of these, the **monetary base scheme**, requires the banks to keep a minimum proportion of their deposits in base money (bankers' deposits at the Central Bank) though it is possible 'till money' might be allowed to count. If the Central Bank could thus control the 'base money' and if there was a known relationship between base money and total bank deposits, the Bank would be able to control the money supply (M3). After describing some alternative base schemes, and the technical problems they would cause, the Bank concluded that they would be unlikely to secure control of M3 and would be therefore of doubtful value.

(*e*) **The 'Indicator' System.** This is another proposal. It calls for the automatic adjustment of interest rates whenever the money supply varies by a given amount—the indicator. Thus if the indicator was 1 per cent growth in the money supply per month, and the money supply exceeded this rate of growth, interest rates would be required by law to rise to choke off the extra demand.

At present there is a 'bias towards delay' over such adjustments, with a 'wait-and-see' policy which enables inflation to creep up. There is something to be said for a control which is known to operate, and which would not arouse political clamour. At present measures instituted to control the money supply invariably lead to political criticism. Unfortunately a mechanistic approach is insensitive to anything but the trigger designed to operate it, and at times its action might be positively the wrong 'cure' for the situation that had developed. It seems unlikely that an indicator system could be introduced without the Bank of England reserving the right to override the trigger. This would only revive the debate as to whether the trigger should, or should not, be overridden at any particular time. In calling rather forlornly for more ideas from the banking community the Green paper reflected the intractable nature of the problems.

(*f*) **Assessing the Liquidity of Banks.** Although not fully discussed in the Green Paper, the question of bank liquidity is referred to, and a parallel document has been issued about the matter. This discussion paper seeks opinions from the banking community about the best way of assessing the liquidity of banks.

The problem of bank liquidity is as old as banking itself. If banks are to be able to create credit they must be able to maintain public confidence in the banking system. This means that they must have sufficient liquidity to be able to meet all conceivable demands upon them by depositors. With greater sophistication in the banking community generally, but also on the part of the general public, it is becoming popular to switch deposits around rather more rapidly than in the past, with the possibility that banks can be caught in an illiquid position. The Bank is therefore seeking an improved knowledge of the liquidity position of banks, and a system of controls designed to ensure day-to-day liquidity.

Traditionally the system has been for banks to keep a certain 'cash ratio', and a further 'liquidity ratio' of liquid assets to liabilities based on the statistical probabilities of deposit withdrawal. More recently, since cash flows are now more varied and can be more quickly identified, the system has been to maintain the same sort of ratios but in a more dynamic way. This involves matching cash flows in and out, not only on a day-to-day basis but for the future, with flows being anticipated and matched on a rolling programme into the foreseeable future. Whilst such activities are no doubt carefully watched by the head offices of banks for prudential reasons, the Central Bank is hard put to monitor such dynamic events. It therefore proposes to introduce a test which will reveal at any given time whether a bank is within the liquidity limits deemed appropriate. This requires a more careful identification of bank commitments, the probabilities that difficulties will arise, etc.

The trouble with expressing a liquidity ratio in minimum terms is that banks—for fear of going below the minimum—maintain a margin above the minimum which influences their general operations. Instead the Bank proposes that the ratios should be expressed as 'norms' rather than 'minima'. This would bring a desirable degree of flexibility into a bank's arrangements and permit it to take account—in its daily calculations of liquidity—of both the total levels of its deposits and assets and their maturities.

To improve the definitions of assets and liabilities the Bank distinguishes as follows:

(*a*) *'Maturity-Certain' Liabilities and Assets.* With these the exact date of liability or the date when the asset will become available is known and can clearly be planned into the cash-flow position without any uncertainty. Examples are fixed-term deposits and loans due for repayment on a contractual basis either in one lump sum or as part of a repayment schedule.

(*b*) *'Maturity-Uncertain' Liabilities and Assets.* Here there is no definite contractual basis for repayment, deposits may be on demand or at short notice which is customarily waived, and loans may be in the form of overdrafts (which may, or may not, actually be used).

(*c*) *Marketable Assets.* These are part of (*a*) above in that they are 'maturity-certain' assets but because of their readily marketable nature they can in fact be realised if necessary sooner than the maturity date. Clearly a bank that has this type of asset can realise them if it comes under pressure, though perhaps at some marginal cost. Examples are Treasury bills, certificates of deposit, bank bills and other marketable securities.

The Integrated Measure of Liquidity. In the discussion paper the Bank proposed that the degree of liquidity required to provide adequate asset cover against its total range of liabilities should be aggregated as follows:

(i) *Maturity—uncertain liabilities.* A 'norm' of 25 per cent (not so very different from the old 28 per cent liquidity ratio).

(ii) *Gross deposits from banks up to one month.* 100 per cent cover.

(iii) *Irrevocable standby facilities, as yet undrawn, given to banks.* 100 per cent cover.

(iv) *Maturity Certain Liabilities* (*Net of Assets*)

Up to 8 days	90%
8 days to 1 month	75%
1–3 months	50%
3–6 months	25%
6–12 months	15%
Over 1 year	5%

This aggregation gives a figure for liquidity. Assets should be available to the extent shown—but in what form? The Bank's conclusion is that 40 per cent of a bank's sterling requirement should be available in **primary liquid assets** (see below), the balance being in the form of **secondary liquid assets.** This separation of liquid assets into primary and secondary groups is an important development.

Primary Liquid Assets are assets which are immediately available. They include the following (all sterling assets; foreign assets do not count):

(i) Cash; (ii) balances at the Bank of England (but not Special Deposits which are sequestrated from bank use); (iii) money at call with the discount houses; (iv) UK and Northern Ireland Treasury bills; (v) local authority bills; (vi) bank bills eligible for discount at the Bank of England; (vii) Government stocks with less than a year to run to maturity.

The distinguishing nature of these primary liquid assets is that the authorities are always ready to buy them or accept them as security for 'last resort' lending to help a bank in difficulties.

Secondary Liquid Assets are assets which are near-cash or readily marketable at very close to their balance sheet values. They may be either sterling or foreign currency, and comprise:

(i) Market loans to other banks up to one month; (ii) money at call with recognised Stock Exchange money-brokers and gilt-edged jobbers; (iii) loans to local authorities up to one month; (iv) non-eligible bills with less than three months to maturity; (v) Certificates of Deposit and certain other marketable securities with less than three months to run to maturity; (vi) British Government stocks with 1–5 years to maturity, including stocks of nationalised industries guaranteed by HM Government; (vii) Northern Ireland Government stocks, local authority and public corporation securities with less than five years to maturity; (viii) gold; (ix) irrevocable undrawn standby facilities from other banks.

The effect of all this is that a bank's liabilities will be known and the probability of cover being required has also entered into the consideration of the amount of liquidity to be provided. Then an adequate amount of this liquidity (40 per cent of the sterling amount) has been provided in primary liquid assets, while the rest is provided in secondary liquid assets. In the actual calculation, when running a check on a bank's liquidity, the Central Bank will not be unduly alarmed if the liquidity is below the norm, so long as tests at other times reveal an above norm figure. The aim is to achieve a norm, without being too frenetic about a 'minimum'.

(*g*) **The Reserve Assets Ratio**. As explained earlier, the intention is to allow the reserve assets ratio to lapse as soon as the banks' prudential controls are instituted; in the meantime it was reduced from 12½ per cent to 10 per cent in January 1981.

(*h*) **The Cash Requirement System.** At present the commercial banks are required to keep cash available at the Bank of England to the extent of 1½ per cent of their eligible liabilities. This requirement is to be extended to all banks and deposit-taking institutions. This would enable the Bank to exert a wider influence on short-term interest rates as these institutions sought funds on a day-to-day basis to achieve their 1½ per cent cash requirements.

Monetary Control—the Conclusion to the Green Paper

The Bank's new policy was announced in a paper 'Monetary Control—Provisions' issued on August 5, 1981, and implemented on August 20. The Bank has kindly permitted the full text to be reproduced herewith, and this permission is gratefully acknowledged. In order to assist the reader a few 'Authors' Notes' have been added. These are of course entirely the authors' opinions and are not in any way authoritative as far as the Bank of England is concerned.

Monetary Control—Provisions

(*Reproduced by courtesy of the Bank of England*)

Introduction

1 On 24 November 1980, the Bank published a Background Note describing a number of improvements to be made to the existing framework of monetary control. On 12 March this year (1981) in a paper entitled "Monetary control: next steps", more detailed proposals on a number of the subjects covered in the Background Note were sent to all recognised banks and licensed deposit-takers (LDTs). The present paper sets out the

provisions resulting from discussions since then with the various associations, as well as with a number of individual institutions.

The cash ratio

2 A substantial part of the Bank's resources and income in recent years has been provided by the average of $1\frac{1}{2}\%$ of Eligible Liabilities (ELs) maintained by the London clearing banks in non-interest-bearing accounts at the Bank. This sum has also served as a fulcrum for money market management. The Bank's paper in March proposed that this latter purpose should in future be served by the volume of operational funds which the London clearing banks would retain voluntarily at the Bank for clearing purposes, while the Bank's resources and income should additionally be secured primarily by a uniform requirement on all banks and LDTs to hold non-operational, non-interest-bearing deposits with the Bank. The provisions set out in this section have accordingly been designed to provide, in aggregate, broadly the same amount of non-interest-bearing funds initially as did the previous arrangements with the London clearing banks alone.

3 This non-operational requirement will be $\frac{1}{2}\%$ of an institution's ELs and will apply to institutions covered in paragraph 16(i)–(iii) below having ELs which average £10 million or more in the latest period over which the requirement is calculated. The level of an institution's non-operational balance will be set twice a year in relation to its average ELs in the previous six months. Thus a deposit calculated in, say, May would relate to the monthly average of ELs from November to April inclusive.

4 For institutions not on the present statistical list of banks and whose business mainly comprises the provision of fixed rate finance for periods in excess of one year, the Bank accepts that the introduction of the $\frac{1}{2}\%$ cash ratio may present a special transitional problem. The Bank will be prepared to consider individual representations from such institutions for some temporary alleviation of the requirement. In addition, in recognition of the special conditions in Northern Ireland, the Bank has reduced to $\frac{1}{4}\%$ the cash ratio to be observed by institutions for which Northern Ireland is the principal place of business in the United Kingdom. This concession will apply in respect only of the ELs of their Northern Ireland offices and will run for two years, when it will be reviewed.

(*Authors' Note: To prevent any confusion the reader is reminded that the 'cash ratio' referred to above is not the same thing as the 'cash ratio' referred to in Economics, i.e. that percentage of the depositors' funds kept in cash by the banks to meet customers' day-to-day requirements. It refers solely to the $1\frac{1}{2}$ per cent kept by the clearing banks with the Bank of England for clearing purposes. This is now to be a matter of voluntary arrangement between the Bank of England and the clearing banks, but in addition to whatever sums are deemed to be necessary for clearing, $\frac{1}{2}$ per cent of eligible liabilities is to be levied on all banks and deposit-taking institutions as a 'non-operational requirement'. This means that the non-clearing banks and deposit-taking institutions, contributing for the first time to these non-operational resources, will now not be able to use this $\frac{1}{2}$ per cent in their day-to-day activities and consequently their liquidity will be marginally reduced.*)

5 ELs are to be redefined to reflect the changes set out in this paper. In future, offsets will be allowed in the calculation of ELs in respect of:

(i) funds (other than cash ratio deposits or Special Deposits placed with the Bank) lent by one institution in the newly defined monetary sector (see paragraph 6 below) to any other.

(ii) money at call placed with money brokers and gilt-edged jobbers in the Stock Exchange, and secured on gilt-edged stocks, Treasury bills, local authority bills and eligible bank bills.

6 ELs will be calculated in uniform fashion for all reporting institutions except:

(i) members of the London Discount Market Association (LDMA), whose ELs will be calculated as the total of sterling deposits other than from institutions within the monetary sector and from money-brokers and gilt-edged jobbers in the Stock Exchange.

(ii) certain banks with money trading departments, who will be allowed to omit from their ELs secured money at call placed by other banks with these departments, up to a limit set by the Bank. The banks concerned are: Algemene Bank Nederland, Banque Belge, Charterhouse Japhet, Leopold Joseph and Samuel Montagu. Hitherto, funds placed on this basis, up to a limit set by the Bank, have counted as reserve assets.

The adoption of a uniform system for all reporting institutions means that the present arrangements for those finance houses which have observed a 10% reserve asset ratio since 1971 will lapse.

7 It would be contrary to the objective of these agreed arrangements for any institution to reduce its ELs deliberately or artificially on reporting dates. The Bank accordingly reserves the right to make a spot check on the level of an institution's ELs on days when it would not normally report.

Special Deposits

8 The Special Deposits scheme remains in place and will apply to all institutions with ELs of £10 million or more at the latest make-up day for which figures are available. Hitherto only banks on the statistical list and finance houses observing a reserve asset ratio have been subject to Special Deposits. As hitherto, calls will be set as a percentage of ELs. The scheme for Differential Special Deposits has lapsed. Details of this scheme can be found in the Bank's *Quarterly Bulletin* for March 1973.

Eligibility

9 As set out in its March paper the Bank has judged applications, by recognised banks wishing their acceptances to become eligible for discount at the Bank, according to the following criteria:

(i) whether the applicant has and maintains a broadly based and substantial acceptance business in the United Kingdom;

(ii) whether its acceptances command the finest rates in the market for ineligible bills;

(iii) whether, in the case of foreign-owned banks, British banks enjoy reciprocal opportunities in the foreign owners' domestic market.

A first list of eligible banks is attached. (*Authors' Note: This list has not been reproduced—there are 96 of them.*)

10 A bank may apply for eligibility at any time. An eligible bank which wishes to renounce its eligibility is free to do so on giving notice to the Bank.

Undertakings by eligible banks

11 From 20 August 1981, each eligible bank undertakes to maintain secured money with members of the LDMA and/or secured call money with money brokers and gilt-edged jobbers (see Note at end of 12 below)—all at market rates appropriate to the nature of the lending—such that:

(i) the total funds so held normally average 6% of that bank's ELs (as defined in paragraph 5);

(ii) the amount held in the form of secured money with members of the LDMA does not normally fall below 4% of ELs (as defined in paragraph 5) on any day.

12 In relation to the above undertaking, each eligible bank will

(i) aim to meet the daily average ratio over either six or twelve month periods (having first notified the Bank of its choice of period), the ratio on any particular day in a banking month being calculated as a proportion of ELs at the last but one make-up day. For example, the relevant ELs figure for each day in banking September will be those as at make-up in banking July.

and

(ii) to provide monthly returns of its daily figures, which the Bank will use to assess the bank's performance relative to its long-term commitment.

A bank will go below the minimum only in exceptional circumstances and will be ready to explain such action to the Bank when the relevant monthly return is made.

Note: The Bank's concern with the adequate availability of funds for the efficient functioning of the gilt-edged market was noted in 'Monetary control: next steps'. There are six recognised money-brokers—James Capel & Co, Cazenove & Co, Hoare Govett (Moneybroking) Limited, Laurie Milbank & Co, Rowe & Pitman Money Broking and Sheppards and Chase. Secured call money with these firms has hitherto counted as a reserve asset. The amount of such money which these firms can take will continue to be limited by the Bank.

13 The Bank will be prepared to review these undertakings, in consultation with eligible banks and the LDMA, when sufficient experience of the operation of the arrangements has been gained, covering at least a year. The Bank will also be prepared to discuss particular difficulties, as they arise, with any party to the arrangements.

Prudential considerations

14 The Bank has received the assurances required in its paper of 12 March "The liquidity of banks", and mentioned in the Chancellor's Budget Speech, that those institutions in the United Kingdom to whom the reserve asset ratio has applied will discuss with the Bank, in advance, changes in their policies for the management of their liquidity and its composition. The Bank is resuming discussions with the banks on the measurement of liquidity as the basis for continuing supervision.

Statistical changes

15 The present banking sector, as defined for the purposes of calculating the monetary aggregates, contains those institutions included in the statistical list of banks and the list of discount market institutions. These lists were drawn up prior to the Banking Act and are no longer appropriate to current circumstances. They exclude a number of recognised banks, many LDTs, and also the trustee savings banks (who will become subject to cash ratio and Special Deposit requirements when they are authorised under the Banking Act).

16 A new monetary sector will therefore be defined, to include

(i) all recognised banks and LDTs;
(ii) National Girobank;
(iii) those banks in the Channel Islands and the Isle of Man which opt to join the cash ratio scheme described earlier in this paper;
(iv) the trustee savings banks (TSBs);
(v) the Banking Department of the Bank.

17 Although the population of the monetary sector will be considerably larger than that of the 'statistical list', the statistical effect will be comparatively modest since the present business of many of the new contributors is relatively small. In total, the initial once-for-all adjustment to the stock of the main monetary aggregate, £M3, will probably be of the order of £8 billion (13%), of which the TSBs account for around £6 billion (9½%).

18 Institutions in the monetary sector having either eligible liabilities totalling £10 million or more, or a balance sheet of £100 million or more, will be asked to supply the full range of statistics (comprising both the monthly and other returns); other institutions will be asked to report only at end-calendar quarters.

The TSBs will continue, for the time being, to make returns on the existing consolidated basis.

The timetable for change and the transitional arrangements

19 The essential features of the new arrangements can be brought rapidly into effect. This section sets out the sequence of developments.

20 On 20 August 1981:

(i) the Reserve Asset Ratio will be abolished;
(ii) the acceptances of all banks in the list of eligible banks will become eligible for discount at the Bank;
(iii) all the banks covered in (ii) above will begin to observe the undertakings set out in paragraph 11 above;
(iv) the agreement with the London clearing banks, whereby they keep an average of $1\frac{1}{2}\%$ of their ELs at the Bank, will lapse;
(v) the Bank will receive the first deposits under the cash ratio requirement.

21 On this date, the first cash deposits will be placed by institutions on the present statistical list of banks and by members of the LDMA; the statistics necessary to include other institutions are not yet available. These initial deposits will relate to the average of institutions' ELs on the monthly make-up days in the period January–June 1981 inclusive, ELs being defined on a transitional basis: i.e. calculated for 'statistical banks' as at present except that offsets will be allowed in respect of all lending to the discount market and all secured money at call placed with money-brokers and gilt-edged jobbers and money-trading banks. These initial deposits will remain unchanged until sufficient figures using the new definition of ELs are available (see paragraph 22 below). Thereafter, these deposits will be adjusted every six months. The undertakings by eligible banks as set out in paragraph 11 will take effect on 20 August 1981, based on the transitional definition of ELs and in respect of their level as at 15 July.

22 As soon as possible thereafter (probably in respect of the make-up day in banking November) currently reporting institutions will be asked to produce figures for one reporting date both on the basis used hitherto and on the basis of the enlarged list of institutions comprising the new monetary sector. At the same time, those seventy or so institutions which are not currently on the statistical list of banks and which are above the cut-off points for full statistical reporting will join the full reporting network. They will be asked to place cash deposits with the Bank when two months' figures have been obtained, if their ELs are £10 million or more on average.

23 Monetary aggregates will be calculated on both bases for this one reporting date; thereafter statistics will only be collected on the basis of the new monetary sector.

24 The remaining institutions not currently reporting and below the cut-off points set out in paragraph 18 will be brought into the reporting network only when the current review of banking statistics has been completed (which is unlikely to be before the second half of 1982).

It is not easy to see that much has come out of the public discussion of the Green Paper other than the things the Bank of England was determined to implement anyway. Thus the Reserve Assets Ratio at 10 per cent of Eligible Liabilities has been abolished. Instead we have an undertaking by all eligible banks to keep funds available (secured call money) with the LDMA and/or the gilt-edged market, to the extent of 6 per cent of ELs. The intention was that this should happen only when the individual bank's prudential controls had been instituted. As section 14 above says, the Bank has now received assurances about the prudential controls being instituted by individual banks. These will reinforce the 6 per cent requirement by further in-house controls.

There is no 'monetary base' control, which the Bank was known to believe would be ineffective in controlling Sterling M3. The 'Indicator System' mentioned in the Green Paper has been disregarded, presumably because of its mechanistic approach and the need for the bank to reserve the right to overrule the trigger if necessary.

The method of calculating eligible liabilities is crucial to the question of controlling the money supply. A redefinition is promised, though some preliminary offsets are mentioned in Section 5. A new definition following the guidelines in the Green Paper seems desirable and would be a determined attempt to quantify liabilities on some sound basis of probability.

The essential thing in securing monetary control is that those who lend money shall be closely watched and punished by the imposition of penal rates when they get into illiquid situations and have to borrow from the Central Bank. A 'wide-open window' is no control at all, and even an announced rate (Minimum Lending Rate or Bank Rate) has the defect that it lets those lending money know how far they can go. A weekly announcement of MLR is out of date in a world where banks regularly advertise that they can get money anywhere in the world in five minutes. The crucial point for control has always been the 'lender of last resort' facility extended to the LDMA by the Bank of England. Since banks in illiquid positions can recall their money from the discount houses, it is they that get forced into the Bank and face the penal rates. This has in the past been very unfair at times. The new 'undertaking' (Section 11) by eligible banks to maintain a minimum level of secured money with the discount houses, and to offer an explanation for any failure to do so, will be a salutory control on the eligible banks. As ever the discount houses, at the sharp end, will face penal rates if they are forced into the bank, and will therefore keep the rates they charge high enough to avoid official displeasure—thus restricting the lending they do and controlling the money supply.

The decision to cease the weekly announcements of MLR, given at the same time as the issue of the document reproduced above, seems therefore to be sound. MLR is not quite abandoned, but will be retained as a residual power to be used by the Bank when it feels the market needs a very clear signal. Indeed, within a month of the changes being implemented the Bank exercised this option and announced a Minimum Lending Rate which raised interest rates by 2 per cent on September 14, only 25 days after the new system began. This was in spite of a major innovation, the introduction '*via the main press agencies, of up-to-date information about the Bank's dealings in the money market. . . . The Bank's objective, with this development, is to provide all market operators with access as rapidly as possible to relevant information about the Bank's activities and daily forecasts.'* (Bank of England *Quarterly Bulletin, September 1981, page 333*)

Describing the Bank's new techniques (the same reference as above), the *Quarterly Bulletin* says:

Essentially, as foreshadowed in November 1980, the Bank has been trying to smooth out day-to-day shortages or surpluses of cash by means of open-market operations, rather than by direct lending to the discount market. In dealing with shortages, the Bank has usually either bought bills outright or, if the shortage was to be followed before long by a day of prospective surplus, it has bought bills for resale on that day. When the market has been in surplus, the Bank has sought to sell Treasury bills set to mature on a day of prospective shortage. Where large transactions could be estimated in advance—notably oil tax payments or calls on part-paid gilt-edged stocks already sold—operations have been framed accordingly (as with the issue in July and August of Treasury bills to mature on 1 September). All these operations were conducted within the context of a general objective for very short-term interest rates. Where the Bank dealt in longer-term bills, it did so to change the market's cash position on the day of the transaction and hence to influence very short-term interest rates. The Bank did not aim to affect rates on longer-term bills themselves but, rather, operated at appropriate market rates to avoid giving a signal which could otherwise have had undue influence on the market.

Clearly these developments constitute an extension of the meaning of 'open-market operations', and the Bank is seeking to control day-to-day events by the most careful forecasts of the flow of funds. Despite this, and the widest circulation of up-to-date information, it found it necessary to make a positive MLR announcement of what it deemed to be desirable for interest rates. Clearly, the institutions are not as sensitive as the Bank to what is necessary as far as interest rates are concerned.

Day-to-day events cannot be chronicled in a textbook. The reader is urged to follow developments in the financial press.

A note on 'prudential controls'. The document issued to the banking fraternity about prudential controls over the banking system is not available to the general public. It apparently calls for discussion with the banks about the measures they are taking individually to meet their obligations as they fall due, or are called. The obvious measures to ensure liquidity are the keeping of cash, or liquefiable assets, and arranging a profile of maturing assets to meet liabilities as they arise. In an article in the *Quarterly Bulletin* (March 1981) the Bank stresses that in assessing the degree of prudence displayed by a particular bank it will take account of the quality of the assets available. These should provide adequate access to liquidity without suffering excessive costs of liquidation. In cases where a bank has derived some protection by securing a right to bid for deposits if required, the costs of bidding should not be excessive (since it would be imprudent to rely on such deposits for liquidity).

Since the Bank believes that the primary responsibility for ensuring liquidity rests on the management of each particular bank, it does not propose to implement across-the-board liquidity controls. It will monitor liquidity procedures for each bank as part of its general supervision, and taking account of each bank's particular characteristics and activities.

12.5 The Revival of Monetarism

The interest of the UK authorities in improved financial control of the money supply coincided with a revival of monetarism elsewhere in the world. In the US pressure for the adoption of monetary policy had been building up throughout the 1960s as the 'New Monetarists' gained influence. Their chief spokesman was Professor Milton Friedman from the University of Chicago, and the appearance of serious inflation on both sides of the Atlantic hastened the acceptance of the ideas he popularised so effectively. By 1970 monetary policy was once more 'respectable' in both the US and the UK. There was widespread acceptance of the view that a link existed between the quantity of money in circulation and the level of economic activity. As the 1970s progressed the link was seized upon by policy-makers who increasingly were finding fiscal policy inadequate in dealing with the major evil of the decade—persistent inflation.

In the UK a reassessment of the place of monetary policy was hastened by balance of payments difficulties. These difficulties meant recourse had to be made to the IMF, and the Fund, naturally, wanted some assurance that its financial assistance would be put to good use. It therefore proposed to monitor the growth of money supply in the UK and as early as 1968 was influencing the Government's monetary policy. This influence was eventually to affect the very way in which money supply was measured, the use of the domestic credit expansion measure being largely attributable to the IMF. It is against this background of a resurgence of monetarism, both internationally and within the UK, that the more recent measures outlined above have been introduced. There is still intense interest in monetary policy and monetarism as a philosophy, and whilst the latter has yet to prove its efficacy and permanency, the former has been used with a fair degree of success for decades and is likely to continue being so used in the future.

12.6 Revision Test

Answers	*Questions*
—	**1.** Why did the Government operate a cheap money policy after the Second World War?
1. In order to stimulate investment and hold down the cost of Government borrowing.	**2.** Why was it abandoned?
2. Because of the difficulty of disposing of undated $2\frac{1}{2}$ per cent Stock in 1947.	**3.** Why did monetary policy make a comeback in 1951?
3. (*a*) Because of the election of a Conservative Government. (*b*) Because it was believed that monetary policy would be more effective in dealing with the inflation of the Korean War.	**4.** What did the Radcliffe Report do for monetary policy?
4. Consign it to a secondary role.	**5.** Why?
5. Because it was believed that the quantity of money had little effect on spending.	**6.** What policy instruments did come out of the Radcliffe Report?
6. The use of the rate of interest and direct controls to restrict credit, particularly hire purchase controls.	**7.** Why was Competition and Credit Control introduced in 1971?
7. (*a*) To bring about more competition between banks. (*b*) To give a more equitable means of controlling the activities of a wider range of financial institutions. (*c*) To provide a more effective means of control.	**8.** How was control to be more effective?

Answers	*Questions*
8. (*a*) Through the use of a new $12\frac{1}{2}$ per cent eligible reserve assets ratio. (*b*) Through the application of a reserve ratio, special deposits, etc., over a wider range of financial institutions.	**9.** Did the system of controls work?
9. Only in part—the introduction of the corset scheme in 1973 indicated that fairly clumsy direct intervention was still required.	**10.** Was there more competition in banking?
10. In the long run, no. (*a*) The banks can compete only to a limited extent on the rate of interest—they must 'keep in step'. (*b*) Even the Bank of England found it required Minimum Lending Rate as a market-leading force	**11.** Now try the written questions in Appendix 1.

Part 4

INTERNATIONAL MONETARY RELATIONS

13

THE BALANCE OF PAYMENTS

13.1 The Nature of International Monetary Relations

We live in a world where sovereign national states exist side by side, each seeking the best advantage for its own people, or at least its own rulers—if people and rulers are distinct. No nation is completely self-sufficient, though some very large nations, such as the USA and USSR, could in an emergency produce most of the things they need. Many of the smaller nations have not been generously endowed by Nature, or have used up their original endowments to a considerable extent and must trade with other nations to obtain many of the items they require. Some are almost totally dependent on trade, not only for luxury items but for absolute necessities. The outstanding examples are Singapore and Hong Kong, where tiny territories with huge populations are kept prosperous by a constant and restless activity, importing raw materials for manufacture and exporting the finished goods thus made available.

The distinctive feature of all such foreign trade is that it poses a monetary problem as well as the ordinary problems of buying, manufacturing and selling. Manufacturers who sell their output within the nation state can use the money obtained from customers to pay for raw materials, wages and overheads. The same manufacturers selling to a foreign customer cannot use the foreign currency received without first exchanging it into the home currency. Thus if a British manufacturer sells a machine to a German customer, the customer's deutschemarks are of no use in Great Britain, and must be exchanged for pounds. This exchange is effected on the foreign exchange market, which is subject not only to market forces (the demand for and supply of deutschemarks and pounds respectively) but also to the activities of the monetary authorities in West Germany and the UK. These authorities may deliberately manipulate the market for their own ends, but this is today against the spirit of the International Monetary Fund, and is therefore less probable than formerly. More likely, the activities of the monetary authorities in their own countries, for purely domestic reasons, will have side effects on the foreign exchange market, affecting imports and exports and consequently the quantities of their currencies being offered or demanded.

The activities of the governments and national monetary institutions of nation states can be arbitrary and capricious. They can also be devious and cynical. Their activities need to be monitored by the banking authorities of nations which are open and fair, and for this reason a study of international monetary relations is essential to students in the banking field.

International monetary relations therefore consist of a pattern of relationships to effect the exchange of currencies with one another, on an enduring basis over the years. The analysis of the pattern of relationships can be reduced to five areas of study:

(*a*) **The balance of payments of a nation state.** What are the component parts of a balance of payments, and how can a surplus or deficit be dealt with at the end of any accounting period?

(*b*) **The Foreign Exchange Market.** How are the world's currencies exchanged, and at what rate do they exchange one with another? What market forces are at work and can national authorities interfere on the market to 'manage' the exchange rates?

(*c*) **How Shall a Disequilibrium on the Balance of Payments be Cured?** Any imbalance of payments that results from the import–export activities of nations means the accumulation of claims by citizens of one country on citizens of another. In other words, some nations become debtor nations and others become creditor nations. Unless a mechanism exists to eliminate these imbalances trade will cease, the creditor nation being unwilling to supply further goods or services to the debtor nation.

(*d*) **What International Reserve Asset Shall we Use?** In order to eliminate balances using the mechanism mentioned in (*c*) we need an international standard reserve asset which can be used for the settlement of debts between nations and also as a unit of account in which currency values can be expressed. This could be gold, or a powerful national currency like the dollar, but today it tends to be a **currency basket.**

(*e*) **What Supranational Institutions have been Developed?** We shall see that a system of settlements between nations is much easier to arrange if multilateral trade is taking place, not bilateral trade between only two nations. In a situation where multilateral payments arrangements are being made a supranational body which can supervise and arrange payments and 'manage' the international monetary system is likely to be helpful. These institutions are described in Chapter 14.

13.2 The Balance of Payments of a Nation State

Using the UK as an example of a nation state which has some reason to be concerned about its balance of payments, we find that the position is monitored by the Central Statistical Office, and an annual publication entitled *United Kingdom Balance of Payments* appears in August–September, giving the position at the end of the previous year. Thus the edition available at the time of writing is the 1981 edition, with details up to the end of 1980, and the tables in this book are therefore based on the 1980 figures.

There are four major divisions of monetary movements taking place in international trade, visibles, invisibles, capital movements and official financing:

Visible trade is trade in items which can actually be seen passing through our ports (raw materials, fuels, manufactured items, foods, beverages, etc.). The payments for these, which are valued on f.o.b. terms (free on board, disregarding freight and insurance charges), result in a visible balance (or imbalance).

Invisible items are charges for services, as distinct from goods. These cannot be seen visibly moving through our ports, but result in payments from overseas for services the UK renders to foreigners, and payments by the UK for services foreigners render to us. The most important services are banking, insurance, communications, sea and air transport and tourism, but earnings from interest, profits and dividends are a very important item too. Another group of invisible payments concerns 'transfers'—for example, immigrants frequently arrive with funds from abroad, or send funds back to support families overseas, while inheritances flow in and out as deaths occur.

Both these classes, visibles and invisibles, are referred to as 'current account' items. The reader who is familiar with book-keeping will appreciate that the phrase 'current account' refers to an item which has to be settled within the current year, whereas capital expenditure refers to expenditure the effects of which will be felt over several years. Thus if the UK sells a Nigerian business-man a piece of machinery which the latter will pay for on arrival that is a current account item, whereas if the UK makes a loan to the Nigerian Government which is repayable over 15 years that is a capital transaction.

The result of the movements on visibles and invisibles gives us a 'balance on current account', which is shown in the published accounts as 'Current balance'.

Capital movements. As explained above, these are loans made to foreigners, or received from foreigners. Such loans are repaid over a period of years, often with interest. Taking a loan by the UK to a developing country, the movement out of the capital at the commencement of the loan is an adverse movement on the balance of payments. The repayments in future years by instalments, with interest, are a series of favourable items in the balance of payments accounts, though the interest will probably be recorded as an invisible item and only the element of repaid capital will appear as a favourable item on the capital movements section of the accounts.

In Table 13.1 below it may be seen that on Capital Account a great many capital transactions are taking place. Not only are foreigners investing in UK firms but also in the public sector (by buying Government bonds, etc.). When we read in the popular press of Arab oil interests buying hotels and office blocks in the UK this is a favourable item in the balance of payments figures. By contrast, the UK Government is lending and giving money to foreign governments for a variety of reasons, while private sector firms are also investing and lending abroad. These are adverse items on the balance of payments (but in years ahead will earn interest which will come in as invisible earnings on current account).

The 'balancing item' is the sum of all the unidentified items in the accounts. It seems a very large sum, but in fact over the years the balancing items tend to average out, and since the figures in many cases are estimates made about payments and receipts which are subject to movements on the foreign exchange markets a high degree of accuracy cannot be achieved.

In any given year the result of all these movements, both 'current account' and 'capital account' items, must result in either a favourable balance, or an unfavourable balance. At a time of unfavourable balance, the nation state is in the same position as the ordinary householder whose expenditure exceeds income—it is necessary to finance the imbalance somehow. The householder may phone a bank manager, or visit a moneylender, or perhaps a pawn shop, but somehow funds must be raised to tide the household over its difficult period. As far as the nation state is concerned, this balance is called the 'balance for official financing' and the nation's housekeeper—the Chancellor of the Exchequer—will take official action to finance the deficit. Just what the action might be is explained later; first let us look at the most recent set of figures available. These are given in Table 13.1, in slightly more detailed form than the 'summary' accounts in the official publication, but all the figures come from the official handbook, and are reproduced by courtesy of the Central Statistical Office.

Table 13.1 The UK Balance of Payments (1980)

Current Account

The Balance of Visible Trade

Debits (debts to foreigners)	£m	Credits (debts by foreigners)	£m
Imports (valued free on board)	46 211	Exports and re-exports (valued free on board)	47 389
Favourable balance on visible trade	1 178		
	£m 47 389		£m 47 389

The Balance of Invisibles

Invisible imports	23 736	Favourable visible balance	1 178
Favourable balance on Current Account	3 206	Invisible exports	25 764
	£m 26 942		£m 26 942

Capital Account

The Balance of Capital Items

UK bank lending to foreigners	2 462	Favourable balance on Current Account	3 206
Government loans to foreign governments (net)	290	Foreign investment in UK private sector	568
Private sector investments in, and loans to, foreign firms	7 829	Foreign investment in UK public sector	4 081
Trade credit given to foreign customers	907	UK bank borrowing from foreign banks	2 024
Payments in advance to foreign suppliers	238	Additions by foreigners to sterling balances	2 569
Other transactions	237	Movements into reserves	1 246
Balancing item	539	Allocation of SDRs	180
Favourable balance for official financing	1 372		
	£m 13 874		£m 13 874

Official Financing

Loans to overseas monetary authorities (net)	140	Favourable balance for Official Financing	1 372
Repayments by public sector to foreign creditors	941		
Additions to reserves	291		
	£m 1 372		£m 1 372

Official Financing

In a year when the nation is in debt to foreigners, with an unfavourable balance on its balance of payments account, there are several ways of dealing with this balance. They are:

(*a*) Pay up the outstanding balance out of reserves, if there are any. After all, that is what reserves are for.

(*b*) Borrow from any official lender who is prepared to lend money. Very often the central bank of a friendly nation will provide funds, or a consortium of central banks will combine to offer assistance.

(*c*) In a really difficult situation the IMF may be prepared to assist, but it will usually insist on government action to correct the imbalance in the years ahead, and thus the sovereignty of the nation-state is interfered with to some extent.

It might seem strange to use the term 'official financing' for the reverse situation, as in Table 13.1, where the UK is seen to be in surplus. The final balance on the accounts was a favourable balance of £1372 million, due to favourable balances on both visible and invisible trade. Capital movements resulted in capital leaving the UK. While foreigners were bringing balances into the UK and leaving them there—a safe haven in an oil-rich country which (paradoxically) was also offering high interest rates—UK capital was moving out to invest abroad. The point about the balance of payments, whether it is favourable or not, is that it does have to be dealt with. The Chancellor must decide what to do with the surplus. Should he make loans available to nations in difficulties, or put the surplus in the reserves, or use it to repay foreign debts, etc.?

It is frequently argued that it is as bad to be a creditor nation with repeated surpluses on the balance of payments, as it is to be a debtor nation with repeated deficits. To be constantly in surplus indicates a very productive industrial system, which produces exports that are highly competitive in world markets and consequently in strong demand. Home nationals prefer to buy home-made goods, so that imports are not sucked in, and a surplus on the balance of payments must result. This is of course fine for the creditor nation, but if it results in permanent adverse balances for other nations they will either endure mass unemployment, or erect barriers against the creditor nation's goods. They must be helped to become competitive again if mankind generally is to make progress, and avoid social—or even international—unrest. To UK ears it is strange to hear the appeals of West German politicians asking German consumers to buy foreign goods. The UK's low productivity has accustomed us to adverse balances on overseas trade and appeals by our Governments to 'buy British'.

13.3 The Foreign Exchange Market

The foreign exchange market does not have any actual market place in the UK, though other centres do maintain the practice of meeting daily in a suitable exchange to establish official quotations for currencies. In the UK the clearing banks and the foreign banks maintain dealing rooms where dealers can keep in touch by telephone and telex with the rest of the market in this country and around the world.

Deals in all the more common currencies are arranged through brokers who match the needs of banks around the world. The situation is that a customer approaches a bank with a particular import or export transaction in mind. An import transaction implies a need to buy foreign currency to pay the foreign supplier at a certain due date; an export transaction implies that a certain sum in foreign currency will become available for exchange into sterling at a due date. A bank which has two customers in exactly opposite positions, with one due to receive a certain sum in a certain currency on a certain date and the other due to pay the same sum in the same currency on the same date, could match them against one another. This is a fairly unlikely circumstance, however, and there would still be the chance that one or the other of these transactions was held up for some reason. By dealing through one of the brokers the bank can establish absolutely reliable arrangements.

The foreign exchange market is a world-wide market with instantaneous communications to all the dealing centres around the world. The result is that a system of world-wide prices prevails, since if a particular currency is cheaper at one centre than at another the brokers would buy on the banks' behalf in that centre, thus raising the price, and would not buy in the more expensive centres, thus lowering the prices prevailing there. This is called **arbitrage**—the tendency to equalise and settle. The days when private fortunes could be made by arbitrage dealings have passed now that the telephone and telex link all centres. Formerly speculators with better knowledge than others could deal with centres whose prices were widely different because of poor knowledge of prices elsewhere in the market. For major international banks arbitrage is still a useful source of profits.

In dealing with the brokers the banks always act as principals, buying and selling in their own names and not as agents of their customers, the importers and exporters. The brokers, on the other hand, act for the banks as intermediaries, matching banks wishing to buy with banks wishing to sell. Deals may be both **spot** and **forward**. A 'spot market' makes bargains which become effective immediately; a 'forward market' makes bargains which will not become effective until some future time.

The need for a forward market developed after the collapse of the Bretton Woods Agreement in 1970, and the Smithsonian Agreement in 1971. The years when these agreements were in force were times of fixed exchange rates. Between 1945 and 1970 there was little expectation that exchange rates would vary in the future other than the small fluctuation permitted either side of par. This was about 1 per cent under the old Bretton Woods Agreement, so that with the pound sterling at £1 = $2.80 from 1948 to 1967 it could only fluctuate from £1 = $2.82 to £1 = $2.78. After 1967 the exchange rate was £1 = $2.40 and fluctuations were permitted between £1 = $2.42 and £1 = $2.38. Imagine an exporter who makes an export sale on which there is a 33⅓ per cent profit: if the exchange rate deteriorates by 1 per cent this will still make a 32.3 per cent profit and will not represent a serious loss. A forward exchange transaction would not be worth bothering about. The same could not be said in a period of floating exchange rates. Exporters now stand to lose a considerable part of their profit, and it will be prudent to deal on the forward exchange market and thus anticipate any change in the rate of exchange.

One of the chief fears about the change to 'floating exchange rates' was that trade would decline as traders found it impossible to strike bargains which would be mutually beneficial. It was feared that an adverse change in the exchange rate might completely erode profit margins on one side or the other. In fact, two ways of covering future exchange risks were developed. The first was the use of the forward exchange market, the second was to deal on the Eurocurrency market.

Forward Exchange Dealings

Suppose an exporter contracts to sell a machine to an American importer for £10 000 payable in three months' time. Suppose the exchange rate is £1 = $2.20, so that if the bill was to be paid today the exporter would receive $22 000. If sterling is falling on the foreign exchange market he will lose $100 for every cent it falls. Suppose the pound came under severe pressure and fell to £1 = $2.10 before the three months' period was over. The American customer would need to pay only $21 000 for the £10 000. The exporter would lose $1000 on the deal.

To prevent this happening the exporter can sell the dollars forward on the foreign exchange market, through his banker. Forward rates are quoted as follows:

	Three months forward
USA	0.83–0.78 c. premium
Italy	18–23 lire discount

This means that dealers expect the lira to fall in the next three months by between 18–23 lire per pound, whereas the dollar is expected to rise between 0.83 and 0.78 of a cent. If the exporter's bank can sell his dollars forward—say at £1 = $2.1920, i.e. a premium of 0.80 cent—the exporter will receive $21 920 for his machine, which means he has limited his possible loss to $80. Whatever happens to the pound the forward exchange dealer will have to honour his bargain at $2.1920 = £1.

Eurocurrency dealings

Instead of covering its customers' anticipated currency receipts on the forward foreign exchange market the bank can borrow an equivalent amount at the same maturity on the Eurocurrency market. This money will be repaid when the customer honours the bargain at the due date, but in the meantime the bank has obtained the foreign exchange at once, and can sell it on the spot market at prevailing spot prices.

Speculation and the Foreign Exchange Market

In their evidence to the Wilson Committee on the functioning of the financial institutions, the clearing banks stated categorically that they never speculated in foreign exchange. They then went on to state that 'they do, however, execute orders for the purchase and sale of foreign currencies from their customers in so far as this was permissible under the exchange control regulations'. Of course the exchange control regulations have now been abandoned and we do not know whether the clearing banks engage in any speculative activity in the freer situations that prevail today. What we do know about speculative activity is that it is sheer madness not to join in if you hold large reserves of a currency which is falling on the market. The organisation which, for whatever reason, holds tight in a deteriorating situation is likely to finish up out of pocket.

The market, in peaceful times, is a laudable place where those who engage in international trade can change foreign currencies into domestic currencies at minimum cost. At times when a particular currency comes under pressure the market may deteriorate to a place where those who have reserves of that currency sell it to less sophisticated buyers and buy it back later at the cheaper price, and the devil take the hindmost. Since the market in the UK was freed from exchange control we have not seen one of these massive crises of confidence, but one is sure to occur sooner or later. There are many factors at work to produce uncertainty about future values of particular currencies. The obvious example is the manipulation of oil prices by the OPEC countries, which may prejudice a particular country's whole economic position. Others are changes in gross national product, gross national product as a percentage of international trade, the terms of trade as between advanced nations and developing nations, political stability, crop failures, interruptions of world transport and many more. These are economic rather than financial problems but they have the greatest impact upon the value of particular currencies.

The Authorities and 'Dirty Floating'

In the years between 1931 and 1939 a system of floating exchange rates was introduced. Under such a system a balance of payments should be achieved by allowing a currency to float to a position where it achieved a balance of payments automatically. Thus a country with outdated equipment, incompetent managers and dispirited workers would display low productivity and poor-quality goods. This would mean that its products would not be in demand, even by home nationals. There would be poor exports, high imports and a surplus of its currency available. The currency would therefore fall on the foreign exchange market, its goods would become cheaper, and foreigners would buy more, while imports would become relatively more expensive.

It was then found that other forces could be brought to bear on the value of a currency which had effects which were *not* justified by the country's productivity performance. Speculators could act against a currency, selling it to force a drop in price so it could be bought back again at a cheaper rate with a profit to the speculator. The solution was found to be the establishment of a large fund of foreign exchange to buy the currency whenever it was being sold by speculators. They were paid in whatever currency they wanted, but the price of the home currency did not fall because the authorities were in the market 'supporting' the currency that was under pressure. In the case of the pound sterling the fund was called the **Exchange Equalisation Fund.** Sometimes, when the speculator had to buy back because he really needed the sterling he had previously sold, he found the price had risen and the final result was a loss. This was called 'burning the speculators' fingers'.

After the collapse of the Bretton Woods Agreement, and the Smithsonian Agreement that followed it, the world returned to a system of floating currencies in 1972. The new system faced the old problem in a new form. Governments began to use an exchange equalisation fund not just to protect their currencies, but as a means of managing the exchange rate to achieve greater penetration of export markets and to impede the flow of imports. All floating today is to some extent 'dirty floating', with the authorities stepping in to achieve national aspirations at the expense of other nations. To reduce this activity members of the IMF have agreed not to pursue 'beggar my neighbour' policies, and to reduce interference with their currencies if the result will be to affect other member nations adversely.

13.4 Adjusting a Disequilibrium

If a nation has a temporary adverse balance on its balance of payments the problem can be solved in the way described in the section on 'Official Financing' above. The debtor nation either pays up out of its reserves, or borrows from friendly nations to tide over the period until it again achieves a favourable balance. What happens when the adverse balance repeats itself year after year, and there is a danger that all the reserves will be used up and the nation's credit with other nations will be exhausted? What mechanism exists to adjust a permanent disequilibrium in the balance of payments?

A permanent disequilibrium in the balance of payments reflects an imbalance between what the nation is producing and what the nation is consuming. If a nation is well-endowed by nature with resources, or pursues a policy of dominating other nations who can be compelled to yield up their resources, and if her industrial system is strong and productive, her people can enjoy a high standard of living. Imports will be cheap, and chiefly in raw material form, because home nationals prefer home-made goods. Exports will be reasonably priced because industry is productive, and consequently foreigners will demand them strongly, so that a favourable balance of payments results. The situation will be very different in a country which is poorly endowed with resources, has no vassal states and has a weak industrial system with low productivity. Imports will be high and it must pay world market prices for raw materials, while home nationals prefer foreign goods which are cheaper and better. Exports will be few in number, since home-made goods are expensive and unattractive to foreigners. The result will be an adverse balance of payments.

How can this adverse balance be corrected? There are only two ways, apart from raising economic output by greater productivity and efficiency. One way is to lower the home standard of living; the other is to lower the exchange rate.

If we lower the home standard of living we reduce the price of goods in domestic currency. The rewards paid to the factors of production (land, labour and capital) are reduced and consequently the unit cost of the goods and services provided are lowered. At the lower prices our goods will be more attractive to foreigners, while at their lower level of incomes our home nationals will be unable to afford many of the things they previously enjoyed and imports will fall. A balance of payments will be re-established.

If we lower the rate of exchange it does not affect money rewards to land, labour and capital, and the owners of these factors of production—the landlords, the workers and those with accumulated savings—enjoy the illusion that their incomes are the same as before. The rate of exchange is used to lower the price of exports, and at the same time it makes imports more expensive to home nationals. Exports therefore increase, and imports are less attractive to home nationals who buy home-made goods instead. They do experience a reduction in living standards indirectly, because they find that things made from imported raw materials are more expensive and they must now make do with expensive and, to them, less attractive home-produced goods.

The alternative mechanisms over the years to achieve these two solutions have been as follows:

(*a*) **The Gold Standard**—a mechanism which throws the full burden of curing a disequilibrium on the home standard of living, cutting domestic prices to restore a balance.

(*b*) **Floating Exchange Rates**—a mechanism which achieves equilibrium by allowing the exchange rate to sink to a point where it will make home-produced products good value for money in export markets and preserves the illusion that the home standard of living is not affected.

(*c*) **Managed Flexibility**—between these two extremes, but yielding a result closer to (*a*) above than to (*b*). The 'managed flexibility' system of the Bretton Woods Agreement permitted a small fluctuation in exchange rates but then required the currency to be supported on the foreign exchange market by the monetary authorities, while the domestic economy was forced to bear the burden of correcting the imbalance, with lower incomes for citizens. The resulting policies came to be called 'Stop-Go' policies, though it would have been better to call them 'Go-Stop' policies. The economy was allowed to 'Go' until the country got into balance of payments difficulties, when all the economic brakes were applied to arrest progress while the disequilibrium was corrected.

A detailed look at these three systems is now desirable.

The Gold Standard Mechanism

(*a*) All currencies are linked to gold. When a country is on the gold standard its currency can be exchanged freely for a given weight of gold, and the number of notes on issue must be restricted to the amount of gold in the reserves (although in the UK the Bank Charter Act of 1844 did permit a small **fiduciary issue**). In 1914 the pound sterling was worth 113.0016 grains of fine gold, and the US dollar was worth 23.33 grains. The rate of exchange between two currencies, both of which were on the gold standard, was therefore related to the quantity of gold that each was worth, and this was called the 'mint par' of exchange. In 1914 the rate of exchange between the pound and the dollar was a little over \$4.86 = £1. To simplify things in the following discussion we will pretend that the pound was worth four dollars.

(*b*) Currencies cannot fluctuate because gold will be shipped. When currencies are tied in this way to gold it is impossible for the value of the currency to fluctuate outside very fine limits (called the gold points) because if this was allowed to happen it would pay a businessman to change his money into gold and ship the gold. Consider, for example, the following circumstances:

(i) £1 = \$4 at the mint par of exchange.

(ii) Because British goods are not selling to America and American goods are popular in Britain the price of the dollar is steadily rising: £1 = \$3.99; £1 = \$3.98; £1 = \$3.97, etc. The more the dollar rises the fewer we get for the pound.

(iii) It costs 1 cent to ship gold weighing 113.0016 grains to America.

How would a businessman who owes \$10 000 to an American businessman pay the money? The following alternatives are available, when the rate of exchange is, say, £1 = \$3.97.

(i) Buy dollars on the foreign exchange market at \$3.97 = £1:

$$\text{cost} = \frac{10\,000}{3.97} = £2519$$

(ii) Exchange £2500 into gold and then pay to ship it:

$$\begin{aligned}\text{cost} &= £2500 + £6.25 \text{ shipping charges}\\ &= £2506.25\end{aligned}$$

Clearly it is cheaper to ship gold, and as gold is not difficult to obtain the businessman would buy the gold and ship it. The result is that a currency cannot fluctuate outside the limits set by the cost of shipping gold. So £1.00 will never fluctuate outside the limits \$4.01–3.99. Beyond these points gold will be shipped.

It follows that a change in the balance of payments cannot be achieved by altering the exchange rate. The old standard mechanism was one of rigidly fixed exchange rates where the burden of curing the disequilibrium on the balance of payments fell on the home market—in the above example on the UK domestic economy. Gold is being withdrawn by businessmen and shipped abroad. The gold reserves fall and currency which has been circulated will have to be recalled. Moncy will become tight, wages will be cut, rents will fall and unemployment will rise. The standard of living will fall, and the price of British goods will be lowered on world markets, while imports will be demanded less, especially now that so many people are unemployed. Exports will rise, imports will fall and equilibrium will be restored by the gold standard mechanism.

Meanwhile, how is the creditor nation affected? Gold flows in; extra notes can be printed; money is plentiful; businessmen will be able to borrow to expand their businesses; unemployment will fall; the standard of living will increase; American goods will become more expensive and less attractive to foreigners so that exports fall; imports will increase as affluent citizens demand more British goods which are now cheaper and therefore more attractive. The favourable balance will be eroded by the gold standard mechanism, and a balance of payments will be restored.

The failure of the gold standard method of adjusting a disequilibrium occurred in the years between the wars. Briefly it broke down because the chief creditor nation, the USA, failed to allow its economy to expand in the way required. As gold reserves rose it should have issued more currency to expand the economy, a process which would have reduced the competitiveness of its goods and services and given other nations a chance to export to America. Instead it simply took the gold into its reserves at Fort Knox. This meant that the debtor nations, like the UK, were depressing the home economy to no real purpose, for no matter how savage the depression the balance of payments could not recover. A new system was required, and currencies began floating.

The Floating Currency Mechanism

There is little point in discussing the 1931–9 period of floating currency although as economic history it is very interesting, and the development of the Exchange Equalisation Fund during those years laid the foundation for the Bretton Woods System and the IMF to be described in Chapter 14.

The modern system of floating currencies began in the early 1970s with the collapse of the Smithsonian Agreement. The idea was that a currency should find its own level, which in fact represented the true state of its national output and productivity relative to the other nations of the world. No matter how highly it paid its factors of production in rents, wages, interest and profit, the exchange rate would operate to lower the export cost of its goods. In fact, as already described, the floating tended to be **dirty floating** with governments manipulating their currencies to some extent to achieve export objectives and impede the flow of imports. This called for some measure of control, and in an alteration to the Articles of Agreement of the International Monetary Funds, it was provided as follows:

Article IV, Section 1. General obligations of members

Recognising that the essential purpose of the international monetary system is to provide a framework that facilitates the exchange of goods, services, and capital among countries, and that sustains sound economic growth, and that a principal objective is the continuing development of the orderly underlying conditions that are necessary for financial and economic stability, each member undertakes to collaborate with the Fund and other members to assure orderly exchange arrangements and to promote a stable system of exchange rates. In particular, each member shall:

(i) endeavour to direct its economic and financial policies towards the objective of fostering orderly economic growth with reasonable price stability, with due regard to its circumstances;
(ii) seek to promote stability by fostering orderly underlying economic and financial conditions and a monetary system that does not tend to produce erratic disruptions;
(iii) avoid manipulating exchange rates or the international monetary system in order to prevent effective balance of payments adjustment or to gain an unfair competitive advantage over other members; and
(iv) follow exchange policies compatible with the undertakings under this Section.

Each member state undertakes to collaborate with the 'Fund' and other members to assure orderly exchange arrangements and to promote a stable system of exchange rates. However, the article also recognises that stable domestic conditions are a necessary prerequisite for stable international conditions, and therefore the members further agree to foster orderly economic growth with reasonable price stability. Clearly some countries around the world find this a difficult target to meet, and few honour the obligation to the fullest extent. The best that can be hoped for is that nations will not make changes in their own internal economic policies if the results will adversely affect other nations.

The fact is then that there is really no such thing as 'freely floating' currencies; international obligations can still impinge on national economic policies, and by contrast manipulation of 'internal' controls over such things as interest rates can have a substantial impact on international rates of exchange. Businessmen complain to the Government that 'the pound is too hard' and can suggest remedies that will weaken it and make exports more competitive, while calls by trade unions for higher pay and shorter hours still have to be resisted by Governments anxious to keep home-produced goods cheap and attractive not only to foreigners but also to home consumers.

Table 13.2 shows the exchange rate of the pound sterling against the US dollar, on average during the years shown.

Table 13.2. Exchange rates

Year	*Rate of exchange (£1 to US dollars)*
1971	2.4445
1972	2.5015
1973	2.4526
1974	2.3402
1975	2.2200
1976	1.8049
1977	1.7455
1978	1.9197
1979	2.1225
1980	2.3281

(Source: *United Kingdom Balance of Payments*)

The Managed Flexibility Mechanism

In the middle of the Second World War, the Allies began to prepare for peace. The climate was one of international understanding. The Atlantic Treaty had placed human rights in the forefront of Allied aims, including the obviously economic aim of freedom from poverty. The achievement of such an ideal was impossible unless some of the barriers between nations could be removed, and barriers to international trade associated with international exchange problems were among the best recognised. Accordingly, a great conference of the Free World's monetary authorities was held in the US at Bretton Woods, near Washington. It resulted in the Bretton Woods Agreement, 1944, and the General Agreement on Tariffs and Trade, 1947.

The Bretton Woods Agreement. The conference at Bretton Woods in 1944 recognised that some system better than the gold standard and better than the floating exchange rate method was necessary. World trade was out of line with the volume of gold to back it, and while gold could have been revalued upwards to get over the difficulty this would have benefited certain nations unfairly. On the other hand, freely fluctuating exchange rates made trade subject to sudden and unpredictable changes which ruined profitability of enterprise, so that merchants would not take the risks. What was needed was a system of 'managed flexibility' so that if a country was suffering from an adverse balance of payments of a permanent nature it could give notice to merchants and devalue its currency, but if it was merely being put under pressure by speculators its reserves would be large enough to withstand the pressure, and eventually 'burn the speculators' fingers'.

The nations required an international Exchange Equalisation Fund which could give any country under massive speculative pressure huge reserves to defeat the speculation. The International Monetary Fund was born!

The arrangements made at Bretton Woods for the establishment of an International Monetary Fund were as follows:

(*a*) By an agreed date all members should declare the par values of their currencies. Great Britain declared that the £1 should be equal to US $4.03, for example. This agreed rate of exchange would be permitted to fluctuate by up to 1 per cent on either side of the agreed parity figure. Because of two devaluations, in 1949 and 1967, the pound last stood at £1 = $2.40. Until August 1971 it was allowed to fluctuate between $2.42 and $2.38, or 1 per cent of its agreed parity. It follows then that except for very abnormal times, like the devaluations mentioned, a foreign businessman making a contract knew that he was unlikely to lose more than 1 per cent of his contract price by exchange fluctuations. As profit margins are much greater than 1 per cent, the proportion of his ultimate profit at risk was very small. World trade continued to expand under this system in a thoroughly satisfactory way.

(*b*) All currencies should be freely convertible on current transactions within five years. In fact this proved impossible, but by 1958 it had been achieved as far as non-residents were concerned, though UK citizens were not allowed to buy foreign exchange freely until 1979.

(*c*) Changes of exchange rate should not normally be permitted; but if the change was of less than 10 per cent and deemed absolutely essential, a country could depreciate its currency without prior consultation with the Fund authorities. If the devaluation was to be greater than 10 per cent, the Fund authorities must sanction the arrangement.

(*d*) The IMF, following the idea of the Exchange Equalisation Account, is a huge reserve of currency and gold collected on a quota basis from all the members of the Fund. Great Britain's original contribution was $1300 million. This was raised in 1959, and again in 1965. Finally, in February 1970 a further revision raised Britain's contributions to $2800 million. One quarter of the quota had to be contributed in gold; the other three quarters were contributed in a country's own currency. During the 1970s some of the gold was sold off to earn funds for aid to developing countries.

Originally there were 39 members of the Fund. By the beginning of 1980 there were 140 members, comprising almost the whole of the free-enterprise world. Switzerland is a notable exception.

Use of the Fund when a Disequilibrium occurred

When a country suffered an adverse balance of payments and its own reserves appeared to be inadequate to withstand the speculative pressure, the members exercised drawing rights against the Fund, in a series of 'tranches' (*tranche* is the French word for 'slice'). The first slice, originally called the gold tranche, is its own contribution of gold plus any shortage of the member's contribution to the Fund. For example, the UK quota was 25 per cent gold and 75 per cent sterling; suppose some other member, wishing to buy British goods, had borrowed sterling from the Fund. The UK would be entitled to put in enough pounds to take out not only its gold share, but any extra currency it wanted up to the limit of its full quota. The Fund would now hold 100 per cent of the UK quota in sterling, and the UK would go back to its battle to support the pound armed with these extra reserves. If they proved insufficient it could return for more 'tranches'—four more slices of 25 per cent each of its quota. By this time the Fund would be holding 200 per cent of its quota of sterling. However, while the gold tranche was available as of right, the successive further tranches would mean more and more stringent guarantees from the borrowing nation that it was really doing something adequate to cure its balance of payments problems. A speculation that persisted as long as this must mean some fundamental weakness in the nation's economic affairs (e.g. over-generous welfare arrangements) and the fund authorities could refuse further help unless corrective measures were taken. This means of course that under the Bretton Woods System of managed flexibility the burden for curing an adverse balance of payments fell, except for very minor movements either side of the agreed parity level, on the domestic economy of the country. Adjustments in the domestic level of prices had to be achieved by management policies designed to reduce economic activity, reduce employment and render exports more attractive to foreigners.

13.5 The International Reserve Standard

If countries are to be able to settle their international indebtedness there must be some standard asset which can be placed in the reserves or taken from reserves as required. The traditional international reserve standard was gold. Despite arguments and proposals, notably by J. M. Keynes, for another standard independent of a commodity such as gold the Bretton Woods Conference could not agree to accept Keynes Bancors (the word was meant to mean Bankers' Gold). Gold therefore continued to be the means of top-level international settlement and was valued at $35 to the ounce.

At one time gold was an everyday currency which passed freely from hand to hand, but the minting of coinage is an expensive business while payment in coins involves a great deal of counting and carrying, with all the attendant risks of theft, embezzlement and loss. The development of banking systems made the use of monetary gold unnecessary within a country. Citizens were content to settle their debts in paper money, or better still by cheque, while even the banks themselves were content to settle their mutual indebtedness through accounts at the central bank. Gradually all the gold in a country became centralized at the central bank, and wealth, for the ordinary citizen, consisted of balances deposited at a bank.

Unfortunately the same system could not apply to international settlements, because large countries preferred to keep their reserves in a form which was intrinsically 'valuable' and not susceptible to influences or pressures from outside the national territory. Many smaller nations tied themselves to the currency of a 'great' neighbour, usually the pound sterling in the nineteenth century and the US dollar after the Second World War. Indeed, all nations kept considerable balances in a variety of foreign exchange holdings in the 'Bretton Woods' era, when the volume of gold available was small relative to the international trade that had to be financed. Sterling was a major reserve currency, but much of it was in the form of 'blocked sterling balances'. These were accumulated debts owed by the UK for goods supplied during the war, which could only be used gradually as the British economy was re-converted to peacetime production. More importantly, the US dollar became a major reserve currency, and the Swiss franc, German mark and Japanese yen later came to play a part in the reserves of many nations.

Difficulties arose when the dollar itself began to come under pressure, and its convertibility into gold was finally ended. In order to provide extra liquidity a new type of reserve asset was introduced by the IMF on January 1, 1970. These were called **Special Drawing Rights (SDRs),** and they were allocated to the various nations in proportion to their contributions to the fund.

SDRs are an official international reserve asset created by the IMF, which can be transferred between official authorised holders only. Their supply, valuation and the interest payable on them are all determined by the IMF. Great Britain's share of the 3½ billion created on January 1, 1970, was 402 million, each one equivalent to a US dollar. A further 3 billion were created in 1971 and again in 1972. A further creation of 12 billion SDRs was made in 1979–81.

A country wishing to use Special Drawing Rights will notify the Fund that it wishes to exchange some for usable foreign currency. The authorities will then designate which countries are to make currency available, and take SDRs instead. Clearly they will choose the countries whose balance of payments positions are strong. While this has proved to supply some strengthening of reserves, the pace of events overtook the introduction of SDRs. The serious deficits in the British balance of payments led the UK to 'float' sterling in 1972 and by 1973 all currencies were floating. In a system of floating currencies the use of IMF reserves, including SDRs, is not of such importance as when a system of fixed exchange rates is operating.

A further difficulty now arose as the weakness of the dollar produced nervousness and uncertainty in international payments. The SDR units had been defined as equivalent to one US dollar on their introduction in 1970. With a dollar that was falling in value it became desirable to establish an independent

Table 13.3. Composition of the SDR unit of account before 1981

Currency	*Weight (per cent)*	*Amount (in units of each designated currency)*
US dollar	33.0	0.40
deutschemark	12.5	0.38
Pound sterling	9.0	0.045
French franc	7.5	0.45
Japanese yen	7.5	26.0
Canadian dollar	6.0	0.071
Italian lira	6.0	47.0
Netherlands guilder	4.5	0.14
Belgium franc	3.5	1.60
Swedish krona	2.5	0.13
Australian dollar	1.5	0.012
Danish krone	1.5	0.11
Norwegian krone	1.5	0.099
Spanish peseta	1.5	1.10
Austrian schilling	1.0	0.22
South African rand	1.0	0.0082
	100.0	

value for the SDR and to give this unit the status of an international unit of account. Accounts have to be kept in some sort of money terms, but if all currencies are floating how shall we keep our records accurate if no stable currency unit is available? The answer was found by making the SDR a currency basket.

Currency Baskets

The idea of a currency basket is that an official body designates a 'unit of account' which is made up of a 'basket of currencies' and not a single currency. The SDR was originally a basket of 16 currencies, with all the world's major trading currencies represented. The actual composition was altered within a short while of the 'basket' being introduced and was then maintained for some years at the figures given in Table 13.3.

Since the weighting chosen reflected the share of world trade which each particular currency enjoyed, and these currencies were the major currencies involved, a fall in value in any one currency resulted in a relative rise in value of the others. This means that the value of the SDR kept very close to the average value of all currencies.

Towards the end of the decade it seemed that the daily calculations required were excessive for the benefits derived from the incorporation of so many currencies, some of them with only nominal weighting. It was therefore decided to change to a simpler system, and from January 1, 1981, the SDR unit has consisted of a basket of only five currencies, as shown in Table 13.4 below.

Table 13.4. The new Special Drawing Rights unit

Currency	*Weight (total 100)*	*Amount (in units of each designated currency)*
US dollar	42	0.54
Deutschemark	19	0.46
Pound sterling	13	0.071
French franc	13	0.74
Japanese yen	13	34.0

With regard to interest rates on SDRs, the original quantity created by the Fund and given to members do not rank for interest. However, a member nation which accepts SDRs in exchange for usable currency is entitled to interest on the excess of SDRs held over its original allocation. A member which has used its allocation of SDRs to obtain usable currency for balance of payments transactions must pay interest on the shortfall of SDRs in its account. The rate of interest paid is calculated on a basket of short-term interest rates prevailing in the major trading countries.

13.6 The Balance of Payments and the Domestic Economy

The contradiction of twentieth-century society is that we have a system of nation states forced by economic necessity to trade internationally. This trade is so extensive that a more cooperative and supranational organisation is really required if the optimum economic performance for all is to be achieved. Unfortunately there are factors which make any attempt to 'manage' the world economy extremely difficult. Among them are the different stages of development of the nations, the existence of a Communist bloc which will not co-operate for ideological reasons on economic programmes and a North–South split where enormous disparities exist between the developed North and the less developed South. It is not possible therefore to operate as if we all lived in one world. Such 'management' as is possible can only be as extensive as the nation states will permit, and it is still largely true, as it was in ancient Greece, that 'the strong will take what they want while the weak yield what they must'.

The balance of payments was the single most important factor in the development of the domestic economy of the UK during the Bretton Woods era from 1945 to the final defection of the UK from the Smithsonian Agreement in 1972. A summary of the situation, and the associated political events is given in Table 13.5. The early years have been excluded since the existence of blocked-sterling credits and the turmoil of conversion from a wartime to a peacetime economy distorted the figures.

Table 13.5. The balance of payments and the UK domestic economy, 1954–80 (£ million)

Year	*Visible balance*	*Current balance*	*Surplus or deficit over-all*	*Economic 'Stop–Go' events in UK*
1954	−204	+117	+126	
1955	−313	−155	−229	
1956	+53	+208	−159	Industrial stagnation —Stop (1956–58)
1957	−29	+233	+13	
1958	+29	+344	+290	
1959	−115	+155	+18	Boom expansion—Go
1960	−401	−245	+325	Industrial stagnation —Stop (1960–62)
1961	−140	+22	−339	
1962	−100	+128	+192	
1963	−80	+131	−58	Boom expansion—Go
1964	−500	−355	−695	Industrial stagnation —Stop (1964–66)
1965	−223	−26	−353	
1966	−66	+101	−547	
1967 (Devaluation year)	554	−298	−671	Slow growth but increased unemployment (1967–68)
1968	−667	−272	−1410	
1969	−156	+460	+587	Stagnation (1969–71)
1970 (Pound floated)	−25	+773	+1287	
1971 (Smithsonian Agreement)	+280	+1084	+3146	
1972 (Pound floated)	−702	+154	−1265	Stagnation (1972–73)
1973	−2334	−736	−789	

Year	*Visible balance*	*Current balance*	*Surplus or deficit over-all*	*Economic 'Stop–Go' events in UK*
1974	−5350	−3379	−1646	Slumpflation
1975	−3333	−1674	−1465	
1976 (IMF standby arranged)	−3927	−1116	−3628	
1977	−2279	−284	+7362	
1978	−1546	+620	−1126	
1979	−3404	−1863	+1710	Slumpflation
1980	+1178	+3206	+1372	

(Source: *UK Balance of Payments*)

Periods of expansion and prosperity alternated with periods of economic restraint, higher taxes and 'credit' squeezes of various sorts. This succession of 'Go–Stop' policies caused considerable frustration to certain sections of the labour movement in the UK. The watershed can be firmly fixed at 1964 when a Labour Government with a small majority was elected on a programme which was based upon determination to end these periodic setbacks in the domestic economy. The call was for earnings-related welfare benefits (such as unemployment pay) and earnings-related standby payments when factories were on short time. The argument was to the effect that it was unfair to expect the unemployed and the under-employed to shoulder the burden of these industrial setbacks, which should be borne by the community at large. This may have sounded reasonable, especially to those who were to benefit. It proved to be wildly inflationary. The burden of extra personal taxation could only be pushed so far; attempts to load burdens of every sort on to the business sector (particularly as Selective Employment Tax, training levies, redundancy payments, equal pay, etc.) caused prices to soar and both home and export markets to be lost as higher prices permitted a flood of imports to replace home produced goods. It became uneconomic to invest in the UK, and growth fell to a bare 1 per cent per annum, or even lower. First there was stagnation, then stagflation and finally slumpflation. **Stagnation** implies that there is no growth. **Stagflation** implies that there is no growth in the economy and at the same time prices are rising, so that a lower standard of living must result for those on fixed incomes. **Slumpflation** implies that unemployment rises seriously at the same time that an absence of growth and rising prices are already adversely affecting many citizens.

A problem that had started with an imbalance of payments thus became one that was to plague the UK economy for a decade and a half, and seems likely to cause difficulties for many years to come. This probem is inflation. To control inflation the major industrial countries have instituted monetary (and fiscal) control policies which have seriously hampered growth in their economies and caused widespread unemployment. Refusal to accept 'Go–Stop' policies has resulted in 'Stop–Stop' policies, and a decline in the whole moral climate of society. The noble sentiments which called for the solution of social problems in the general interest of all have been to some extent at least debased by the intrusion of narrower, more sectarian interests.

13.7 Revision Test

Answers	*Questions*
—	**1.** What two types of transactions occur in international trade?
1. (*a*) The sale of goods and services. (*b*) The exchange of currencies to arrange payments for the goods and services.	**2.** What are the elements in any balance of payments?
2. (*a*) Visible trade; (*b*) invisible trade; (*c*) capital movements; (*d*) official financing.	**3.** What is visible trade?
3. Trade in goods, primary and secondary production of every sort.	**4.** What are 'invisibles'?
4. Services performed for others, such as transport, banking, insurance, communications and tourism.	**5.** Visible trade and invisible trade together, yield . . .?
5. A balance on current account which may be favourable or adverse.	**6.** What types of capital transactions occur on the balance of payments?
6. (*a*) Official loans to or from foreign governments. (*b*) Official movements to or from the IMF. (*c*) Private loans to or from foreign firms. (*d*) Private investment abroad, or by foreigners in the UK.	**7.** What is the final result of all current and capital movements?
7. A balance on the balance of payments, which may be favourable or adverse.	**8.** What is 'Official Financing'?
8. It is the process by which adverse or favourable balances on the balance of payments are dealt with.	**9.** How can we deal with an adverse balance?
9. (*a*) Pay up out of the reserves. (*b*) Borrow from foreign central banks to tide the nation over into the next period. (*c*) Borrow from such bodies as the IMF.	**10.** How can we deal with a favourable balance?
10. (*a*) Collect the balances due and put them into the reserves. (*b*) Lend the balances to 'debtor' nations facing difficulties. (*c*) Use the favourable balance to clear up long-term debt outstanding.	**11.** How may an exporting firm due to receive foreign money in the future safeguard itself against currency depreciation?

Answers	*Questions*
11. (*a*) By a 'forward transaction' on the foreign exchange market. (*b*) By borrowing the currency on the Euro-currency market at the same maturity and exchanging the currency borrowed on the spot market today. The loan will be repaid with the foreign money when the foreign customer settles his account.	**12.** What have been the chief methods of adjusting a disequilibrium on the balance of payments? Where do they take effect?
12. (*a*) The gold standard mechanism—the impact is on the home economy and the home standard of living. (*b*) The Bretton Woods system of managed flexibility. The impact was only to a small extent on the profit margins of the exporter: then control of the home economy had to begin—a 'Go–Stop' policy. (*c*) Floating exchange rates—the impact is largely on the exporter but eventually the home economy has to be controlled.	**13.** What has been the result of abandoning 'Stop–Go' policies?
13. Inflation has largely resulted from this, and the response has been fierce monetary controls. The problem is complex—God proposes (remedies) but man disposes (we are getting better at avoiding them).	**14.** Go over the page again until you are sure of the answers. Then try some of the questions in Appendix 1.

14

EUROPEAN AND INTERNATIONAL MONETARY INSTITUTIONS

14.1 The International Monetary System

Despite the existence of organisations such as the United Nations there is no truly international body, and the world consists of a collection of 'nation states' each of which seeks an optimum position in the economic community. Some states are bound together in a tight union such as the USA and the USSR. Others are members of more loosely knit organisations such as the European Economic Community or the European Free Trade Association. Free peoples are very loath to give up their sovereignty, and dictatorships even more so. If there can be no truly international political system there can equally be no truly international monetary system, for any agreement on monetary matters means constraints upon national policies which represent a loss of sovereignty. What we do have is a system where some very important groups have agreed to work together to reduce some of the worst effects of 'beggar my neighbour' policies, while other groups remain outside. In particular the Communist bloc does not have a genuine 'money' system as it is practised elsewhere, and cannot enter into the international monetary system in the same way as other nations.

Those nations which do play a part in the international monetary system do so because it is now widely realised that national prosperity depends to a considerable extent on international prosperity. A government which pursues policies which take no account of international monetary arrangements will soon find itself in difficulties and the optimum level of national prosperity is more likely to be achieved within a framework where all are seeking solutions to common problems.

The present inernational monetary system began in 1944 while the Second World War was still raging. The Bretton Woods System has already been described (see p. 181). Its system of fixed exchange rates, with only 1 per cent fluctuation allowed either side of the declared parity, meant that central banks had to step in and support their currencies whenever the limit of fluctuation was reached. To fight speculation the International Monetary Fund was available to lend 'tranches' of foreign exchange to members under pressure, but was able to exert strong pressure in return for a reform of their domestic economies to correct the imbalance of payments from which they were suffering.

What the Bretton Woods System did not attempt to do, for which the need is obvious to us now, was to take any direct steps towards the balanced development of the world economy. This is not suprising. At the end of the Second World War the emphasis was naturally enough on rebuilding shattered national economies: it has only become obvious in recent years that closer harmonisation of economies is the most likely way to resolve economic difficulties. The two major institutions of the Bretton Woods System were the International Monetary Fund and the International Bank for Reconstruction and Development.

14.2 The International Monetary Fund

The original establishment of the IMF has already been described (see p. 182). Its functions have now changed to such an extent that the 'founding fathers' might find it difficult to recognise their brain-child. The shift from the Bretton Woods system of 'managed flexibility' to floating exchange rates has reduced the demands made upon the Fund by the major economies who largely formed the membership (of 39) in 1947. The much enlarged membership today (140 in 1980) has a preponderance of 'Third World' nations whose economies are either OPEC economies, running huge balance of payments surpluses, or poor, energy-deficient economies running corresponding balance of payments deficits. The size of these surpluses and deficits (about £50 000 million in 1980) would have been unthinkable in 1947, when the vast majority of trade was bilateral trade.

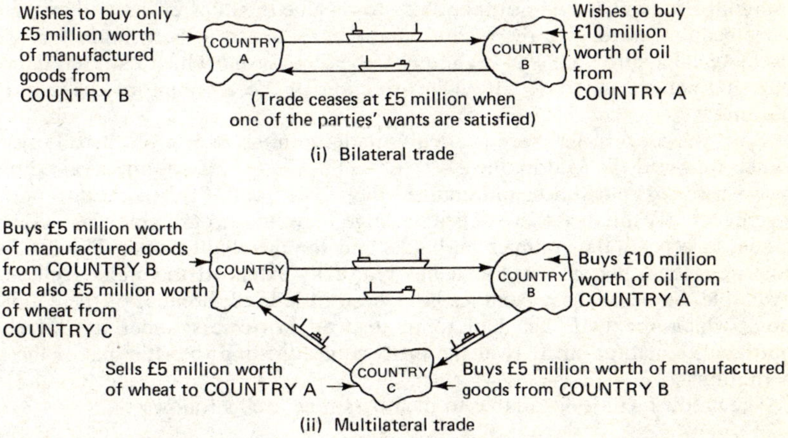

Fig. 14.1. Bilateral and multilateral trade: (i) bilateral trade—trade ceases at £5 million; (ii) multilateral trade—trade rises to £10 million.

Notes

(i) With bilateral trading agreements trade can only continue to the point where one country's requirements have been satisfied. In part (i) of the above diagram, Country B would like to import a further £5 million of oil from Country A but cannot do so because Country A does not want any more of Country B's manufactures. Trade could continue if Country B could pay the balance in gold, or some acceptable currency such as dollars, but in 1947 few nations could do so.

(ii) With multilateral trade the desire of Country C to buy goods from Country B enables world trade to rise in volume. Since Country A is willing to buy wheat from C, she will sell further oil to B, who will pay for it with manufactured goods delivered to C, who will pay for them by shipping wheat to A.

(iii) Clearly the more nations involved in world trade the better, and hence the IMF's interest in encouraging a multilateral trading arrangement between member nations.

One of the main aims of the IMF system was to put an end to bilateral trade. The objection to it is illustrated in Fig. 14.1, which shows why multilateral trade is preferable.

Despite problems in the early years, by the end of 1958 the free convertibility of currencies among major trading nations had been achieved and a period of prosperity based on multilateral trading began. It was to last until 1971. World trade grew by almost 10 per cent per annum, real incomes in the advanced nations doubled and inflation scarcely reared its ugly head.

There were some problems though. The first problem was that a decline in world liquidity became apparent as international trade expanded. It had already been noticed that a nation whose reserves fell to about 20 per cent of its international trade was extremely vulnerable to speculative pressure, and might need to borrow to finance its ordinary deficits. A General Agreement to Borrow was arranged in 1961, with the 'Group of Ten' leading banking nations extending credit facilities to one another (chiefly the UK) through the IMF. Later it was decided to create Special Drawing Rights (SDRs) to provide a further source of liquidity. These have already been described (see p. 184).

The second problem was the imperfect arrangements made at Bretton Woods about the solution of fundamental disequilibrium problems. The ability of debtor nations to devalue their currencies when faced with a fundamental disequilibrium on their balances of payments was of little help to them if creditor nations would not take steps to revalue their currencies and expand their economies to give the creditor nations a chance to earn more foreign exchange. The problem was beginning to be seen as one which required international action—not just national correction of the economy of the debtor nation.

Both these problems were suddenly made infinitely worse by the oil crisis which followed the Middle East War of 1973. The OPEC countries raised oil prices three or four times, and plunged the whole non-OPEC world into massive deficit. To finance these deficits a huge recycling programme was undertaken, largely by the commercial banks and the merchant banks. The IMF's role was not a major one, but it has gradually extended the credit facilities available. Some of these facilities have been little used, because of the conditions which the IMF has had to impose on borrowers under its (largely outdated) constitution. It is in the process of adjusting to criticisms of these conditions.

The credit facilities available to members now are as follows:

(*a*) **Ordinary credit tranches.** These have already been described (see p. 182).

(*b*) **The Compensatory Financing Facility.** A facility available to countries whose export earnings fall for temporary reasons only (crop failures, natural disasters, etc.).

(*c*) **The Extended Fund Facility.** This is available to countries who require longer than usual to repay—they have up to eight years to repay the funds borrowed.

(*d*) **The Gold Sales Trust Fund.** This fund was set up from the sale of gold when the IMF's constitution was changed so that gold was no longer required. One sixth of the gold was sold on the open market, the profits being used to establish a trust fund for the use of less developed countries (LDCs) facing balance of payments difficulties due to the oil price increases. The fund stands at present at about $4.5 billion, and to date almost 1000 million SDRs have been paid out to less developed nations to assist them with balance of payment difficulties.

(*e*) **The Supplementary Financing Facility.** This facility was raised from the oil-producing nations to assist countries placed in difficulties by the oil price rises.

(*f*) **The Bufferstock Facility.** This facility exists to help nations prepared to stockpile commodities at times when they are cheap because of a lack of demand in the recession currently prevailing.

This wider range of facilities has been helpful in bridging balance of payments deficits for many nations, but the Fund has come under criticism for its harsh borrowing conditions—i.e. the requirements it makes for countries to control their domestic economies so as to be able to repay the sums borrowed and avoid adverse balances of payments in the future. Often the money can be borrowed just as easily from the ordinary banking system without any conditions. It seems likely that the IMF will experiment with different kinds of conditions, which might make a positive rather than a negative approach to the economy. Thus if instead of the usual credit squeeze conditions it could insist on borrowers developing export industries or import-substitution industries it might help them to achieve a balance of payments in a more positive way. If we have a nation with a good clay soil importing bricks for construction projects the Fund might insist they develop a brick-making industry. One agency helping a developing country found this to be the case, and earned the enduring gratitude of the government concerned by showing them how easy it is to make bricks.

14.3 The 'World Bank'—the International Bank for Reconstruction and Development

The other major creation of the Bretton Woods Conference in 1944 was the World Bank, the International Bank for Reconstruction and Development, or IBRD for short. The Bank initially received capital contributions from members, but its loan activities are financed by floating bonds designated in dollars, against the security of its capital which currently stands at $80 000 million. Only 10 per cent of this has actually been supplied by members; the other 90 per cent may be called if necessary.

The original plan was for the Bank to evaluate projects put up to it by national governments and provide the funds at competitive rates of interest (because the Bank as a prestige borrower can borrow at very competitive rates). The project itself must be capable of repaying the interest and the capital over an agreed period. Apart from the immediate post-war years when reconstruction was important, the chief activities are in the developing world. The Bank faced a dilemma with many of its early projects, in that they tended to be 'prestige' projects which were sophisticated and capital-intensive, whereas the developing nations need generally less sophisticated, labour-intensive industries. Frequently the fundamental educational level of the less developed countries leaves them unqualified to operate the prestige projects which the Bank formerly tended to sponsor. A sophisticated project operated by a few expatriates does little to help a developing nation seeking to develop basis skills among a large and growing population.

The Bank has therefore turned to sponsoring more 'grass-roots' projects, basic training programmes, population-control schemes, improvements in basic agriculture, etc. These projects may call for research into the general development of an economy if the full implications are to be appreciated (and the loan successfully repaid).

The IBRD itself arranges the actual loans and supervises repayments. It had approximately $5000 million out in loans at the end of 1980. Its role is to approve projects proposed by government or government-backed institutions, and to find the funds.

Two other bodies supervise activities in less-developed countries (LDCs) and play a more direct part than the IBRD, although they are part of the World Bank group. They are:

(*a*) **The IFC (International Finance Corporation).** This corporation acts in the private sector in LDCs, attempting to develop and encourage private enterprise businesses. It takes a share in the equity capital of companies, securing finance for them and acting as adviser.

(*b*) **The IDA (International Development Association).** This association is active in the poorest countries, lending funds for approved projects at heavily subsidised interest rates and with repayment periods as long as 50 years. Many of its projects are for developing the infrastructure of a developing nation, roads, waterways, ports, airports, power supplies, irrigation, telecommunications, etc. Although project spotting is still the main basis of these activities the evaluation procedure tends to be too slow, and the trend is towards 'programme' lending, in which a general programme is outlined and aspects can be started upon at once, while the larger projects are evaluated and approved.

14.4 The General Agreement on Tariffs and Trade (GATT)

Among the major examinations of international monetary and trading arrangements held during and after the Second World War was a convention at Geneva which resulted in the General Agreement on Tariffs and Trade. The agreement was signed in 1947, by 23 nations; the number has now reached 70. The convention's aims had been as follows:

(*a*) To reduce existing trade barriers between nations.
(*b*) To reduce discrimination against particular nations.
(*c*) To promote international confidence in tariff policies by promoting consultation rather than unilateral action as a means of deciding tariffs.

Although not strictly speaking an institution, GATT has had a very powerful influence on the trading behaviour of the signatories. The US made very generous reductions in tariffs as a result of the 1947 negotiations, and these enabled European nations in particular to penetrate the North American market. This policy of the 'good creditor' enabled Europe to recover from many of its post-war difficulties.

In 1963 President Kennedy persuaded the American Congress to cut American tariffs if other nations would agree to do so by June 1967. This initiated a new round of discussions called the **Kennedy Round,** which ended in 1967 with massive tariff reductions by the industrialised nations. Some 70 per cent of their dutiable import tariffs were cut, and in two thirds of the cases the cuts were of 50 per cent. A 'product-by-product' basis was the most successful method of agreeing these tariff cuts; chemicals, pulp and paper, transport equipment, machinery, base metals and many more commodities had extensive cuts made. The one major flaw in the agreements was the extent to which primary producing countries were unable to gain concessions about agricultural products. Almost all nations have strategic or social reasons for not reducing agriculture. Developing nations tend to be agricultural, but the

Kennedy Round did not prove helpful in allowing them to specialise in the activities at which they have a comparative advantage. Instead the refusal of advanced nations to cut back their agricultural programmes has given developing nations an added incentive to diversify and industrialise their economies.

One principle of GATT is that the member countries agree to give 'most-favoured-nation' treatment to all members. This means that if Britain cuts her tariff on American-manufactured electrical goods by 10 per cent she will do the same for all GATT members. With 70 nations in the Agreement it means that practically the whole world shares in the tariff cut. Such tariff cuts are made much less likely as a result.

A major criticism of GATT comes from the 140 LDCs who object to it as a 'rich man's club'. They have put concrete proposals before the developed nations through the UN for a general system of free and preferential entry of manufactured and semi-manufactured goods from the LDCs to the developed countries. The suggestion was made to the second plenary session of the UN Conference on Trade and Development (Unctad) at New Delhi in 1967. The idea was to replace aid, which has unsatisfactory emotional, psychological and political overtones, with trade. A limited programme of unrestricted entry for some products began in 1971, against some opposition. The programme is called the **Generalised System of Preferences.** In 1974 a UN Report called for an extension of the system to include all textiles, leather and agricultural produce.

A new round of GATT negotiations, called the **Tokyo Round**, began in 1973. The US wanted major powers, particularly EEC countries, to abolish tariffs on industrial goods. Europe might have been prepared to consider this in return for American consent to give industrial preferences to the 'LDCs'. Europe proposed a deadline of 1975 for implementing these negotiations, but they were not concluded until 1979, and took effect on January, 1, 1980, except that one clause was not implemented until January 1, 1981. This clause opens non-military government procurement to foreign competition.

The liberalisation of trade is all very well, and a noble sentiment, but incredibly difficult to achieve in fact. Despite the great advances made under GATT the subtle avoidance of obligations can be achieved in many ways—for example, goods can be 'dumped' abroad by subsidising remotely. This means that producers are given indirect help in manufacture to cut prices overseas—cheap energy in the USA has undercut British synthetic fibres and caused 7000 redundancies. This is an effective breach of the GATT rules, as is child labour in Italy, South America, etc. The 1979 agreement for the first time entitled countries to introduce emergency safeguard action against 'disruptive imports'.

14.5 The European Monetary System (EMS)

The Bretton Woods monetary system collapsed in 1970, and was followed by the Smithsonian Agreement of December 1971. It proved impossible to maintain these new parities, and by June 1972 the pound sterling was floating. By February 1973 the dollar was under severe pressure and a further round of discussions produced a revaluation of the yen and the deutschemark—to no avail. By June 1973 flexible exchange rates were the order of the day, and 'managed floating' had arrived as a permanent feature of the monetary scene for the rest of the decade.

By late 1973 the first OPEC oil crisis had raised oil prices drastically around the world, and it is possible that floating exchange rates played some part in enabling the advanced nations to survive the drastic payments imbalances which resulted. Other factors were just as influential—in particular the sophisticated financial activities of the banking sector around the world in recycling oil funds to prevent a major world recession. The orders lost to industries from nations rendered impecunious by the rise in oil prices were replaced by orders from the oil-producing nations, as ports, airports, industrial plant and infrastructures were created. Such temporary activity—which is still continuing today—must eventually diminish, and will leave us with the fundamental dilemma of floating exchange rates: this is that floating exchange rates are an attempt to preserve national positions and achieve national objectives, when what is really required is a concerted international programme to achieve non-inflationary growth.

What is needed to foster growth, restore confidence and reduce unemployment is a planned expansion of world economic activity, achieved through compatible advances in the economic performance of the major trading nations. If expansion proceeds at a uniform rate in the major trading nations the relationships between their currencies (the exchange rates) should be stable. It goes without saying that this is not easy to achieve in a world where a very large Communist bloc exists which does not participate in a normal way in monetary arrangements. In view of the difficulties it seemed that a start could at least be made in the European Community by harmonising growth over a fairly lengthy period, and member governments have been taking steps to implement this policy.

At its inception—originally scheduled for January 1, 1979—the European Monetary System had three elements. First, it set up an exchange rate regime with parities established between pairs of currencies, and intervention margins requiring central banks to intervene to maintain the parity if necessary. Second, it aimed at the progressive convergence of the economies of member nations. Finally, it proposed the establishment of a new European currency, the **ECU (European Currency Unit)** and the eventual establishment of a **European Monetary Fund,** to extend credit to member nations in difficulty with their balances of payments. The UK does not yet participate in the scheme, the start of which was delayed for a few months until March 1979.

The European Monetary System is therefore a zone of monetary stability set up in March 1979 in which all the EEC countries except the UK participate, although the UK is not entirely outside the system.

14.6 Currency Parities

The zone of monetary stability is being achieved by the use of two types of parity: a grid of currency parities one with another, and an ECU parity in association with a new international currency basket—the European Currency Unit (ECU).

A Grid of Currency Parities. Of the 10 member nations of the EEC, Great Britain and Greece have not yet joined the EMS and Luxembourg has a currency that is tied to the Belgian franc. Six of the other nations—Ireland, Belgium, Denmark, West Germany, the Netherlands and France—have fixed a parity with one another's currencies, a grid of currency 'central rates' which will not change except for minor fluctuations of 2¼ per cent either side of the central rate. Remember that under the Bretton Woods System the maximum fluctuation allowed either side of parity was 1 per cent. In addition, Italy has arranged a central rate on the understanding that its exchange rate may vary as much as 6 per cent either side of the central rate.

There is a disadvantage about the use of this type of currency grid, in which central rates are laid down between pairs of currencies. This was the system adopted in the 'European snake', and the same measure of divergence, 2¼ per cent either side of the central rate was allowed. The point at which currencies diverge by 2¼ per cent is reached simultaneously by both currencies, but it cannot be determined which currency is at fault. The parity grid system used in the 'snake' required both nations to take corrective action at the same time. The currency which is depreciating relative to the other will be obliged to support its currency and lose reserves in the process; it will also be obliged to reduce its level of economic activity in the domestic market. Clearly this is a real disservice to its home nationals if in fact there is nothing wrong with its exchange rate, and the other country with an appreciating currency is the real cause of the divergence. Under the 'snake' system there was no obligation upon the country with an appreciating currency to do anything at all about the strength of the currency, except put away into its reserves the favourable balances it was achieving. Excessive (and even unnecessary) correction at the deflationary end of the scale by a weak country, and no counterbalancing expansion by the prosperous country, meant that overall the 'world' economy was declining. This lack of symmetry in the obligations imposed by the parity grid is corrected in the EMS system by a new device. To signal which nation really is at fault, an early warning system, called a **divergence indicator,** has been devised. This is achieved by a second set of parities, the ECU parities. Before these are explained we must first introduce the ECU.

The European Currency Unit (ECU). The introduction of the European Monetary System was marked by the introduction of a new world currency, the European Currency Unit, or ECU. This is a 'currency basket' made up as shown in Table 14.1.

Table 14.1. The European Currency Unit (ECU)

Currency	*Weight (Total 100)*	*Amount in units of each currency*
Deutschemark	33	0.828
Pound sterling	13	0.0885
French franc	20	1.15
Italian lira	10	109
Dutch guilder	10	0.286
Belgian franc	10	3.66
Luxembourg franc	(linked to BFr)	0.14
Danish krone	3	0.217
Irish punt	1	0.00759

This currency unit is used as the unit of measure for all accounts of EEC member states and as the common denominator for presenting financial statements. Actual settlements are made in currencies of the member states, converted from ECUs according to market rates published daily in the *Official Journal of the European Communities*.

The ECU is intended to be not only a unit of account, like its predecessor the European Unit of Account, but an actual currency to be held as a reserve asset and used for the settlement of international debts between central banks. Member banks are expected to surrender one fifth of their total reserves of gold and dollars in exchange for ECUs, and this they have done every three months. Even Britain joined in this arrangement in July 1980. The choice of a three-monthly period for these 'currency swaps' means that the countries do not lose control of their gold and dollar reserves, but resume control of them every three months, though in fact they simply roll them over into ECUs again as soon as the new rate for the ECU has been determined. The reserves are revalued every three months, and the 20 per cent is then taken up again in ECUs. Consequently a country's holding of ECUs does not get out of step with its actual reserves.

The intention was to proceed to Phase II of the EMS system, in which the policies of member countries would converge to promote the European economy, in March 1981—two years after the system started—with a genuine pooling of reserves and the creation of a European Monetary Fund. To date (early 1982) these plans have had to be shelved, and the policies of member states show little sign of converging.

ECU Parities. We now come to the ECU parities. Besides the central rates agreed between pairs of currencies, which form the currency grid described above, there is also an ECU central rate which ties each currency to the value of the ECU. It might seem unnecessary to have two systems of parity rates, one with the ECU and the other a parity grid with the other currencies. Because the ECU is a currency basket, any movement in a currency also moves the ECU, but to a smaller extent because the currency that has moved is only a small part of the ECU. Thus the deutschemark, which is 33 per cent of the ECU, moves the ECU by one third of any fluctuation in deutschemarks, while the movement of the Danish krone, which is only 3.1 per cent of the ECU, moves the ECU by only about one thirtieth. Consequently the parity with the ECU has to be calculated carefully for each currency, since the influence it will have is different. Central banks are rather secretive about exactly what ECU rate they are using.

If a currency starts to drift away from its agreed central rates on the parity grid this fluctuation is permitted, but when it gets three quarters of the way to the limit of $2\frac{1}{4}$ per cent it is in danger of reaching the limit of its fluctuation against the ECU. This alarm bell rung by the ECU limit is known as the **divergence indicator** and raises a presumption that the currency which is diverging must be brought back towards centre by action within its own domestic economy. The divergence from the basket of currencies (the ECU) clearly identifies which currency is at fault and must take corrective action. This also recognises the criticism much voiced under the Bretton Woods System that it is just as bad to be a creditor nation as to be a debtor nation. If the divergence from the ECU is evidenced by a weakening of the currency it is correct to contract the home economy and solve its adverse balance of payments problem. If the divergence is evidenced by a stronger currency, the correct thing to do is to expand that economy, and correct its favourable balance of payments problem. No longer can the strong nation claim, as West

Germany did under the Bretton Woods System, that it is for the 'sick to take the medicine'. It is just as bad to be too healthy—if what we are aiming at is convergent economies. (This is further explained below.) The strong must give the weak a chance, by allowing their imports to come in, etc.

In the first three years of operations four countries (Denmark, Belgium, France and Italy) rang the alarm bells as their currencies weakened, and had to take corrective action. Had the UK been a member it would have been the only nation to ring the alarm bells as its currency rose in value, and would have had to expand its economy—the very reverse of the policy of the Thatcher Conservative administration at the time.

14.7 Economic Convergence

The introduction of the EMS requires that member nations shall take steps to ensure stable exchange rates. This is believed to be possible only if the economies are of similar strengths, and the intention is that steps to strengthen the weakest economies shall be taken. This involves transferring resources to them, which will place some burdens on the stronger members. Studies are being undertaken to achieve a better understanding of the requirements for economic convergence.

Economic convergence cannot be achieved by any system of exchange rates, but must be achieved by an adequate coordination of economic policies. This is not easy because some countries like France, with a strongly centralised authority, can implement plans and projects more quickly than countries like Britain, where particular programmes have to be introduced adroitly against a barrage of complaints by interested parties, and where a particular government may be opposed to central planning of any sort. All countries are agreed that one important step is a convergence of inflation rates at a moderate level of inflation only, but this is by no means easy to achieve.

14.8 Stage II of the European Monetary System

The original plans for the introduction of the EMS envisaged a further stage in development which should have taken place within two years after the commencement, i.e. by March 31, 1981. This stage will set up the European Monetary Fund as a genuine supranational reserve fund to be used like the International Monetary Fund as a huge reserve to which any nation could turn whose currency was under speculative pressure. This fund would be a permanent one, unlike the three-month 'currency-swap' arrangement operated at present. The member nations would each give up 20 per cent of their gold and dollar reserves, and the same amount of their own domestic currencies, to form a pool of reserves to which all could turn when under pressure. In return for these currencies the nations would receive ECUs, but only half of them (those given in exchange for gold and dollars) could be used at once; the rest would be blocked, and only available in certain circumstances, with the approval of the governors of the central banks, as medium or long-term loans.

The full development of these ideas is awaited, but the deadline has long been passed. The plans to pool resources had to be shelved.

14.9 Intervention Arrangements in the European Monetary System

(*Note: A full account of these arrangements is given in the Bank of England Quarterly Review, June 1979, page 190*)

Whereas the European Unit of Account was defined as a fixed weight of gold, and unaffected by the exchange rates of the currencies contained in it, the ECU value depends upon the exchange rates of the currencies in the basket. Its value in dollars is found by taking the amount of each currency and converting it to dollars at the prevailing rate of exchange. Thus the 8.85 pence in the ECU when sterling is at £1 = £2.40 dollars is worth $0.2124. If the other currency contents in the basket are converted to dollars and then added, we might finish up with an ECU valued for the day at 1 ECU = $1.54. Once this dollar rate for the ECU is known it is possible to calculate the ECU value of any other currency from it. Thus the pound sterling at £1 = $2.40 dollars must be equal to

$$£1 = \frac{\$2.40}{\$1.54} \text{ ECUs}$$

$$= 1.558 \text{ ECUs}$$

Intervention and the Parity Grid. The theory of intervention on the parity grid is that the agreed 'central rates' may not be varied from by more than 2¼ per cent (Italy 6 per cent). Thus if 2.5 Deutschemarks are equivalent to 1 ECU and 6 French francs equal 1 ECU, the parity between the two is

$$2.5 \text{ DM} = 6 \text{ FF}$$

$$\text{or} \quad 1 \text{ DM} = 2.4 \text{ FF}$$

This gives us in Germany 1 DM = 2.4 FF and in France 1 FF = .416 DM. Each central bank is required to intervene to keep the market rate of its currency within 2¼ per cent of the cross-parity shown above, so that the Deutschemark must be kept between 1 DM = 2.454 FF and 1 DM = 2.346 FF. It would do this by announcing selling and buying rates for the French franc as shown, and expressing its readiness to deal in unlimited amounts with any bank at these rates. No one is going to sell Deutschemarks for less than 2.346 French francs when they can be sold to the Bundesbank for this figure, and no one is going to buy Deutschemarks for more than 2.454 French francs when they can be obtained from the Bundesbank at this rate.

Clearly, if all the rates of one currency with other currencies are written down, and then the margins either side calculated, we can build up a matrix of intervention rates at which the central bank must intervene. In practice the requirement to intervene would exert a stronger influence than at first appears, since a currency has 'central rates' fixed against all other currencies. If all currencies were at their parity points and the Deutschemark began to weaken, the Bundesbank would need to intervene if the rate fell to 1 DM = 2.346 FF, but if other currencies were themselves not at their parities the Deutschemark might hit the intervention point against one of these other currencies before it hit the intervention point against the French franc.

Intervention and the ECU. Although the ECU is a new European currency it is a currency that can only be used by central banks. Therefore a central bank cannot intervene to buy or sell its currency simply by publishing buying and selling prices and expressing its willingness to deal. It is alerted by the 'divergence indicator' not to the need to enter the market and buy or sell its currency, but to the need to control its economy. This means that its reaction to the ringing of the alarm bell is to raise interest rates or take other action to correct an adverse trend (a depreciation of its currency) or to lower interest rates and take other action to correct a 'favourable' trend (an appreciation of its currency). Once again the word 'favourable' is questionable—the country with an appreciating currency may be favourably placed, but it is doing a disservice to other nations because its economy needs to be adjusted to assist them with their deficits.

14.10 The European Investment Bank

The European Investment Bank (EIB) was created by the Treaty of Rome, which came into force on January 1, 1958, establishing the European Economic Community. The members of the European Investment Bank are the 10 member states of the Community, who have subscribed to its capital which stood at 7087.5 million units of account at December 31, 1979, the amount paid in or to be paid in being 911.25 million.

The EIB raises the bulk of the funds required for financing its lending operation on the capital markets of the Community and non-member countries, and on international markets. An independent public institution within the Community, the Bank's basic function under Article 130 of the Rome Treaty is to contribute, on a non-profit-making basis, to the balanced development of the Community. The EIB grants long-term loans from its own resources and furnishes guarantees to enterprises, public authorities and financial institutions to finance projects contributing to regional development, projects for converting undertakings or creating fresh activities, and projects of common interest to several member states or the Community as a whole.

Since 1979 the Bank has also, acting as agent for the Community, granted loans from the resources of the **New Community Instrument for Borrowing and Lending (NCI)** to finance infrastructure and energy projects deemed eligible by the Commission of the European Communities, and designed either to reduce regional imbalances to make the Community less dependent on outside energy supplies or to improve its self-sufficiency. The Bank also acts as agent in appraising and administering Euratom loans approved by the Commission.

Article 18 of the Bank's Statute, which forms a Protocol to the Treaty of Rome, provides for financing operations in non-member countries (on special authorisation from the EIB's Board of Governors). Authorisations are decided on a case-by-case basis for loans for certain types of project of particular importance for the Community—for example, in terms of its energy supplies. They are expressed as ceiling amounts when they concern loans in individual countries or groups of countries to be granted under Community agreements, conventions or decisions on financial cooperation with various non-member countries. Over the years, the Bank's theatre of operations has been extended to include Turkey, 58 states in Africa, the Caribbean and the Pacific which are signatories to the Lomé Convention, Portugal, Yugoslavia, Malta, the Maghreb countries (Algeria, Morocco and Tunisia), and the Mashreq countries (Egypt, Jordan, Lebanon and Syria), Israel and Cyprus. Apart from loans from the EIB's own resources, the Bank furnishes most of these countries with concessionary aid drawn from budgetary funds and managed on behalf of the Community.

Enterprises, public authorities or financial institutions wishing to contact the European Investment Bank apply directly to the Head Office of the Bank, or, in the case of projects located in Italy or the UK, to its Rome or London offices. Contact with the bank may also be made through the promoter's own bank.

14.11 Revision Test

Answers	*Questions*
—	**1.** Why are international monetary institutions necessary?
1. Because the interests of nation states conflict, and yet trade is essential.	**2.** What is the function of the IMF?
2. To assist member nations facing balance of payments problems.	**3.** List the facilities available to assist members.
3. (*a*) Ordinary credit tranches, (*b*) the Company Financing Facility, (*c*) the Extended Fund Facility, (*d*) the Gold Sales Trust Fund, (*e*) the Supplementary Financing Facility, (*f*) the Bufferstock Facility.	**4.** What is the chief objection raised by borrowers to IMF assistance?
4. Conditionality. The IMF insists on lending its funds only on condition that steps are taken to correct the imbalance of payments.	**5.** How could this criticism be met?
5. By taking a more positive approach to the needs of the economy in difficulty, rather than a negative approach of credit restriction and demand reduction.	**6.** What institutions form the 'World Bank Group'?
6. (*a*) The World Bank itself (IBRD), (*b*) the International Finance Corporation (IFC), (*c*) the International Development Association (IDA).	**7.** What are their functions?
7. The IBRD makes loans to national governments and officially-sponsored organisations. (*b*) The IFC promotes private enterprise by taking an equity share in approved firms. (*c*) The IDA offers 'soft' loans to the very poorest nations (subsidised rates of interest and long repayment periods).	**8.** What is GATT? What are its aims?
8. The General Agreement on Tariffs and Trade. It seeks to reduce tariff barriers and free trade from protectionist barriers.	**9.** What is the European Monetary System?

Answers	*Questions*
9. A zone of monetary stability in the European Community.	**10.** What are the basic elements in the EMS?
10. (*a*) A grid of currency parities with limited fluctuations either side of the central rates specified. (*b*) A new European currency, the ECU. (*c*) A system of ECU parities which lead to a divergence indicator when any currency begins to rise or fall. (*d*) A policy of 'convergent economies' which seeks to keep currencies together by strengthening weak economies.	**11.** Now try some of the written questions in Appendix 1.

15

EXCHANGE RATE SYSTEMS

15.1 Introduction

In theory there is very little difference between the trade which takes place between persons within regions of the same country and trade with foreigners. However, there is one complicating factor as regards foreign trade; the nation states use different currencies. This necessitates two sets of transactions when foreign trade occurs, one involving the goods or services, and another involving the currencies concerned. Generally this increases the degree of uncertainty surrounding transactions, and over the years international institutions have developed with the aim of reducing this uncertainty.

This is an area where governments may also find themselves involved, since stable trading flows are assisted by the reduction of risk. Some forms of official insurance, such as Export Credit Guarantees Department insurance, are designed to reduce risks in the export trades which ordinary insurance organisations are not prepared to cover.

Government activities in directing the economy of a nation are also affected by the exchange rate system adopted, since the choices open to the Government vary—some systems, it is claimed, having an automatic element of adjustment for achieving a balance of trade and payments built into them.

Generally debate in the area of international exchange and payments polarises around two considerations:

(i) Will there be fixed, or free, rates of exchange?

(ii) How will sufficient amounts of acceptable liquidity be provided for trading purposes?

Of course the two areas are not independent of each other!

15.2 The Theory of Rates of Exchange

Since different economies use different currencies, the relative valuation of these currencies becomes a matter of importance for businesses, governments and economists. If economies were completely closed, i.e. self-contained with no contact outside their own boundaries, then the problem of exchange rates—rates at which different currencies exchange for each other—would never arise. In the real world economies are not self-contained and some level of trade with 'outsiders' is a feature of all but the most primitive of societies. It should come as no surprise, therefore, to find that the *basic* determination of a currency's rate of exchange depends upon the volume of external trade in goods and services. There are, of course, complicating matters such as capital movements for both investment and speculative purposes, but the process can best be illustrated by temporarily ignoring these.

Any economy engaged in international trade will have a flow of imports and a flow of exports. With the exception of those instances where barter is being used (and barter is more common in international than in domestic trade) the flow of imports will have to be paid for in currencies acceptable to the country of origin. Payment for the flow of exports will usually be demanded in the form of the exporting country's own currency, or some other acceptable currency. This does not mean that traders themselves actually handle foreign currency which they have acquired. Instead, they normally work through their bank and/or their trading partner's bank. The bank or banks involved have very close contacts with the **foreign exchange market**—the market where currencies are traded for each other. An example based, for simplicity, on only two countries—the UK and the Federal Republic of Germany—will serve to illustrate how the foreign exchange market operates.

The demand for Deutschemarks will be a reflection of the demand for German goods by British customers, but the supply of Deutschemarks will be a reflection of the demand for UK goods by German customers. Conversely, the demand for sterling will mirror the demand for UK goods by German customers but the supply of sterling will reflect the demand for German goods by British customers. Fig. 15.1 shows the way in which the exchange rate between the two countries will be determined, so far as the basic trade in goods and services is concerned.

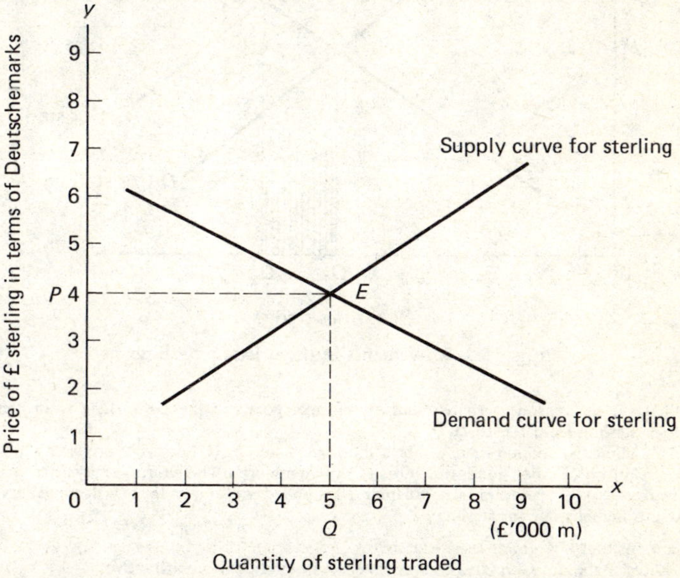

Fig. 15.1 Determination of the rate of exchange for sterling against Deutschemarks.

Notes

(*a*) The supply curve for sterling slopes upwards to the right. This indicates that few UK citizens wish to buy German goods when the value of the pound is low in DM, but as the value of sterling rises more and more pounds are attracted onto the market.

(*b*) The demand curve for sterling slopes downwards to the left. This indicates that when sterling is very highly priced (£1 = 7 DM) few Germans wish to buy British goods, but when sterling is very cheap (£ = 2 DM) the quantity of sterling demanded is very large.

(*c*) Where the two curves intersect at E, the equilibrium exchange rate position, the demand for sterling and the supply of sterling will be in equilibrium, and the price will be fixed at £1 = 4 DM, with a quantity of £5000 million of sterling being exchanged for DM.

(*d*) This is the basic way a rate of exchange is determined reflecting the volume of goods and services which citizens of the two countries wish to trade.

The rate of exchange, P is the equilibrium price of sterling. Like any other equilibrium price it will persist until the basic factors which underlie it change. Suppose that some of the factors affecting the demand for pounds change *in favour of the pound*, e.g. the prices of UK exports fall relative to those goods and services available from competitors, or supplies from competitors fall in quantity or become erratic. This has the effect of increasing demand for sterling—that is, of shifting the demand curve for the currency to the right, more being asked for at every price than in the previous situation. Fig. 15.2 illustrates this and the notes explain the diagram.

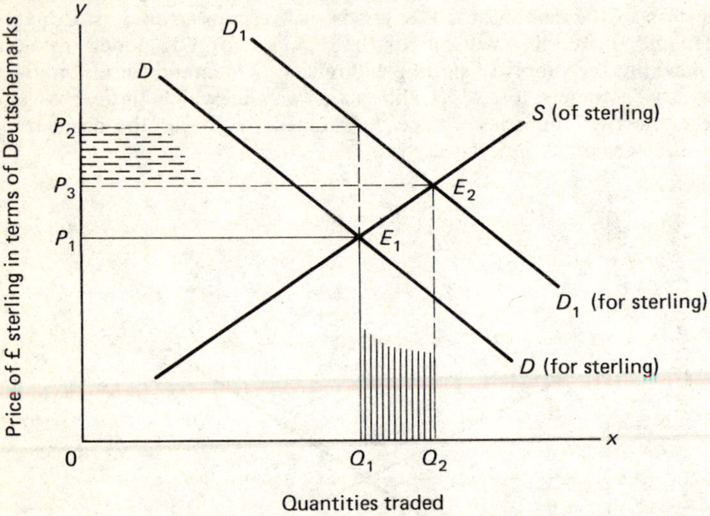

Fig. 15.2. Movements in the price of sterling.

Notes

(*a*) Whatever the reason (perhaps relatively cheaper goods in the UK), there is an increase in demand for sterling from DD to D_1D_1.

(*b*) In the immediate period there will be a shortage of sterling (UK citizens preferring to purchase their own, relatively cheaper, goods rather than German imports). This shortage may drive up the price of sterling from P_1 to P_2, the point where a quantity supplied of Q_1 meets the new demand curve D_1D_1.

(*c*) At this higher price for sterling:

(i) Germans find UK goods less attractive.
(ii) UK residents find German goods cheaper and therefore more attractive.

Therefore there is a gradual increase in demand for German goods which extends the supply of sterling. As the supply of sterling rises from Q_1 towards Q_2 the price of sterling falls from P_2 towards P_3. This induces Germans to take more UK goods—to demand more sterling as the price falls.

(*d*) Eventually a new, appreciated, equilibrium price is arrived at which occurs at point E_2, price P_3.

(*e*) The new equilibrium exchange rate of E_2 causes (at least in theory), through the adjustments outlined in (*c*) above, an equilibrium between the value of imports and the value of exports, i.e. a balance on the balance of payments.

The Elements of Price in Goods from Abroad

Goods purchased from another country have two elements in their price:

(i) The domestic price—in other words, the price quoted in domestic currency. For example, a woollen sweater might have a price in the UK of £8.

(ii) The exchange rate calculation. Those who buy from other countries must normally take into account the exchange rate between their own currency and that of the country from which they are buying. Variations in the exchange rate can cause 'price' changes even though the domestic price does not change at all. Suppose a German purchaser wishes to buy a UK woollen sweater. The UK domestic price is £8, but the German purchaser is interested less in the sterling price than in the amount that has to be paid in Deutschemarks. If £1 exchanges for 4 DM, then the price of a sweater is 32 DM. If, however, the sterling price does not change but the pound sterling appreciates to £1 = 5 DM the same sweater now costs 40 DM. This clearly will be a factor discouraging German purchasers of UK goods, but is likely to *encourage* UK purchasers of German goods. A German cassette recorder costing domestically 240 DM under the old exchange rate would cost £60 to a British customer but under the new exchange rate only £48.

15.3 Floating Exchange Rates

When countries allow the exchange rates of their currencies to move up and down in response to factors relating to trade in the fashion outlined above, their currencies are said to be **floating freely.** The original concept of a 'free float' was that market forces would prevail in the foreign exchange market, and achieve an automatic balance of payments. If sterling, for example, was in weak demand because foreigners believed British goods to be too highly priced for their quality, its price would automatically fall against other currencies. This fall in sterling would continue until the effective price of British goods was lowered to the point where foreigners believed them to be good value for money.

This concept has proved to be rather naive, because of the presence of speculators in the market. The fact is that in a sophisticated market like the foreign exchange market there is no special class of speculators; all holders of foreign exchange are potential speculators. Any attempt to force down the price of a currency like sterling, which many institutions and nations are holding as part of their reserves, will damage those holding the currency, if they do not join in. In any massive speculation against a currency those who hold it must join in unless someone—a central bank—is prepared to step in and protect them by 'managing' the currency. The aim should be to prevent the currency falling if the pressure upon it is purely speculative, but to allow it to fall if the decline in value is simply due to weak demand for British goods and services.

It follows that very few countries have indulged in a completely free float, feeling that the external values of their currencies are too important an issue to leave to market forces over which they may exercise no control. Therefore when a country allows the external value of its currency to vary, or is forced to allow it to vary, it normally chooses one of the following modified methods:

(i) **The Managed Float.** This is similar to the free float in that a country's currency will move according to market forces, but the authorities intervene in the market when they feel it is in the nation's interest. At certain times they will sell their own currency—if they feel its value is rising too much relative to other currencies. At other times they may buy their own currency in order to push up its relative value. By agreement amongst members of the IMF, such interventions are only made to protect a currency when it is unjustifiably under pressure, and are not made to pursue narrow national objectives of a 'beggar-my-neighbour' nature.

(ii) **The Crawling Peg System.** Here the exchange rate follows market forces, but only very slowly. Essentially, the crawling peg limits the degree of movement possible in any period by restricting the permitted movement in the value of the currency to a specific percentage per period—say a year. In subsequent periods the march of the currency with market forces will be allowed but again only by the specified amount per period.

(iii) **The Adjustable Peg System.** Under this system rates of exchange are allowed to move either side of the chosen parity by a stated amount. However, if a persistent disequilibrium occurs on a country's balance of payments, a new parity can be adopted through a devaluation or revaluation.

(iv) **The Fixed Peg with Minor Fluctuations.** Here a parity is adopted and only small fluctuations either side of this parity are allowed, e.g. 1 per cent up or down.

The above methods illustrate descending degrees of flexibility. There remains, of course, the complete opposite of the free float: the situation in which countries do not allow the external value of their currencies to vary at all. This is the **absolute fixed peg.** The state of the nation's trade is rarely stable over long periods, and so the choice of fixed or almost fixed exchange rates imposes some problems for an economy. These relate to the methods by which equilibrium on the balance of payments can be achieved. With floating rates the value of a country's currency can vary and bring about price changes which can eradicate both balance of payments deficits and surpluses. With fixed rates of exchange this method of adjustment is of course not available. Alternatives therefore have to be found. A favourite is for governments to intervene and affect either the demand for, or the supply of, their own currency. Fig. 15.3 illustrates how they might do this.

Fig. 15.3 might suggest the idea that fixed rates of exchange can only be operated with continuous government intervention, either in the domestic economy or in the foreign exchange market using funds such as the Exchange Equalisation Account. However, the best-known and longest-running fixed exchange rate system, the Gold Standard, had virtually no positive role for the governments which subscribed to it, and was famed for its supposed 'automatic equilibrium' on balance of payments. (The workings of the Gold Standard and other systems have already been described—see Chapter 13.)

15.4 A Role for Gold

The problems surrounding international liquidity outlined above have prompted many commentators to argue for a return to a system based upon gold. The agreement at Bretton Woods was effectively the introduction of a gold exchange standard based upon the dollar, where countries held their reserves partly in gold, but increasingly in the form of convertible currencies. Members of the IMF linked their exchange rates to the dollar (convertible into gold) and agreed to deal in gold only at the official price—this was $35 an ounce between 1934 and 1971. In 1968 at Washington, a meeting of central bankers agreed on a two-tier pricing structure—one for the 'commercial' market, to be determined by market forces, and an official rate (still $35) at which central banks would deal with each other. The weakness of the dollar eventually culminated in the ending of its convertibility into gold in 1971, at which time official price of gold rose to $38 an ounce, and in 1973 to $42 an ounce.

During the 1970s the IMF decided that gold should be 'demonetarised'—effectively that the official price should end and free dealing in gold between

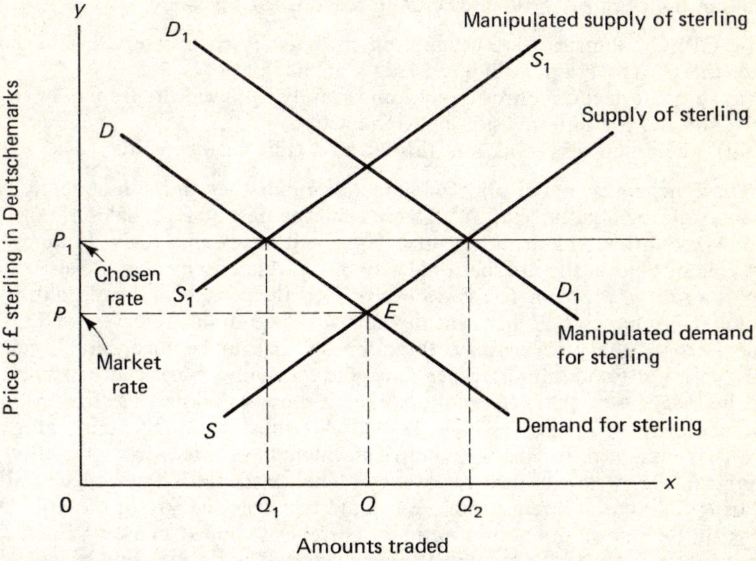

Fig. 15.3. Government influence on the exchange rate.

Notes

(i) The chosen rate of exchange for the UK is P_1.

(ii) P_1 is a higher rate than the market feels is correct for sterling; the equilibrium point according to the market is at the point where the demand and supply curves intersect, *E*, giving a price of *P* and a quantity traded of *Q*.

(iii) The monetary authorities have two alternatives:

(*a*) They can enter the market with a reserve of foreign exchange (in this instance DM) and purchase pounds, thus pushing the demand curve to the right to D_1D_1 and establishing a market rate which is identical to the chosen rate. The pounds it purchases will be taken into the reserve fund (in the case of the UK the Exchange Equalisation Fund). The difficulty with this alternative is that the authorities might have to go on supporting the pound against continuing (possibly increasing) pressure and they may not have a bottomless fund of reserves. In this case they may eventually have to devalue, i.e. choose a lower rate than P_1, and bow to the pressure of the market.

(*b*) The second alternative is to work on the supply curve of pounds, not the demand for pounds. This requires the authorities to force a contraction of the supply of pounds reaching the foreign exchange market. This can only be done by reducing the effective standard of living at home. Direct reductions could be achieved by prohibiting foreign travel or the import of foreign goods, but these invite retaliation from other countries. The more usual method has been the reduction of total monetary demand by increases in taxation, reduced government spending, higher interest rates, etc. The effect of such actions is to move the supply curve of pounds to the left (S_1S_1 on the diagram) and achieve the chosen exchange rate at quantities of Q_1 traded at the chosen price P_1. The difficulty with this exchange rate is that the need to depress the home economy may be inappropriate for the domestic social and political state of affairs, with high unemployment and vociferous opposition from those affected.

central banks be allowed. Such a policy benefited those central banks which had accumulated gold and ended a debate over the revaluation of gold which was prominent in the 1960s, but rejected then on the grounds of conveying advantage on producers and hoarders. The UK benefited little from the freeing of gold, having moved most of its reserves into dollars.

One of the startling developments in the late 1970s was the rapid rise in the value of gold, which shot from $200 an ounce in London in early 1978 to $850 an ounce in early 1980. The main reasons for this were:

(i) OPEC countries were attempting to diversify their reserves, especially after the US Government blocked Iran's dollar holdings.
(ii) A great deal of confusion and uncertainty followed the Iranian crisis in 1979 and the Russian invasion of Afghanistan.
(iii) The dollar was weak and this led to a transfer into gold.

These increases in the price of gold (although they did subsequently fall away from the high price of $850) were achieved despite large sales of gold by the IMF and the American treasury. The result has been a revived interest in the role of gold in the international economy, which many economists would see as a retrograde step. The EMS has revived the official status of gold, with members exchanging 25 per cent of their gold and dollar reserves for ECUs. The rise in the gold price has made these deposits, held in the European Monetary Co-operation Fund, about 75 per cent gold and only 25 per cent currency.

The IMF has no plans to sell more gold at present and may use the revalued balance of its gold reserves to back a 'dollar substitution account'. This account is designed to enable countries which have excessive quantities of (depreciating) dollars in their reserves to exchange them for a new type of SDR bearing full market interest rates. We could therefore see a return to gold as a backing for international and national currencies, but at market values, not fixed values as under the Bretton Woods System. The result would be a victory for the critics of fixed gold values, particularly the French in the 1960s, and a great benefit to gold producers (Russia and South Africa—two nations which critics would say do not particularly deserve rewards from the international community of nations). Developments in these changing attitudes to gold and SDRs are taking place month by month, and the reader should refer to the financial and economic press for developments.

15.5 Revision Test

Answers	*Questions*
—	**1.** What is the basic factor determining the rate of exchange between countries?
1. The volume of external trade in goods and services in which nations engage.	**2.** What determines the demand for a currency such as sterling?
2. The desire of foreigners to buy British goods and services or to hold sterling in their reserves.	**3.** What determines the supply of a currency such as sterling?

Answers	*Questions*
3. The willingness of UK citizens or Governments to buy foreign goods and services, and to invest or lend money abroad.	**4.** Suppose there is an imbalance in the demand for, and the supply of sterling, at a time of floating exchange rates. How will a balance of payments be achieved?
4. The pound sterling will float to an equilibrium point where demand and supply are in equilibrium?	**5.** What would happen if exchange rates were fixed?
5. Pressure would develop for a devaluation (or revaluation) of the currency and the Government would be forced to take action to control the domestic economy.	**6.** List the methods of achieving a balance, in descending order of flexibility.
6. (*a*) A free float, (*b*) a managed float, (*c*) the crawling peg, (*d*) the adjustable peg, (*e*) the fixed peg with minor fluctuations, (*f*) the absolute fixed peg.	**7.** Are you sure what each of these means?
7. See Section 15.3 for the answers.	**8.** What role might gold yet play in the exchange system?
8. It seems certain to be regarded as a valuable element in the reserves of any country, and to act as a backing for the SDR, the ECU and any similar international currency basket.	**9.** Now try the written questions in Appendix 1.

16

CAPITAL MOVEMENTS AND INTERNATIONAL AID

16.1 Introduction

In Chapter 13 capital movements were briefly mentioned in relation to the balance of payments. There it was stated that an inflow of capital amounted to a plus item on the balance (virtually an export) whilst the outflow of capital amounted to a minus item (virtually an import). It is intended in this chapter to examine capital movements as a whole, and international aid in particular, in more detail.

In general, foreign currencies are demanded and supplied for capital transactions in order that investing and lending can take place across frontiers. Such capital movements can be classified into two broad groups, long-term capital movements and short-term capital movements. Some of these movements are said to be **autonomous**, by which we mean that they take place because of the needs and wishes of firms and governments to invest in long-term projects and carry out capital construction programmes. They have a life and purpose of their own, and are not simply **accommodating** capital flows of borrowed funds to meet deficits on the balance of payments, or surpluses loaned to foreigners in temporary difficulties. Thus an official loan to Nigeria to help finance a hydroelectric scheme is an autonomous flow which takes place because of the need for capital for the project. An official loan to Nigeria to finance a temporary deficit in the Nigerian balance of trade with the UK would be an accommodating flow, part of the 'official financing' referred to in Chapter 13.

16.2 Long-term Capital Movements

Long-term capital movements are generally regarded as 'autonomous' in nature; they play a part in the active shaping of the balance of payments rather than merely responding to other flows. Thus direct investment in an overseas automobile manufacturing and assembly plant has an immediate effect upon the balance of payments in the year of investment, where it constitutes an adverse movement as the capital flows out, making the balance of payments less favourable. Of course, in the years ahead it will have a series of favourable effects upon the balance of payments because it gives rise to a flow of dividends over time. Such invisible flows of investment income can have very significant effects upon the national income and on the investment policies a country is able to pursue. In the years before 1914 Britain invested half of the annual growth in capital available to her overseas, but there was no drain apparent in the balance of payments, since overseas investments provided an income of roughly the same amount—her new investment abroad was in fact financed by past investment abroad.

A great deal has been written on the likely effects of capital outflows on an economy, and the following are points worth noting:

(*a*) An investment in a key domestic area will always increase the level of national income more than an investment abroad, providing of course that the domestic economy is not fully employed. This is because the multiplier effect of domestic investment is greater than overseas investment; the former produces incomes for all factors whilst the latter yields only profits. Full employment, though, makes domestic factors scarce and expensive, while the eventual inflationary effects might also reduce the attraction of investment at home.

(*b*) When capital movements are made in the form of direct investment abroad (in the sense of direct business investment) the effect upon the home economy depends upon the level of technology which the investment utilises. Where direct investment overseas involves the export of new processes or products, the fruit of developing technology, it is likely to have the greatest effect in stimulating exports and the least effect in deterring them. If a 'standard' industry only is being established then the call on equipment from the home country will probably be at a minimum. In such circumstances the investment should be regarded (from a purely economic standpoint) only in respect of its rate of return—the beneficial effects which flow from it in the form of further export orders are likely to be difficult to calculate. Probably the rate of return is the 'correct' criterion for non-direct or 'portfolio' investment in overseas financial securities also.

(*c*) Military expenditure overseas usually involves a very low automatic feedback of demand to the home economy. A great proportion of such expenditure often represents installations abroad where materials, labour, etc., are procured locally. Even the personnel from the 'investing' country are likely to spend the bulk of the capital transferred to them in the country in which they are stationed.

(*d*) One of the most hotly debated areas in the field of capital transfers is the question of overseas aid. It is a matter of much argument as to which party receives most benefit from aid—the donor or the recipient. The focus for this dispute is the balance of payments of the donor country. Recipients claim that donor countries more often than not give aid in tied form and that such a method of 'giving' guarantees the maximum favourable effect upon the donor's balance of payments. This is an important area and will be considered in more detail later.

16.3 Short-term Capital Movements

Short-term capital movements are generally regarded as having an important role in the UK balance of payments. The main reasons are:

(*a*) The position of sterling as an international currency—a 'key' currency.
(*b*) The position of London as an important international financial centre.

Short-term capital flows become important for government because of their size relative to official reserves and because of their volatility.

The impact of short-term capital movements relative to the size of the official reserves is a problem faced particularly by countries operating with a fixed exchange rate. Here reserves are necessary in order that the country can buy its own currency and thus maintain its value on the foreign exchange markets. If the potential movements in short-term capital seem likely to 'swamp' the reserves available then the brunt of adjusting to such capital movements falls upon the internal economy—a change in demand management policy is necessary. Should there be a 'run on sterling', with the UK on a fixed exchange rate, the result would be a policy to contract domestic demand and restore 'confidence'.

If the economy operates with floating exchange rates, however, movements in short-term capital are likely to be felt primarily in the form of variations in the exchange rate rather than in reserves. An outflow of capital will cause the depreciation of sterling and an inflow will cause sterling to appreciate. However, the effects of these exchange rate changes will in the end be the same as devaluations/revaluations brought about by deliberate policy. They are likely to have important internal repercussions for the economies concerned.

A further problem with short-term capital flows is their volatile nature. Generally, short-term capital movements can be split into two types:

(*a*) Speculative flows.
(*b*) Non-speculative flows.

Speculative capital movements are those made in order to take advantage of anticipated changes in spot exchange rates; in other words, they are made in order to gain profit from expected variations in a country's rate of exchange over time. A hint of, say, a sterling devaluation or depreciation is likely to cause those who hold sterling assets to switch into foreign currencies—with the intention of switching back again later when a greater amount of sterling can be obtained (once the rate of exchange has depreciated).

Non-speculative capital movements depend upon traders' and investors' views of the interest rates to be earned around the world, and the security of the haven offered to their funds. Thus high interest rates in a stable country like the UK will attract short-term capital inflows, which will flow out elsewhere if interest rates fall or the economy appears to be weakening. Non-speculative flows are also influenced by investors' views of how the future rate for a currency might be expected to vary from its spot rate. The object here is to minimise the risks involved in potential variation, rather than to take advantage of variation (as in the case of speculation).

The volatility of short-term capital movements can thus be seen to depend upon a complicated collection of factors amongst which perhaps the most important is expectations. Official financing will always play a large part in short-term flows, to 'accommodate' surpluses and deficits on international payments.

16.4 Government Influences over Capital Movements

In a situation where capital movements can have profound influences not only on the current balance of payments but also on the balance of payments in the years ahead, what can a government do to control or influence capital flows? The answer is that governments do not seem to have a great deal of room to manoeuvre. The UK abandoned foreign exchange controls in 1979 after 40 years of restrictions. This change of policy is discussed below, but clearly outright control of all foreign exchange movements by home nationals is one answer to the problem.

The other options are:

(*a*) To vary the domestic interest rate. This has a strong influence upon the attraction of a country as a resting place for short-term funds. There are problems in the use of this device. The first of these is that there may be a conflict between the rate of interest called for by conditions within the domestic economy and that needed to bring about the required capital movements. The second is that if other countries vary their own rates of interest then the object of the exercise can be defeated.

(*b*) The government's agencies can attempt to manage the forward exchange rate and therefore take out some of the risks attendant upon holding a currency such as sterling. The intention is that the risk-free nature of the currency in the 'short-term' future will prove attractive to those with funds to place on short-term deposit.

It has already been stressed that such management policies must be carried out within the spirit of the IMF's charter, and consideration must be shown for the impact of the policies on other countries.

Experience in the UK has suggested that neither of these measures is effective when a currency comes under severe strain. Severe speculative pressure is of course strongest when a country has a fixed exchange rate, but it is still possible to be under a great deal of pressure when exchange rates are floating if a currency is an influential world currency.

Exchange Control

For 40 years, from 1939 to 1979, a system of exchange control operated through the Bank of England which effectively rationed the use of foreign exchange as far as British nationals were concerned. Although this gave the Treasury a tight control over the movements of currency by domestic firms and individuals, it could not be effective over the activities of foreign nationals holding sterling. For the first 30 of these 40 years sterling was still a major 'reserve' currency, with other countries holding at least some of their reserves in sterling. The temptation for foreign individuals, banks and governments to switch these reserves about whenever the UK economy faltered or recovered brought massive speculative pressure on sterling.

The main reasons for exchange control are to conserve UK gold and foreign currency reserves, monitor the balance of payments and support sterling's role in the world as a major trading currency, and to some extent—still—as a reserve currency. The situation in 1979, as North Sea oil came on stream, was that sterling was rising in value as a petro-currency, and also as a reflection of avowed 'strong' Government policies in the domestic field. This strength of sterling coincided with increased pressure from membership of the EEC to relax controls over certain foreign exchange movements—notably direct investment overseas, portfolio investment overseas and movements connected with emigration, gifts and dependants' payments. These relaxations would give greater freedom to individuals and business firms and permit economic choices denied under exchange control.

By late 1979 the relaxations had revealed that a total dismantling of control procedures might as well take place, and they were finally abandoned on October 24, 1979, except for controls affecting Rhodesia at that time. For the first time in 40 years foreign exchange was readily available for all the following purposes:

(*a*) Outward direct investment for projects in overseas countries. In addition, the requirement on companies to repatriate two thirds of all foreign profits was removed. Companies were also free to arrange repayments of foreign loans as they thought fit, and not within a limited time scale as previously.

(*b*) Outward portfolio investment. This permitted the purchase of foreign stocks and shares without restriction, and also the borrowing of foreign currencies to purchase them. Interest on such loans could now be paid in a perfectly free way; formerly it had to be financed out of the foreign earnings from the investment.

(*c*) Gold coins. The restrictions on dealings in gold coins, medals, etc., were removed in June 1979.

(*d*) Personal transactions. It is now possible to obtain such foreign currency as an individual wishes for personal travel, emigration, purchase of private property abroad and cash gifts, dependant's allowances, etc.

Although the dismantling of controls opened new avenues of investment to business, it left the Bank of England somewhat less informed than previously about balance of payment affairs, and certainly led to heavy movements of British capital abroad, but the drain was more than offset by foreign capital moving into the UK.

16.5 Capital Movements for Overseas Aid

About 140 countries of the world are classified as LDCs—less developed countries. Of this number approximately 20 are NICs—newly industrialised countries. That the NICs reached their relatively high status is partly due to capital transfers from developed countries, in the form of overseas aid. If the remaining 120 are to have any real hope of increasing the living standards of the bulk of their populations, they too will require assistance from developed countries. They really need large transfers of resources in order that they can implement capital investment programmes necessary for growth.

It is possible for developed countries to offer assistance in a variety of ways:

(*a*) **Technical Aid.** Most technical aid involves the recruitment of skilled personnel in the donor country and its subsequent employment in the recipient country, the whole being paid for by the donor. Such aid can be very important since specialists not available in the developing world may be required to plan and implement programmes.

Another way of providing technical aid is for the donor country to undertake the education of personnel from the developing country in the donor country's own educational institutions.

(*b*) **Commodity Aid.** This form of aid can be vitally important from the point of view of keeping populations alive. Many famines are prevented or their effects mitigated by the hasty provision of food aid, particularly where war or national disaster has aggravated the already dire conditions which are the normal lot of much of the world's population. However, commodity aid of this type does little for the process of long-term development (rarely is commodity aid in the form of energy or essential raw materials). It might postpone the Malthusian crisis and encourage the country to support a population which is larger than the one it can hope to support from internal resources. Such an increased population might also necessitate the diversion of scarce resources from development to survival. Further, if the donor countries, who perhaps have surpluses of the commodities they give (without adverse effect upon reserves of foreign exchange!), later reduce the finance they *would* have provided, commodity aid becomes positively unhelpful to the long-term process of development.

(*c*) **Financial Aid.** Perhaps the most useful kind of aid is the provision of foreign exchange by the donor country in order that the recipient can purchase the materials and services it needs for development. In theory the most useful manner in which this provision can be made is one where the recipient has the use of such foreign currency entirely without 'strings'. However, because most financial aid is provided on a bilateral basis (donor directly to recipient) it is easy for 'obligations' to be imposed along with the granting of aid. The most frequent of such obligations involves the tying of aid. This means that the recipient receives a 'credit' from the donor and this credit must then be spent in the donor country or in a country of the donor's choosing, and perhaps even upon items which the donor specifies!

The advantages from the point of view of the donor are obvious. There is a favourable balance of payments effect (the items sold offsetting the loan or 'gift' of aid). Other effects are the reduction of stocks of unwanted items (perhaps with employment overtones), political capital if a project is prestigious, and a response to the practice of other countries of tying aid. Long-term political influence and markets may be extended as a result. However, none of these reasons finds much sympathy amongst developing countries who often accuse developed nations of giving aid in order to benefit their own rather than the recipients' economies.

There has been, and still is, a great deal of debate over how international aid should be provided, and also how much official financial aid should be contributed to the poorer nations.

As a 'jumping-off point', UNCTAD (the United Nations Conference on Trade and Development) at its first session in 1964 passed a resolution recommending that the economically advanced countries should supply the developing countries with financial resources which amounted to 1 per cent of their national income, or as close to 1 per cent as could be managed (in the early 1970s 0.7 per cent of national income was regarded as a realistic target). Such assistance is regarded, for target purposes, as being capital flows which are official, for the purpose of development, and concessional in that at least 25 per cent of the sum is in grant form.

Few developed countries, however, have managed to meet even this moderate target. The majority of the Development Assistance Committee countries (an OECD Committee) have throughout the 1970s managed less than 0.7 per cent of Gross National Product (GNP) in the form of official aid. The group comprises Australia, Austria, Belgium, Canada, Denmark, Finland, France, West Germany, Italy, Japan, New Zealand, Switzerland, the UK and the US, the Netherlands, Norway and Sweden. Only the last three have reached or surpassed the 0.7 per cent target.

The recipients of aid, however, are as anxious to influence the way in which aid is given as they are to secure increased amounts of it. It has already been pointed out that the bulk of official financial aid is given in bilateral, tied form. This though is not the only way in which financial aid can be given; the recipients themselves prefer multilateral aid.

16.6 Multilateral Aid and its Institutions

By its nature multilateral aid tends not to be tied. When developed countries pool some of their financial aid resources it becomes difficult for one country to specify how and where the amount it feels to be its 'own' should be spent. This difficulty tends to be increased since multilateral financial aid is channelled largely through a number of institutions, of which the following are the most important:

(*a*) **The World Bank** (the official name is the International Bank for Reconstruction and Development). This institution was established in 1945 along with the International Monetary Fund and is principally concerned with providing development finance for less developed countries. The Bank's funds come from:

(i) *Capital subscribed by member countries.* This amounts to some $31 billion of which 90 per cent is not called but used instead to back bond issues.

(ii) *Bond Issues.* These are either issued to the public in major capital markets or placed with central banks and governments. The Bank's outstanding borrowing amounts to more than $16 000 million.

(iii) *Profits.* The Bank has made a profit on its operations each year since 1948. In the 1970s this profit averaged around $200 million per year. At present the bank has accumulated earnings of more than $2 billion.

(iv) *Repayments.* A constant flow of repayments helps to swell the resources available to the Bank.

The Bank's lending policy is very much one which espouses the ideals of multilateralism. It does not lend in order to facilitate military or political objectives and will not give loans with the specific objective of helping out a developed country's balance of payments. Most of the loans made are for specific development projects in agriculture, power, communications, etc. In the past the Bank has been criticised for conceiving rather grandiose schemes which have been beyond the resources or needs of the country gaining them. That aspect of its lending policy now seems to be under control.

The World Bank tends to lend for 15–20 years, mostly to central governments, but sometimes to state governments and local authorities. There is a careful vetting and evaluation process for intended schemes and the main criterion is that the benefit should outweigh the cost. At present the Bank has approximately $30 billions on loan. Besides its own operations the World Bank has established two major subsidiaries:

(*b*) **The International Finance Corporation (IFC).** The IFC was established in 1956 with the object of promoting the development of the private sectors of developing countries. Since the time of its inception it has committed over $200 million. One feature of the IFC is that it does not provide all the necessary capital itself. However, its status is such that it is able to generate local interest and bring forth local capital—approximately four times as much local capital as is provided by the IFC itself.

(*c*) **The International Development Association (IDA).** This organisation was formed in 1960 to help those developing economies where the investment required exceeded the capacity to service such debt. It thus provides capital for the very poorest nations, drawing funds from members (amongst whom number developed countries), and by way of grants from the World Bank.

The terms of loans made are extremely soft and the IDA is often known as the World Bank's soft 'window'. Those who borrow are allowed up to 50 years to repay. During the first 10 years the borrower does not have to make any capital repayment; during the next 10 years only 1 per cent per annum; and after that 3 per cent per annum. No interest is payable but there is an annual service charge of $\frac{3}{4}$ per cent.

The type of loan made by the IDA is similar to those of the World Bank.

(*d*) **The Regional Development Banks.** The following banks make funds available for developing countries within their spheres of influence, though their lending is not necessarily limited to developing countries:

(i) The Inter-American Development Bank.
(ii) The African Development Bank.
(iii) The Asian Development Bank.

16.7 The Very Poor

During the 1960s and most of the 1970s the less developed countries managed a respectable rate of growth per annum of between 3 and 6 per cent. This was a better group rate of growth than the developed world. However, the overall growth statistics for the LDCs hide the fact that there is a 'sub-group' of LDCs with very poor performance and special problems. One of the most pressing problems of the very poor is that they are virtually denied access to the commercial credit sources of the Eurocurrency market, since this market only makes funds available subject to economic performance. The significance of this drawback becomes apparent when it is realised that over 50 per cent of non-OPEC LDCs' indebtedness is in the form of commercial borrowings rather than aid.

The oil crisis and inflations of the 1970s placed an intolerable burden upon the debt servicing of very poor countries and in 1974 45 per cent of these were classified by the UN as **Most Seriously Affected Nations (MSA)**. These countries were adjudged to have borne an 'unreasonable' share of the adjustment to higher oil prices. Along with other LDCs they have suffered as a result of the developed world's practice of raising its prices in order to claw back some of the higher cost of oil. Having no oil and no capacity to provide the high technology goods which they require for development, the LDCs in general and MSAs in particular are placed in a precarious position.

So badly affected have the MSAs been that they have not been able to service their existing debt (provided not by commercial institutions on commercial terms but almost exclusively by governments and international institutions on the softest of terms). This situation has led countries such as the UK to introduce a 'retrospective terms adjustment'—effectively loan cancellation—for 17 of the countries receiving aid and in the worst circumstances. This provides a temporary respite but does not solve the problem of long-term development.

16.8 Conclusion

The ending of exchange controls seems certain to draw more long-term capital from the UK mostly for the purpose of direct investment in other economies. Whilst we have oil and a relatively stable economy (and the prospect of attractive interest rates) this movement will probably be balanced by short-term flows of capital. It remains a moot point as to whether the countries really in need—the poorest less developed ones—are recipients of much of the long-term capital leaving the UK.

16.9 Revision Test

Answers	*Questions*
—	**1.** Why does capital flow abroad?
1. To facilitate investing and lending.	**2.** What are the two main types of capital flow?
2. 'Autonomous' flows and 'accommodating' flows.	**3.** Are long-term flows autonomous or accommodating?
3. Autonomous, and consequently they play a part in the active shaping of the balance of payments.	**4.** Why do short-term capital movements have an important impact on the UK balance of payments?
4. Because sterling is a key currency, and London is an important financial centre.	**5.** Why are such short-term movements important to UK governments?
5. Because they are volatile in nature and affect the size of the official reserves.	**6.** What can a government do about short-term capital movements?
6. It can vary the domestic interest rate, and exert some influence on the forward exchange rate.	**7.** What did exchange control do?
7. It rationed the use of foreign exchange as far as UK nationals were concerned.	**8.** Why do developing countries need aid?
8. In order that they may have access to the resources they need for development.	**9.** What forms does aid take?
9. (*a*) Technical aid, (*b*) commodity aid, (*c*) financial aid.	**10.** How is aid usually given?
10. In bilateral aid tied to the donor country.	**11.** Now try some of the written questions in Appendix 1.

17

INTERNATIONAL BANKING

17.1 The Pattern of International Banking in the 1980s

Today the pattern of international banking is changing rapidly, and a situation of global competition is developing. The major national commercial banks are entering the merchant banking and investment banking fields, which were formerly the province of smaller, specialist banks. Barriers are everywhere breaking down and there is an accelerating tendency for traditionally domestic banks, for example in the US, to enter international markets. For half a century banks have been protected, even in the most ardent free-enterprise countries, from the competition that has faced other firms in manufacturing, transport, etc. The fears of bankruptcies, like those of the great crashes of 1929–31, have ensured that governments have shielded banks from the rigours of competition by limiting the areas in which they have been allowed to operate and the prices they have been permitted to offer for deposits. Depositors are not risk-takers like shareholders; they have to be protected. Suddenly, this protectionist attitude has changed, and the banks are moving out of their domestic enclaves, to trade in wider international markets.

In the 1980s the dominant role in international money markets is being assumed by the former 'slumbering giants', the big national banks which had previously been chiefly concerned with lending to their own domestic markets. Examples are the British clearing banks, France's Crédit Agricole (about to be nationalised), the German savings banks, and Asian banks such as Overseas Chinese Banking Corporation and Bank Bumiputra. These banks have been putting pressure on the formerly dominant **universal banks**, such as the German Deutsche Bank and the Swiss Union Bank of Switzerland. These universal banks undertake all types of banking activities: underwriting bond issues, executing foreign exchange transactions, confirming letters of credit, providing funds to finance international trade, placing Euromarket securities with retail customers building portfolios, managing international deals and floating international bonds. The ability of the 'universal banks' to offer the same skills as the traditional British merchant banks and the American investment banks, from a bigger client base, put these traditional institutions under pressure in the mid-1970s. Now the universal banks are under pressure themselves from the commercial giants. What are the causes of the changed climate today?

17.2 Forces for Change in Banking Today

Among the forces at work to make banking more competitive we may list:

(*a*) Increased confidence in the banking network's ability to withstand financial difficulties.
(*b*) Saturation of domestic banking outlets.
(*c*) The growth of international business, especially in recycling petrodollars.
(*d*) The inflationary acceleration.
(*e*) Contracting economies in the advanced nations.

(*f*) Increased customer sophistication.
(*g*) Microchip technology.

We must deal with each of these in turn.

(*a*) **Increased confidence in the banking network.** The traditional fear of banking authorities was loss of liquidity leading to a run on the bank and bankruptcy. In such a situation—for example, in nineteenth-century British banking—the tendency was for other banks dealing with a bank in difficulties to withdraw whatever assets were at risk and thus precipitate the collapse of the weakling.

Today the very reverse is true: the banking community seeks to support the weakling with a 'lifeboat' arrangement, or a deposit-insurance scheme such as the Community-wide proposal being discussed at present. The Bank of England has powers under the Banking Act, 1979, to establish a Deposit Protection Board to levy contributions from banks and deposit-taking institutions. In many countries the nationalisation of banks reduces the risks of bankruptcy to minute proportions, while the unregulated Euromarkets have proved to be able to operate in the most competitive conditions without getting into major difficulties. Indeed, there have been some signs that banks with limited abilities to operate internationally, and fenced into their domestic markets, may be more vulnerable than those able to do business in other areas offering a wider variety of opportunities.

(*b*) **Saturation of domestic markets.** When domestic markets become saturated, so that almost every family has a bank account, there is little opportunity for banks to grow and they can only do so by attracting deposits away from other banks and non-bank institutions. Any sort of protective legislation which excludes banks from engaging in activities which other non-bank institutions are pursuing profitably enough are seen in these circumstances to be unfair. The development of secondary banks in the UK in the early 1970s to the exclusion of more reliable, and more soundly based, commercial banks is a case in point.

(*c*) **The growth of international business.** The oil crisis of 1973, and the annual oil crises since then, have called for an enormous financial effort from the sophisticated banking networks of the advanced nations to recycle petrodollars back into useful wealth-creation. The Eurodollar market had been operating for some 15 years as an off-shore market not subject to the detailed controls of national banking systems. This unregulated, highly competitive market was suddenly faced with the problem of finding safe havens for vast sums of money paid to the oil-rich states, as well as the handling of considerable sums to provide rescue services for 'Third World' nations badly hit by the oil price rises. The consequent expansion of the Eurodollar and Eurocurrency markets gave banks new opportunities to gain expertise in the free markets, while the opening of branches of banks from all over the world in major centres like London brought further contacts with bankers experiencing different types of control. The advantages of a dollar-base for the Eurodollar markets led foreign banks to set up branches in the USA, or to buy their way in by take-over activities. The presence of foreign bankers, free to deal in ways not permitted by the US authorities to their domestic banks, led to calls for a revision of the US domestic banking controls. In particular the requirement that banks should operate in only one State (about as sensible, said one critic, as confining General Motors to Michigan or Du Pont to Delaware) came under fire, since it prevents domestic USA banks achieving the wide credit base so advantageous in international banking. Developments in the US are discussed later in this chapter.

(*d*) **The inflationary acceleration.** In inflationary times everyone gets more sophisticated about money, and especially the legally and financially advised. It is the falling value of deposits in real terms which is a nightmare to savers. Non-interest-bearing current accounts are clearly of no benefit, and even the most unsophisticated savers switch to other savings banks and building societies. Larger firms disintermediate (cease to use the banking system as an intermediary for placing temporary surpluses of spare cash) and use their accountants or other advisers to place funds for them. Special brokers and markets develop to put those with cash in touch with those in need of cash, and interest rates reflect the market and the risk. Monetary authorities, trying to squeeze the money supply, find that they have no control over large sections of it seeping through every unclosed exit from the banking system, and multiplying its way round the economy in every de-regulated way possible. The media available today make everyone his own bank manager; interested parties hear on radio and television advice to sell off savings certificates and similar investments within 24 hours of a change in interest rates which renders them overnight a 'less-than-best-buy'. While the banking authorities ponderously try one policy or another, the general population are scurrying to safer havens, and the financial directors of firms are switching funds faster than anyone.

(*e*) **Contracting economies in the advanced nations.** For 25 years after the Second World War the advanced economies expanded under the influence of Keynesian policies. In expansionary times, even with domestic banking restrictions, slow growth of banking was always taking place. Competition between banks was restricted by feelings that the best policy was for everyone to enjoy a fair share of an expanding monetary cake.

The change in oil prices in 1973 brought tighter monetary policies and fiercer competition for deposits. For the first time banks could grow only by competing funds away from other deposit takers, and this increased the price of credit to borrowers. This in turn choked off marginal projects within the economy which turned expansion into stagnation and inflation into stagflation—a situation where prices are still rising despite the presence of massive unemployment and under-utilisation of capital assets. This again accentuated the competition for funds, and major conflicts between various classes of deposit-taking institutions began to appear. 'Knocking copy' emphasing the superiority of a particular bank's services over other types of service available from competitors is now featured in advertisements, for example.

(*f*) **Increased customer sophistication.** This has already been referred to, but it is a fact that where institutions pursue advertising policies which open a general debate about alternative financial portfolios, the general public becomes more aware of returns on capital invested. Again, the media employ financial advisers who raise the whole level of public understanding to points not dreamed of fifty years ago.

(*g*) **Microchip technology.** Perhaps the most significant development of the last decade is the emergence of a microchip technology which has given financial managers a much more thorough understanding of what happens on the money markets and the trends that are developing. Head offices now know within certain limits the impact of many of their actions upon the banking system, their depositors and their borrowers. Much of the increased confidence in the banking system comes from this advance in control by head offices. They are better informed of the dangers than at any time before; they can build in alarm systems which will be triggered off; and they are about to replace much of their branch banking activities by home services electronically operated from terminals by the housewife's telephone. A housewife will pay her bills by keying in coded account numbers and the sums payable, and a fraction of a second later her account will be debited and the payee's account will be credited. We move one stage closer to the cashless society.

17.3 Universal Banking

The change to universal banking which is taking place today has important implications for all those in banking. What it means is that banks with a broad domestic deposit base will move increasingly into international banking to pursue some of the high earnings both in fees and interest that are available in these markets. To do so they will need to compete more for domestic funds, and this will bid up the rates payable to depositors, and consequently the rates payable by borrowers. Increased competition in banking is therefore a paradox: it does not mean cheaper loans for the man in the street but more expensive rates of interest all round. To keep these down as much as possible head offices will have to pursue cost-cutting wherever possible, particularly in the cheaper (and therefore more easily mechanisable) staff activities. Some savings can also be achieved by reducing the number of branches, and replacing the local branch with telephone banking services operated from regional centres.

Universal banking means that a bank is able to offer every kind of service in every type of financial market. The chief markets are those designated as Eurocurrency markets, a term which includes Eurodollar and Euro-deutschemark transactions, as well as transactions stated in SDRs and ECUs.

17.4 Dealings on the Eurocurrency Markets

Banks which deal on the Eurocurrency markets are lending funds in foreign currencies which they have obtained in some way, perhaps by accepting deposits from a foreign customer. Clearly, to be profitable, there must be a difference between the price at which they borrow the money and the price at which they lend it. This is called the margin or mark-up. Rates are quoted for overnight money, 7 days' notice, 1 month, 3 months', 6 months' and 1 year's bid and offered rates. The bid is the price at which a bank will buy deposits or securities, the offer rate is the rate a bank will charge for lending money, or will sell securities or discount bills.

The chief sources of funds are as follows:

(*a*) A foreign currency current account.
(*b*) A foreign currency short-term notice account.
(*c*) A foreign currency short-term fixed account.

In each of these a deposit is accepted from a foreign national, whether an individual, a firm or a bank, of funds in an account in their bank at home—say in New York if we consider dollars as the currency involved. The funds will be transferred to the bank's account with its New York branch (or correspondent bank) and will be available for use as required.

(*d*) Eurocurrency market deposit.
(*e*) Medium-term non-bank Eurocurrency deposit.
(*f*) Certificates of deposit (tap or tranche).

These are all deposits taken from banks or other individuals, usually for a medium term (2–5 years). In the case of certificates of deposit a certificate is issued which can be sold on the **market in certificates of deposit,** the seller recovering his original deposit with interest from the buyer. The buyer then continues to earn interest on the sum deposited until the certificate matures at the end of the agreed period.

(*g*) Capital notes issue.
(*h*) Eurobond issue.
(*i*) Convertible Eurobond issue.

With all of these capital is collected from those who have funds to spare in return for a note or bond which is usually a long-term investment, of about 15 years, but may be re-sold by the lender on the Eurobond market if he requires to recover liquidity.

A major source of the dollar deposits in the Eurocurrency market has been petrodollars obtained by the OPEC and other oil-producing countries since the higher prices of oil were fixed from 1973 onwards. These funds, when made available to the banks, are lent out in all sorts of ways.

The chief uses to which funds borrowed may be put are listed below. Most of them are loans of one sort or another, but they may take the form of actual investments in an enterprise.

1. Foreign currency overdraft.
2. Negotiation of bills of exchange for overseas trade.
3. ECGD-backed buyer and supplier credit loans.
4. Eurocurrency floating-rate roll-over loans.
5. Eurocurrency fixed-rate loans.
6. Investments in Eurobonds issued by other borrowers.
7. Trade investments in foreign affiliates or subsidiaries.

The major activities are as follows:

(*a*) **Fixed-rate loans.** Fixed-rate loans are usually for up to five years, with a fixed rate of interest. There is no attempt to manage the repayments by a sinking fund; the loan simply becomes repayable in a lump sum at the end of the period. The agreement usually precludes early redemption.

(*b*) **Roll-over loans or floating rate loans.** These are more flexible than the fixed-rate loans described above. Funds borrowed as fairly short deposits (up to about a year) are loaned out to commercial borrowers at a rate of interest which applies for only a few months. The loan will then be renegotiated at the agreed 'roll-over' interval, so that the borrower pays, and the lender receives a rate of interest as prevailing at the roll-over time. It is also possible to build in options, such as a currency-option which will enable the loan to be re-negotiated into a cheap currency if this would be advantageous. One advantage of these roll-over periods is that it enables banks to match the maturities of various loans being made, so that they can keep more easily within safe liquidity limits, and will not be caught borrowing short to lend long.

(*c*) **The syndicated loan market.** Because of the huge size of loans required it is usual for one bank to lead-manage a syndicated loan, finding other banks and financial institutions to take a share of the loan. One bank advertised that it had been asked by Unilever to arrange a $340 million bridging loan to enable Unilever to acquire the National Starch and Chemical Corporation in the USA. Clearly only the very largest banks can be lead managers; other banks take up secondary positions somewhere down the hierarchy of banks who are helping to syndicate the loan. Sometimes banks who agree to provide funds take up co-management positions, reflecting the substantial stake they have in the success of the loan. Sometimes such a position entitles the co-manager to a share in the fees to be earned from the loan. In 1980 out of almost 3000 loans arranged to a total value of $89 billion, Citicorp lead-managed 89 loans to a total value of $4111 million and Chase Manhattan lead-managed 101 loans to a total value of $4090 million. National Westminster, the leading British bank, lead-managed 63 loans worth $2630 million.

Table 17.1 shows the lead-managers in this market in one recent year.

Table 17.1. Lead managers in the syndicated loan market (1980)

Lead managers	*No. of loans*	*Amount ($m)*	*Position 1980*	*Position 1979*
Citicorp	89	4111.41	1	1
Chase Manhattan	101	4090.15	2	3
Bank of Montreal	62	2748.18	3	5
Bank of America	70	2737.42	4	4
National Westminster	63	2629.50	5	14
Crédit Lyonnais	91	2291.99	6	11
Manufacturers Hanover	51	2263.81	7	9
CIBC	40	2114.29	8	30
Morgan Guaranty	42	1985.63	9	8
WestLB	36	1788.19	10	13
Lloyds	74	1711.92	11	6
Merrill Lynch Int Banking Group	11	1559.25	12	39
Société Générale	48	1556.08	13	21
Dresdner Bank	46	1508.36	14	23
Credit Suisse First Boston	20	1497.06	15	37
Shearson Loeb Rhoades Int	13	1404.00	16	28
Royal Bank of Canada	48	1389.17	17	24
Midland Bank	57	1308.55	18	19
Société Générale de Banque Group	36	1191.33	19	25
Banque Nationale de Paris	38	1168.81	20	—

Lead managers	*No. of loans*	*Amount ($m)*	*Position 1980*	*Position 1979*
Bank of Nova Scotia	26	1150.01	21	43
Bank of Tokyo	38	1100.27	22	2
Banque de Paris et des Pays-Bas	25	1084.96	23	—
Kredietbank International Group	23	1067.73	24	35
Orion Bank	35	987.02	25	17
Barclays	43	937.73	26	22
Bankers Trust Company	23	886.17	27	12
Wells Fargo	22	862.13	28	15
Deutsche Bank	26	861.04	29	7
Toronto Dominion Bank	28	852.43	30	48
Crédit Commercial de France	27	806.37	31	29
Chemical Bank	26	793.27	32	10
National Bank of Canada	17	742.41	33	—
Gulf International Bank	33	696.77	34	—
Schroder Wagg	11	671.88	35	—
Banque Bruxelles Lambert	6	654.91	36	—
DG Bank	21	590.79	37	38
Continental Illinois	26	555.49	38	36
Bank Bumiputra Malaysia	3	555.00	39	—
Commerzbank	19	550.50	40	27
Swiss Bank Corporation	19	510.29	41	40
Libra Bank	20	499.43	42	—
International Mexican Bank	8	487.83	43	—
Banca Commerciale Italiana	9	475.14	44	—
Dai-Ichi Kangyo Bank	15	471.21	45	—
Crédit Agricole	13	468.12	46	—
First National Bank of Chicago	20	467.96	47	—
SG Warburg	12	467.74	48	46
Fuji Bank	18	466.11	49	—
Hambros Bank	11	457.70	50	49

(Reproduced by courtesy of Euromoney Publications Ltd)

The greatest care is necessary in documenting these loans, since even the greatest 'names' can get into financial difficulties. The whole range of questions affecting any grant of credit should be asked, such as the purpose of borrowing, the length of time, the repayment terms, the official backing available, how funds to repay the loan are to be generated, what covenants are to be entered into about such matters as the payment of dividends to shareholders, the issue of other loans with priority over the present loan, etc. The record of all the borrower's senior staff should be considered, the exact roll-over terms, and the impact of national controls in the borrower's country over liquidity, capital structure, taxation, foreign exchange, etc.

Loans are usually arranged at a marginal rate above the **Libor** (London Interbank Offered Rate). Thus a UK bank without a retail dollar base must finance the loan in the Eurodollar market, either by accepting dollars from an OPEC member, foreign central bank or multinational corporation or by borrowing at the Libor rate on the London Interbank market. The loan will be repayable at a margin—say $\frac{5}{8}$, $\frac{1}{2}$ or even perhaps only a $\frac{1}{4}$ per cent above Libor rates. Such fine margins do not leave much leeway to the banker, bearing in mind the considerable risks, and margins obviously vary with the creditworthiness of the borrower, most of whom are 'great names' in industry, or nationalised institutions.

(*d*) **The Eurobond Market.** The Eurobond Market is a market which provides long-term capital to 'great names' and national authorities for the finance of major developments. Thus India in 1981 raised \$680 million for the erection of an aluminium project in Orissa at $\frac{1}{2}$ per cent above Libor for the first four years and $\frac{5}{8}$ per cent above Libor for the next six years. The intention is to repay the loans out of the exports generated by the project once it is established. The loan referred to earlier as a bridging loan to enable Unilever to finance the purchase of National Starch and Chemical Corporation, was eventually consolidated by the issue of two \$100 million dollar Eurobonds which provided the long-term capital to finance the purchase.

The borrower appoints a bank to lead-manage the issue. In earlier times this would have been a merchant or investment bank; today it would probably be a universal bank of the type described in Section 17.3 above. The lead-manager will probably seek one or two major banks to provide a large part of the funds required, in return for 'co-manager' status, and to share in the fees (say $\frac{1}{2}$ per cent of the total issue amount) and expenses. The 'managers' would arrange for the issue to be underwritten by a group of major banks, (the banks undertaking to provide the funds if no one else can be found to do so). Once again this calls for a fee of about $\frac{1}{2}$ per cent of the total sum to be issued. A list of financial institutions to be invited to participate in selling the issue is now drawn up. They will be institutions with 'placing power', i.e. they have clients who are looking for investments at reasonable rates of interest and will be able to 'place' some of the bonds with these clients. These investors will naturally want to know who the borrower is, how reliable he is, what the money is to be used for, etc. To answer all such questions a 'prospectus' may be drawn up.

To safeguard borrowers, and ensure that they have someone to speak and act for them in safeguarding their investment, it will be usual to appoint a trustee or fiscal agent to act on their behalf and to monitor the performance of the borrower. This is similar to the role of a debenture trustee in the issue of domestic debentures.

The league table of international bond issues given in Table 17.2 shows the lead managers in the international bond markets during a six month period in 1981. Table 17.3 shows how the market broke down as to the currency of issue, and type of borrower.

The authors express their appreciation for permission to reproduce in this chapter tables from *Euromoney*, a monthly publication devoted to the provision of reliable news about the international money markets. Its articles are informed and authoritative, and the range of statistics provided is enormous. *Euromoney*'s address is 20 Tudor Street, London, EC4Y 0JS.

17.5 A Review of World Banking at the Start of the 1980s

Global banking has become the distinguishing feature of banking in the last quarter of the twentieth century. The universal bank, able to offer all services around the world, has eroded national restrictions on banking. Even the Communist world has been penetrated by banking consortia offering

Table 17.2. Lead managers in the international bond markets

All notes and bonds (excluding New York issues)
Sole lead managers receive full amount of the issue; joint lead managers receive equal amounts

Period: January–June 1981

Position	*No. of Issues*	*Amount ($m)*	*Percentage share*	*Position*	*No. of Issues*	*Amount ($m)*	*Percentage share*
1. Crédit Suisse First Boston	27	1530.0	13.7	21. Yamaichi International	5	131.5	1.2
2. Deutsche Bank	9	656.9	6.1	22. Dillon Read Overseas	2	121.3	1.1
3. Salomon Brothers	10	570.0	5.3	23. European Banking Company	3	120.8	1.1
4. SG Warburg	16	559.6	5.2	24. Daiwa	5	119.1	0.6
5. Morgan Stanley	10	497.5	4.6	25. Paribas	3	116.9	1.1
6. Merrill Lynch	13	489.2	4.5	26. Manufacturers Hanover	3	107.5	1.0
7. Crédit Commercial de France	7	351.9	3.3	27. Société Générale de Banque	4	100.4	0.9
8. Goldman Sachs	3	337.5	3.1	28. Crédit Lyonnais	1	100.0	0.9
9. Société Générale	4	330.1	3.1	29. Long-Term Credit Bank of Japan	2	100.0	0.9
10. Nomura	9	329.2	1.8	30. IBJ International	3	94.6	0.9
11. Banque Nationale de Paris	3	277.9	2.6	31. Caisse dés Depôts et Consignations	3	94.2	0.9
12. Orion Royal Bank	6	213.1	2.0	32. CIBC	1	92.5	0.9
13. Morgan Guaranty	6	210.8	1.8	33. County Bank	2	85.6	0.8
14. Kreditbank International Group	4	192.5	1.8	34. Kleinwort Benson	3	81.5	0.8
15. Swiss Bank Corporation	5	189.9	1.8	35. Nikko Securities	3	65.8	0.6
16. Hambros	3	181.1	1.7	36. Banque de l'Union Européenne	2	60.3	0.6
17. Citicorp	4	167.5	1.5	37. Algemene Bank Nederland	1	58.8	0.5
18. Wood Gundy	4	152.5	1.4	38. Soditic	1	56.3	0.5
19. Chemical Bank	2	150.0	1.4	39. Banco di Roma	1	56.3	0.5
20. Union Bank of Switzerland	3	150.0	1.4	40. Kuwait International Investment Company	1	50.1	0.5

(Reproduced by courtesy of Euromoney Publications Ltd.)

Table 17.3 The market breakdown in the first half of 1981 (excludes New York issues)
$m equivalent: 1980 figures in italics

	No. of Issues	Amount	Percentage of total market	International agencies	Government	Municipalities	Public authorities	Corporations
Sterling	7	325.0	3.2	—	—	—	33.2	291.8
	5	*293.8*	*3.3*	—	—	—	—	*293.8*
Eurodollars	86	5782.5	57.5	865.0	50.0	275.0	705.0	3887.5
	54	*4615.0*	*52.4*	*915.0*	*400.0*	—	*660.0*	*2640.0*
Canadian dollars	1	41.4	0.4	—	—	—	—	41.4
	5	*214.9*	*2.4*	—	—	—	—	*214.9*
Deutschemarks	6	264.5	2.6	94.7	—	—	—	169.8
	20	*1516.9*	*17.2*	*107.2*	*662.3*	*101.0*	*372.4*	*273.8*
SDRs	1	25.6	0.3	25.6	—	—	—	—
	1	*19.6*	*0.2*	—	—	—	—	*19.6*
French francs	8	525.7	5.2	—	—	—	306.9	218.8
	4	*285.2*	*3.2*	*62.9*	—	—	*222.3*	—
Euroguilders	3	106.1	1.1	58.8	—	—	—	47.3
	5	*304.4*	*3.5*	—	—	—	—	*304.4*
Norwegian kroner	2	36.3	0.4	18.8	—	—	—	17.5
	2	*40.4*	*0.5*	—	—	*20.4*	—	*20.0*
Floating rate notes ($)	27	2510.0	24.9	—	100.0	—	825.0	1585.0
	20	*1250.0*	*14.2*	—	—	—	*250.0*	*1000.0*

Floating rate notes (£)	—	—	—	—	—	—	—	—
	2	*163.8*	*1.9*	—	—	—	—	*163.8*
Floating rate notes (SDR)	1	121.3	1.2	—	—	—	121.3	—
	—	—	—	—	—	—	*121.3*	—
EUAs	1	24.9	0.2	—	—	—		24.9
	1	*30.4*	*0.3*	—	—	—		*30.4*
Japanese yen	3	233.7	2.3	166.5	67.2	—	—	—
	1	*69.5*	*0.8*	—	*69.5*	—	—	—
ECU	2	67.6	0.7	38.0	—	—	29.6	—
	—	—		—	—	—	—	—
Total	148	10064.6	100.0	1267.4	217.2	*275.0*	2021.0	6284.0
	120	*8803.8*	*100.0*	*1085.3*	*1131.8*	*121.4*	*1504.6*	*4960.6*

(Reproduced by courtesy of Euromoney Publications Ltd)

massive loans to Comecon countries—at some risk to themselves. In the face of this global activity many of the rigidities of banking in individual countries have been reduced. It is proposed in the short sections that follow to list some of the main areas where changes have occurred.

(*a*) **The USA.** America has a federal system of government, with a division of powers between the federal authorities and the States. This makes it very difficult to alter institutions like banks which have a natural tendency to achieve economies of large scale, and therefore would logically operate most economically on a national, or at least a regional basis, but have been fettered by restrictions on interstate banking. The position became difficult in the 1970s, when the entry of foreign banks, not subject to regulation, brought multi-state banking by foreigners into competition with domestic US banks restricted to their home states. The complaints that arose from the 'banking lobby' led to the **International Banking Act, 1978.**

The International Banking Act, 1978 brought the foreign banks into the federal regulatory network. The effects of this were as follows:

(*i*) Foreign banks were forced to elect a 'home state' and may not accept deposits outside that state. Where foreign banks already had multi-state branches these were allowed to continue, but further expansion is not permitted.

(*ii*) Reserve requirements were imposed on all foreign banks with worldwide resources in excess of $1 billion.

(*iii*) Foreign banks were required to observe the same rules about rates of interest payable for deposits as domestic banks. There is a maximum limit on interest payable. (However, this is being phased out under the 1980 Act referred to later, and should have disappeared by 1986.)

(*iv*) Under the Edge Act of 1919, certain types of banks called 'Edge Corporations' are permitted to be set up to deal in international banking only. The 1978 Act extended the areas in which these 'Edge Corporations' could work, and permitted foreign banks to set up this type of corporation.

(*v*) The foreign banks were brought under control as to the 'non-bank' activities they performed ('new issue' work, for example) which are not permitted to domestic banks. Existing arrangements were allowed to continue, but not to expand.

This Act, therefore, did not do much to liberalise US banking, but it did meet the objections of American bankers to the competition they were facing from foreign banks.

The chief difficulty with America's financial system is its fragmented nature. There are over 40 000 different deposit-taking institutions, of which 14 000 are commercial banks and the rest 'thrift' institutions. These are of three main types: savings and loan institutions (S & Ls), mutual savings banks (MSBs) and the very numerous credit unions. There are over 20 000 of these consumer finance cooperatives.

Restrictions on multi-state banking, restrictions on rates payable for deposits, and on rates chargeable for mortgages, and many other types of restriction have prevented competition in the banking field. It became clear that changes were needed. The result was the **Depository Institutions Deregulation and Monetary Control Act, 1980.**

The Depository Institutions Deregulation and Monetary Control Act, 1980. The effect of this act is to dismantle the barriers restraining competition, and to equalise the ground rules for all types of deposit-taking institutions. The chief changes are:

(*i*) All banks and deposit-taking institutions are brought into the Federal Reserve System and must provide cash ratios of 3 per cent of the first $25 million of transaction balances and 12 per cent on the rest, plus 3 per cent on non-personal time deposits. These reserve rates will be phased in over a four-year period for member banks and eight years for non-members. In return all banks will have access to the Fed's discount window.

(*ii*) All interest-rate ceilings on deposits will be phased out over six years, to allow banks greater freedom to compete for funds. The effect is likely to be a rise in interest rates payable to depositors, and therefore a rise in rates payable by borrowers.

(*iii*) The system of NOW accounts, operated in the New England States, is extended to all States. A NOW account (negotiable order of withdrawal) is a current account on which interest is payable. The rate of interest payable is $5\frac{1}{2}$ per cent at the time of writing, but this may change. The effect is to provide an alternative to chequeing accounts on which interest is not allowed.

(*iv*) State-imposed ceilings on mortgage rates have been over-ridden. Originally these ceilings on mortgage rates (Regulation Q) were designed to ensure that mortgage funds would be available at rates householders could afford. Unfortunately, as soon as market rates of interest rose above the rates payable by Savings and Loan Associations the general public ceased to invest and many of the associations have had to be merged with other organisations, or have gone into liquidation.

The main barrier to full competition is the persistence of State laws on branch banking. There is every likelihood that these obsolete controls will be removed now that electronic banking, non-bank credit and other devices have permitted banking to move over State boundaries in many ways. For example, the customer who banks electronically by dialling coded information into the telephone system can deposit money in any state, and is not concerned with bricks and mortar premises in his/her home town.

(*b*) **The UK.** The British banking system has recently been by far the most profitable in the world. This is because Government policies have maintained high interest rates in recent years—from which the banks inevitably profit. The atmosphere in banking has become very competitive, particularly domestically, where competition with building societies for deposits has increased, and where a variety of new services (mortgage finance, special types of savings schemes, etc.) is being offered. The banks are also facing domestic competition from the foreign bankers now operating in London, who have begun to lend money to institutional borrowers and large companies at favourable rates. The Government itself is a competitor for deposits, offering favourable terms to savers, including index-linked savings which safeguard saving in real terms.

In the international field the UK banks have not all moved in the same directions. Only one of them (Lloyds) was strong in merchant banking with a genuine international presence. Barclays has always been strong in banking in the countries formerly part of the Empire. It has recently moved into the US in the personal, retail field and into consumer finance. Midland has acquired a private bank in Germany, and a commercial bank in the USA. All the banks are playing an active part in the syndicated loan market.

(*c*) **West Germany.** The West German banking system was enormously strong in international markets during the 1960s and 1970s as the German economy continued to out-produce most of its European rivals. The deutschemark was strong, not only because of surpluses on the balance of payments but also because foreign investors, and particularly central banks around the world, wished to hold some of their reserves in deutschemarks, to diversify out of dollars. Germany thus became a country with an international reserve currency, replacing sterling, with 14 per cent of world reserves held in deutschemarks against about 80 per cent held in dollars. Their willingness to play a strong part in international banking was helped by saturation of the home market, where almost every family has a bank account.

The system has come under pressure in the 1980s. The chief cause is the weakening of the Germany economy due to the adverse effects of oil price rises. Germany has been harder hit than most countries, because its dependence on imported oil is that much greater. Import penetration has also had some effect on the balance of payments. The vulnerability of the deutschemark when the dollar is strong is reminiscent of the weakness of sterling in former times when the dollar hardened. There is some evidence that the German authorities do not wish the deutschemark to become a leading reserve currency. A monopoly is imposed by the German **Capital Markets Sub-Committee**—a body which rations the issue of bonds denominated in deutschemarks—so that only German banks may lead-manage deutschemark issues, and the market was actually closed in November 1980 for about three months. In the first six months of 1980 deutschemark notes and bonds totalled 22, to the value of DM3125 million. In the same period in 1981 there were only six issues, totalling DM555 million.

(*d*) **France.** The developments in French banking hinge around the effects of the nationalisation proposals of M. Mitterrand now that the Socialist movement has at last secured a majority. The proposals include compensation for shareholders based on a scheme which is very favourable to the taxpayers—who will have to find the money to pay. Foreign shareholders in French banks are protesting loudly. Foreign banks are not to be nationalised, so that the foreign investor in a French bank is very poorly placed compared with other home nationals who moved into France in other ways.

All this is not very conducive to the development of international banking. Before M. Mitterrand's elections the French banks, particularly three of the huge nationalised banks and Crédit Agricole which had been expanding rapidly outside the national fold, were entering international markets in an increasing way, seeking to become 'universal banks'. The essential feature of universal banking is that it is 'one-stop' banking. Every type of service is available in every branch. The prospects for development were great, and the economics minister was talking of privatisation rather than nationalisation. This has of course been totally reversed, and no doubt considerable confusion reigns as to the direction French banking will take for the future.

(*e*) **Switzerland.** Traditionally the Swiss have been the strongest bankers in the international market and have particular expertise in the bullion market, the securities markets, and the foreign bonds market. The **à forfait market** is a specialist market which refinances supplier credits at fixed rates for the medium term without recourse to the supplier. It generates business on an increasing scale in recession periods and the Swiss have a particular expertise in it.

(*f*) **Canada.** There are 12 nationally chartered banks in Canada, of which five are very big. These are the Royal Bank of Canada, Toronto Dominion Bank, the Bank of Nova Scotia, the Bank of Montreal and the Canadian Imperial Bank of Commerce. The assets of the banks approach $C150 billion, and the big five represent about 90 per cent of this. Under a recent Act, the Federal Bank Act, foreign banks altogether may only loan up to 8 per cent of the domestic assets of the chartered banks, i.e. up to about $C12 billion. The domestic banks therefore have a strong and broad base for their activities and have been active in the international money markets in recent years. All five of the major Canadian banks feature in the league table of syndicated loans (see Table 17.1).

(*g*) **Japan.** Japanese banking is closely controlled by the Ministry of Finance, which is anxious not to allow too much lending of capital abroad. For about a year from late 1979 overseas lending was not permitted at all, and when it was relaxed it was selective. Banks could lend only to international organisations and to borrowers developing raw materials which Japan needs for her industries. There is a move on the part of foreign central banks to keep reserves in yen as an alternative to the dollar and the deutschemark. This offsetting flow of foreign funds into Japan was recently enhanced by the authorities' free-yen accounts, which permitted foreign funds to receive free-market rather than Japanese rates of interest. The resulting flows were so large that the free-yen accounts had to be restricted again, and further increases were not permitted.

(*h*) **Arab banks.** Not surprisingly, Arab financial institutions are beginning to play a significant part in international banking. The aim is to secure a fair share of Middle East banking for Arab banks and to conduct some recycling of petrodollars. A large share of the development work in the Arab world is funded from OPEC funds.

17.6 Revision Test

Answers	*Questions*
—	**1.** Why have banks been generally controlled and protected from the rigours of competition in the twentieth century?
1. To protect the depositors, who are not risk-takers like shareholders. Confidence in the banking system is essential.	**2.** Why is this attitude less influential today?
2. (*a*) The banks have shown their ability to avoid difficulties in competitive situations. (*b*) 'Lifeboat' and deposit-protection schemes are more widespread.	**3.** What is a 'universal bank'?
3. A bank which offers every type of service and is able to operate both in 'retail' and 'wholesale' banking.	**4.** Which banks are best placed to become 'universal banks'?

Answers	*Questions*
4. Broadly-based commercial banks in the advanced and affluent economies, so long as they are freed of domestic controls limiting their operations.	**5.** What are the forces for change in banking today to a more international approach?
5. (*a*) Increased confidence in the professionalism of the banking fraternity. (*b*) Saturation of domestic outlets. (*c*) The need to recycle petrodollars. (*d*) The inflationary acceleration. (*e*) Contracting economies in the advanced nations. (*f*) Increased customer sophistication. (*g*) Better control through microchip technology.	**6.** Why is competition in banking something of a misnomer?
6. Because it implies competition to bid for deposits by offering higher rates of interest—and hence it raises costs of loans. It does not lower the cost of banking services.	**7.** What is the basic process on the Eurocurrency markets?
7. (*a*) Money is borrowed by bankers in a variety of ways (i.e. they accept deposits, or they raise capital by borrowing on the Interbank Market, or even by selling bonds). (*b*) This money is then loaned out to 'great name' borrowers in a variety of ways, with suitable safeguards about repayments.	**8.** What is the syndicated loan market?
8. A market where: (*a*) borrowers appoint a bank as lead-manager to arrange a loan for them, in return for fees and commission; (*b*) the lead-manager finds other banks to join the syndicate—offering some of them co-manager status; (*c*) the managers investigate the creditworthiness of the borrower and devise a scheme with adequate safeguards; (*f*) the members of the syndicate place the loans with investors and monitor developments throughout the life-time of the loan.	**9.** What is the Eurobond Market?
9. A similar market to the syndicated loan market but the outcome is a long-term capital loan to the borrower—effectively a foreign-bond issue, supervised during its life-time by a trustee or fiscal agent.	**10.** Now try some of the written questions in Appendix 1.

Part 5

THE MONETARY ENVIRONMENT

18

BANKING IN ITS ECONOMIC ENVIRONMENT

18.1 The Concept of the Claimant

Every organisation operates within an economic environment. First it will have the framework of national laws within which it is bound to function. These laws will change from time to time; they may be strongly enforced or more honoured in the breach than in the observance. They may include a framework of international obligations which have been enacted as national statutes, such as the British Parliament's enaction of Community laws since joining the EEC, or the Warsaw Rules embodied in the Carriage by Air Act, 1961. Then there will be local laws and bye-laws, on a descending scale of importance, imposing obligations to pay rates or local taxes, to seek planning permission for various projects, to keep open paths and footpaths, etc. Outside this legal framework for the environment of business there will be an infinitely large and minutely detailed pattern of obligations both outside the organisation and within it. Most firms recognise some sort of duty to their own locality and to the environment in general; to their own workforce and the families of their workforces; to their customers and suppliers. All these people constitute 'claimants' upon the organisation.

The survival of organisations in many cases depends upon their proper appreciation of the many claims that are made upon them. They exist to fulfil the purpose for which they were founded, but they can only do so if managers appreciate that those ends have to be met in an environment which presents countless obstacles to be overcome. The least understood element of any organisation is this total environmental framework and the claims which it makes. Countless examples could be quoted of organisations which failed because they were too intent upon their own activities to appreciate the impact they would make upon their environment. We cannot regard responsibility for employees as ending at the factory gate, if we wish to avoid rapid staff turnover and costly training programmes. We cannot proceed with plans if there is a likelihood that governmental opposition or local opposition will be aroused. Capital costs are high, and an abortive project can ruin a prosperous company.

A claimant is an individual, firm or institution which is making, or may make in the future, a justifiable demand upon the organisation, which it would be illegal, morally wrong or merely unwise for the organisation to overlook.

Every banking institution, at whatever level it is operating, has to take account of the environment in which it works and the likely organisations and individuals in that environment who may make a claim upon the bank at any time. We are not considering here a 'financial' claim, though they will frequently be made and are the bank's *raison d'être*. It is just as much a claim upon the Bank of England if the Governor is expected to speak to the annual dinner of the Chartered Accountants as it is if he is required to meet the IMF for an examination of the British economy. A local bank manager who is obliged to take up golf because some of his best clients play golf is assuming an obligation which has been 'imposed' (not too strong a word for a bank manager who hates golf) on the bank by claimants in the environment.

It is a salutary thing to draw up an environmental model for your own organisation in the banking field. This is called an **organisational-claimant model**, and it will vary with every institution. It lists the claimants upon the organisation, the nature of the claim, the proposed method of meeting the claim and the method of conflict resolution to be adopted should it be impossible to reach an agreed settlement. Such an 'organisational-claimant model' is presented in Table 18.1 but the reader should note that it cannot be more than a general model. The crucial thing for the management of any organisation is to draw up such a model in the correct order of priority of claim, specific to the organisation. Such a model will enable management to appraise the various bodies and persons exerting pressures upon the firm; to decide priorities and review the economic, social and domestic implications of various courses of action. The reader should now consider Table 18.1, which has been divided into sections. Some of these sections will apply only to banks at the appropriate levels—not all bank managers will be concerned with international or even national implications of the services they offer. Indeed, these implications may come down to the branches as head office instructions.

18.2 Assessing the Impact of Claimants

Having identified the claimants on his sector of the banking hierarchy, the manager must turn this mental model into quantified details about the impact of each claim upon the organisation. The organisation's planning and decision-making will be influenced by its estimates of the time and money it must spend to meet the present and the developing claims of each class of claimant. It will equally be influenced by the returns it anticipates from the improvements achieved in the process. Thus a strike-free bank should more than offset the cost of achieving good industrial relations; staff fringe benefits may cut labour turnover and the cost of training; customer satisfaction should increase market share; good community relations should increase goodwill and bring reciprocal benefits in such local matters as further education college bias in favour of the training programme; improvements in transport infrastructure, etc.

It may be that claims are unreasonable, or deserve to be side-stepped because they seek to take advantage of the organisation's availability. Local bodies frequently look no further than their local industrialist for financial support, regardless of his need to plan his own cash flow for normal business purposes. Appetite grows with feeding, and a concession to support a particular aspect of local life may snowball into demands to support a wider and wider range of activities. It may be necessary to fend off adverse trends by publicity or appeals to local and central government to reach a more reasonable consensus on measures to be adopted. Organisations cannot fall in with every proposal just because it has been made. The organisation's original objectives are still the reason for its existence. Pressure groups exist to preserve a vested interest and protect it from assailants who may not fully appreciate its value to the community at large, or the extent of the capital sunk in it at great expense to the community as well as to the owners.

The decision-making process therefore involves three elements. First, an **information system** detects the environmental influences at work, or monitors those that have already been located. Such an information system may have a

Table 18.1 Organisational-claimant model

List of claimants	*Nature of the claim*
This is a general list not arranged in any special order. Managers should draw up their own lists in proper order of priority for their own organisations.	Further columns should be added to any chart drawn to suit the claims upon a particular organisation, showing: (*a*) Method of satisfaction envisaged, and (*b*) Method for resolving conflicts, if any.
Banks and the international community	
1. Foreign central banks	(*a*) Claim to consideration as interested parties in the international economy. (*b*) Claim to consideration in the movement of currency values one against the other, especially with regard to: (i) Their own domestic currency. (ii) Other currencies which they may be using as a method of storing international reserves. (iii) The value of gold if this is part of their reserves. (*c*) Claim to assistance with 'official financing' difficulties when in deficit on their balance of payments. (*d*) Claim to be treated as regards (*b*) above in the spirit of the 1976 revision of the IMF constitution as regards 'dirty' floating and 'beggar-my-neighbour' policies.
2. International Monetary Fund	(*a*) Claim that all member countries shall abide by the constitution and pay attention to the needs of the international economic community as well as their own domestic situation. (*b*) Claim to impose conditions on any borrower of credit tranches with a view to correction of the adverse balance of payments being experienced by the borrower. (*c*) Claim to repayment of tranches borrowed by members within the appropriate time limit. (*d*) Claim to representation from the member on standing or *ad hoc* committees.

List of claimants	*Nature of the claim*
3. The World Bank Group	(*a*) Claim to representation and cooperation in deliberations about World Bank aims and policies. (*b*) Claim to call 'uncalled' capital in the event of a particular scheme resulting in a loss—since the Bank's loans are made against the security of its capital, 90 per cent of which is uncalled. (*c*) Claim to have obligations honoured on any project within the member country's home territory.
4. Other foreign banks	(*a*) Claims to have contractual obligations honoured. (*b*) Claims to enjoy reciprocal benefits in matters affecting the conduct of international trade, so that international banking arrangements are mutually profitable.
Banks and the national community	
5. The Central Government	(*a*) Claims to control the banking system in the national interest to achieve the Government's financial targets for the control of the economy, the money supply, etc. (*b*) Claims to the assistance and cooperation of the banking system in the collection of taxes, the disbursements of the spending departments, the management of the gilt-edged market, etc. (*c*) Claim to have the legislative requirements on health, safety at work, trading standards, quality controls, documentation and statistics, codes of conduct in industrial relations, worker participation, disciplinary procedure, taxation, VAT, exporting, etc., met by the bank, like all other organisations. (*d*) Claim to interfere in matters of monopoly trading, price control and other administrative aspects.
6. Local Government	(*a*) Claim to know what the bank proposes in so far as law requires or mutual interest makes this desirable. (*b*) Claim to have rate contribution, as levied, promptly paid. (*c*) Claim to participation of bank in projects of mutual or public importance. (*d*) Claim to release with pay of employees who become elected representatives. (*e*) Claim to service of bank's senior staff on local panels, committees, boards of governors of institutions, etc.

7. The local business community	(*a*) Claim to special consideration as customers. (*b*) Claim to support in financial or practical terms for mutually advantageous schemes. (*c*) Claim to membership and service by bank's officials on local committees and panels.
8. The local community	(*a*) Claims for improper environmental behaviour by the bank. (*b*) Claims for nuisance by parking, traffic access, noise, television interference, etc. (*c*) Claims for provision of local amenities of a social, religious, educational or recreational nature. (*d*) Claims for raising aesthetic overtones of the bank's buildings, grounds, parking lots, etc. (*e*) Claims for participation of bank's officials in local affairs, local institutions, rag weeks, festivals, charities. (*f*) Claims to supply a reasonable proportion of local produce or goods and services by local tradesmen and craftsmen.
Banks and the banking community	
9. The Institute of Bankers and other regional or trade associations	(*a*) Claim to represent the banking industry at all levels. (*b*) Claim to impose levy on members for funds. (*c*) Claim to discipline for breach of agreed codes of practice.
10. Competitors	(*a*) Claim to pursue a line of production or service previously conceded to lie within the bank's brief. (*b*) Claim to diversify into an area which is a manifest duplication and waste of capital. (*c*) Claim to compensation for alleged deliberate poaching of ideas, staff, etc.
11. Unions	(*a*) Claim to represent groups of organised workers. (*b*) Claim to engage in collective bargaining. (*c*) Claim to participate in drawing up job descriptions. (*d*) Claim to participate in drawing up codes of practice for (i) health and safety, (ii) disciplinary procedures and (iii) industrial relations. (*e*) Claim to participate in management and to know full facts on profit calculation and allocation. (*f*) Claim to be informed of all developments likely to affect security of employment, redundancy, expansion, take-overs, etc.

List of claimants	Nature of the claim
12. Personnel	(*a*) Claim to realise self-respect, the respect of others and the full development of individual personality in the working situation. (*b*) Claim to a satisfactory reward for the factor labour, in money form on an appropriate scale and with prospects of economic advancement. (*c*) Claim to be free of arbitrary or capricious behaviour on the part of supervisors and managers. (*d*) Claim to be represented by an appropriate union, and to exercise rights to act freely in accordance with the law in the pursuit of legitimate aims. (*e*) Claim to know the terms of any contract of service and have them in writing. (*f*) Claim to participate in the planning and organisation of his or her own job. (*g*) Claim to participate in management at an appropriate level and be aware generally of the trends within the organisation and its position in the mixed economy. (*h*) Claim to enjoy a safe system of work. (*i*) Claim to enjoy staff welfare facilities and other fringe benefits. (*j*) Claim to an adequate and professional level of training in the general background of banking and in the detailed use of techniques and equipment as they are devised or adopted.
Banks and the investing public 13. Ordinary shareholders	(*a*) Claim to share in the profits. (*b*) Claim to vote at the AGM. (*c*) Claim to a share of the assets on liquidation. (*d*) Claim to take up additional stock offerings. (*e*) Claim to ask for investigation of the company. (*f*) Claim to receive copy of the directors' report and accounts. (*g*) Any other rights accorded in the prospectus or other contractual arrangement with the company, or in legislation such as the Companies Acts, 1948–81.
14. Preference shareholders	(*a*) Claim to receive the agreed rate of dividends if profits are available. (*b*) Claim to vote at meetings if dividend is in arrears or variation of rights is proposed. (*c*) Claim to prior return of capital if authorised by the issue originally.
15. Minority shareholders	(*a*) Claim to fair treatment in dividend policy. (*b*) Claim not to be defrauded under the exceptions to Foss *v.* Harbottle rule. (*c*) Claim for investigation under Section 164 of the Companies Act, 1948.

16. Debenture holders	(*a*) Claim to interest on debenture. (*b*) Claim to secured assets in event of default. (*c*) Claim to receive copy of the directors' report and accounts.
17. The investing public in general	(*a*) Claim to consideration whatever company they are investing in. Thus a bank decision to refuse to extend an overdraft to a firm may enforce liquidation and all investors in that firm will be adversely affected. (*b*) Claim to participate in a sound economy, which banks will not affect adversely for their own partisan reasons.
Banks and their creditors and customers	
18. Secured creditors	(*a*) Claim to receive payment in the agreed manner. (*b*) Claim to petition for bankruptcy and deal with security according to law.
19. Unsecured creditors	(*a*) Claim for payment. (*b*) Claim to petition for bankruptcy and a receiving order.
20. Suppliers	(*a*) Claim to be considered as accredited supplier, especially if the business has been adjusted to suit the bank. (*b*) Claim to be paid in the agreed manner. (*c*) Claim by suppliers of professional services to be treated in a professional manner and possibly with *uberrima fides* (utmost good faith).
21. Customers	(*a*) Claim to the return of all sums deposited as and when required. (*b*) Claim to consideration when loans or overdrafts required. (*c*) Claim to be considered for the fullest use of bank facilities, credit cards, cheque cards, etc.
Banks and the general public	
22. The general public	(*a*) Claims as customers (see above). (*b*) Claims to participate in a sophisticated economy of which confidence in the banking system is an essential element. (*c*) Claims to participate in a sophisticated economy where employment, investment of savings, pension rights, etc., are all dependent on the banks playing their full part in financing and supporting business enterprise. (*d*) Social, environmental and ecological claims of every sort.

formal framework like a Technical Committee on Banking Developments. Alternatively, it may just be the branch manager who has his ear to the ground to detect disgruntled sentiments so that they can be given a quick hearing before anyone 'downs tools'. Secondly, the information has to be processed. **Information processing** takes many forms. It may mean case work in personnel, or consideration by an appropriate committee and reporting upwards and downwards. Finally, there has to be a **decision output**. Decision outputs do not need to come from top level—they can be made at every level. Discretion within a policy is an almost universal practice, which speeds up decisions at any given level, and throws the more difficult decisions up to a higher level, and finally to board level. Routine decisions are made within the agreed policy laid down by the board as it conceived the organisation's objectives at the time. Those cases needing a decision which do not fit the existing policy come up to the board for a top-level decision which is then promulgated as a new policy development.

18.3 Revision Test

Answers	*Questions*
—	**1.** What is an organisational claimant?
1. An individual, firm or other institution which is making, or may make in the future, a justifiable demand upon the organisation, which it would be illegal, morally wrong or unwise to overlook.	**2.** What sort of claims might we envisage?
2. (*a*) Money claims; (*b*) claims for service by the organisation's officers; (*c*) claims affecting the preservation of the natural environment; (*d*) claims for the preservation of social life as we know it.	**3.** What is an organisational-claimant model?
3. It is a chart which attempts to identify all the claimants on a given organisation, and the nature of their claims.	**4.** What are the stages in dealing with claimants?
4. (*a*) An 'information system' to identify claimants and claims. (*b*) A 'processor' to examine the claims, investigate their impacts and make recommendations. (*c*) A 'decision output' to decide exactly what to do and if necessary lay down organisation policy on the matter.	**5.** Go over the page again. Then try the questions in Appendix 1.

Appendix 1

REVISION QUESTIONS

Chapter 1

1. Why is a money system essential to the working of an advanced economy? In your answer refer to specialisation as the source of the wealth of advanced economies.

2. Money need not be intrinsically valuable, so long as it is generally acceptable. Explain.

3. Mark Twain's advice to a beggar read: 'No, you are not obliged to accept greenbacks at par.' Explain this advice, including the joke.

4. Explain the term 'creation of money' as applied to lending by banks to customers.

5. Investigate in any library the varieties of 'money' used, from primitive societies to the modern world.

Chapter 2

1. What are the functions of a central bank? Refer to the Bank of England to illustrate your answer.

2. How does the Bank of England implement the Government's monetary policy?

3. Describe the changes made by the Banking Act, 1979, in the regulatory role of the Bank of England?

4. 'The Federal Reserve System is part of the "separation of powers" in the United States.' Explain.

5. How does the Federal Reserve System differ from the Bank of England's role in controlling the money supply?

6. Why is the Banque de France no longer so influential in the economic affairs of the nation?

7. What is the link between the note issue, the creation of wealth in goods and services, and prices? How would you recommend that this relationship was stabilised?

Chapter 3

1. What is the importance of current account, deposit account and savings account services to (*a*) the general public and (*b*) the banks? How might head offices evaluate the performance of branches with respect to each of these services?

2. Discuss the impact of computerisation on commercial banking.

3. (*a*) 'Too many High Street branches are a waste of resources in a society where prime shopping sites are expensive.' (*b*) 'The banks must increase their competitiveness if they are to resist calls for nationalisation.' Discuss whether there is a conflict in the above statements. What level of High Street service should the banks aim at?

4. 'On-line' banking will be the major development in banking in the 1980s. Explain what 'on-line' banking is and discuss its future development.

5. What are the merits of the further expansion of bank departments for investment, executorship, insurance and similar services?

6. Obtain the Annual Report of one of the major banks in any recent year. Referring to the figures for the whole banking sector provided in the publications of the central bank, assess the relative importance of the bank in the nation's affairs.

Chapter 4

1. What is the function of a bill-broker? What part do bill-brokers play in the financial sector of an advanced economy like the UK?

2. What is the 'lender of last resort' facility? To whom is it extended and why? How does it help the Bank of England to secure control of the short-term money market?

3. What functions does a merchant bank perform for its clients?

4. 'The savings bank movement collects funds from a very large number of relatively poor people.' Who uses these funds? What services do the savings banks provide to their depositors?

5. What is a trustee savings bank? How did the system start and what changes has the Trustee Savings Bank Act, 1976, introduced?

6. Why is the Co-operative Bank well placed to offer banking services to a wide section of the public? What services might it offer more readily than the ordinary commercial banks?

7. 'The building society movement offers services to the general public which are of great value to them.' 'The proliferation of High Street building society branches is a waste of scarce prime retail sites, and a considerable loss to the general public's shopping facilities.' Comment on these views of the building societies' activities.

8. What part do the finance houses play in the financial affairs of the community? How do they obtain funds, and to whom do they lend them?

9. What measure of success has been achieved by National Girobank since its establishment in 1967?

10. Draw up a chart showing the pattern of savings and lending in a sophisticated economy, with the sources of savings, the destinations of ultimate loans and the interrelationships between institutions.

Chapter 5

1. What are the 'money markets'? Where is the market place in each case?
2. Distinguish between 'retail' banking and 'wholesale' money transactions.
3. Why do banks operate in the money markets? What are they hoping to achieve?
4. What are Eurocurrencies? Describe the Eurocurrency market, and explain (*a*) why depositors choose to deposit there and (*b*) why borrowers choose to borrow there.
5. What determines the interest rates payable on (*a*) the inter-bank market, (*b*) gilt-edged securities, (*c*) the discount market and (*d*) hire purchase transactions?
6. Draw up a list of interest rates from such sources as are open to you covering the entire range of markets for money.

Chapter 6

1. How is it that banks are able to create credit? Explain the 'credit creation' process.
2. What is the link between 'credit creation' and the money supply?
3. A common fear in advanced societies is that banks, as a group, can create credit without limit. Is this fear well founded?
4. Why do banks follow a process known as 'keeping in step'? Explain the process.
5. Using the published accounts of any major bank calculate the percentage which the various classes of assets represent to the total of the balance sheet (which is of course the same as the total of the liabilities).

Chapter 7

1. Outline the major points involved in both the 'real' and the 'monetary' approaches to the rate of interest.
2. Is it at all possible to reconcile the 'real' and 'monetary' approaches to the rate of interest?
3. How is the rate of interest determined?
4. 'Hoarding is irrational when a reward can be earned for using funds.' 'Hoarding is rational if the use of funds leads to capital losses.' Explain these two different approaches to hoarding.
5. Draw up a table of interest rates to be earned from the various investment opportunities available. Update these rates monthly over the course of a full year. Plot the rates, using different colours for each type of investment.

Chapter 8

1. What part does money play in the economy? Why is its role today considered to be so significant?

2. Today economic policies are dominated by two schools of thought, 'Keynesian economics' and the 'new monetarism'. Explain briefly each of these approaches.

3. Explain the 'multiplier' effect in Keynesian economics. What effect does it have in times of full employment, when the Government is using fiscal measures to counter the tendency to inflation?

4. What is 'economic modelling'? Why is it possible to argue about the results derived from such a model? Are they, therefore, any use?

5. Explain the term 'velocity of money'. What factors could influence the velocity of money and what would be the effect of (*a*) an increased velocity, (*b*) a decreased velocity of money.

6. As a modern monetarist, what advice would you give to the Chancellor of the Exchequer preparing the next budget?

7. You are an economic consultant at the Treasury. Draft a report showing the relative merits of monetary and fiscal policies.

Chapter 9

1. What have been the chief aims of Government policy since the Second World War? To what extent are they irreconcilable?

2. Distinguish between direct taxes and indirect taxes. What difference is there in their impact upon the taxpayer? What are the problems of indirect taxation for a Chancellor preparing a budget?

3. What is the budget? How has its impact on the economy changed in the twentieth century?

4. What is meant by the term 'Management of the National Debt'? What are the aims of the Treasury and the Bank of England in the management of the debt?

Chapter 10

1. Outline the main problems faced by governments as they pursue their economic objectives.

2. What problems are presented to policy-makers by the lack of direct influence upon their targets?

3. What is meant by 'lags' in monetary control of the economy? Can the problem of 'lags' be overcome?

4. What are the causes of unemployment? How may unemployment problems be solved?

5. In monetarist theory distinguish between targets, instruments and indicators. Give examples of each, referring to the economy of your own country.

Chapter 11

1. What specific techniques may be used by central banks to implement monetary policy?

2. What forces are at work in the economy to encourage financial institutions to cooperate in implementing the monetary policies of a particular government?

3. What is Minimum Lending Rate? Does it differ from Bank Rate? What part does it play in influencing the money supply?

4. Explain the system of Special Deposits. If the Bank of England calls for an increase in Special Deposits of 1 per cent, what is the likely impact on the money supply?

Chapter 12

1. 'Before 1939 monetary policy was all the policy there was; after 1945 fiscal policy was the basis of Governmental control of the UK economy; after 1970 monetarism again became the dominant policy.' Explain.

2. The Radcliffe Report led to the imposition of a 28 per cent liquidity ratio on the

banking system. What was the purpose of this ratio, and why did it eventually prove inadequate?

3. What was the system for control of bank credit set up after the discussion paper *Competition and Credit Control* in 1971. How effective was it?

4. Write short notes about each of the following:

(*a*) The 'monetary base' method of control over short-term money.
(*b*) The 'indicator system' of control over growth in the money supply.
(*c*) Maturity-certain assets.
(*d*) Maturity-uncertain liabilities.
(*e*) Marketable assets.
(*f*) The integrated measure of liquidity.

5. Evaluate the success of monetary policy in the last decade.

Chapter 13

1. What are the elements in the balance of payments accounts? What is the likely result of each in a normal year, and how is the final balance of payments achieved?

2. In a period of floating exchange rates, how may (*a*) an exporter and (*b*) an importer safeguard themselves against fluctuations in foreign exchange rates?

3. How may a central bank operate on the foreign exchange market to manage the value of its currency? What is 'dirty floating', and what measures has the IMF taken to limit it?

4. What is the advantage of a currency-basket over an ordinary currency? How is the composition of a currency basket decided?

5. What have been the causes of slumpflation in the years since 1973, when OPEC first raised oil prices?

Chapter 14

1. Discuss the function of the IMF in the present era. Refer in your answer to the conditions imposed on borrowers, and their appropriateness for the current world economic situation.

2. What part does the World Bank play in the developing countries?

3. 'Project spotting has been the basis of the World Bank's activities in the past. It must now move over to "programme" lending.' Explain.

4. How has the General Agreement on Tariffs and Trade benefited (*a*) the advanced nations and (*b*) the developing nations?

5. Describe the European Monetary System.

6. Write short notes on each of the following: (*a*) the EMS grid of parities; (*b*) the ECU; (*c*) ECU parities; (*d*) convergent economies.

Chapter 15

1. What is the basis of exchange rates? Illustrate your answer by considering the exchange rate between (*a*) the pound sterling and the Deutschemark and (*b*) the pound sterling and the rupee.

2. Describe the system of exchange rates that prevailed under the Bretton Woods System.

3. Write short notes about: (*a*) the 'free floating' of currencies; (*b*) managed floating. What is the IMF's concern about managed floating?

4. Why was gold demonetarised in 1976? Why is it likely to be remonetarised in the future?

Chapter 16

1. How can the developed world help the developing world?

2. Distinguish between 'autonomous' capital movements and 'accommodating' capital movements.

3. What ways are open to the Government to influence capital movements in the interests of securing a balance of payments?

4. What part does the World Bank Group play in providing aid to the developing world?

5. Some nations have been designated MSAs, because they are the 'Most Seriously Affected' by the OPEC price increases. Why are these nations so badly hit, and how can they be helped?

Chapter 17

1. What is universal banking? What is the importance of 'universal banks' in international banking?

2. What factors are tending to reduce controls over banks in the operations they may perform? Refer in particular to US and UK banks.

3. Write short notes on: (*a*) Libor; (*b*) margins above Libor.

4. What factors might enter into the considerations of a major bank asked to lead-manage a huge loan for a multinational company? The loan is to be used to take over a company in a foreign country.

5. What is the Eurobond Market? Describe its main activities and outline how it works.

Chapter 18

1. What is meant by the term 'claimant' in an 'organisational-claimant' chart?

2. 'The bank is not bound to answer for the particular aims, ambitions or ends of its employees, any more than the king is bound to answer for the particular aims, ambitions or ends of his soldiers, for like the soldiers the employees do not purpose their deaths when they purpose their services.' Discuss this statement.

3. What part should a bank play in the locality where it has established a major branch or regional office? If this involves costs, how may the costs be justified?

4. Discuss the case for a code of practice in industrial relations. In your answer refer particularly to the economic implications of such a code of practice as far as a bank is concerned.

5. Draw up an organisational-claimant chart for your own organisation, listing both the claimants and their claims.

Index

Index